HISTORICAL FICTIONS

Essays by

HUGH KENNER

NORTH POINT PRESS · SAN FRANCISCO

1990

The author and the publisher wish
to thank the publications in which these essays
originally appeared: Art & Antiques; Ezra Pound
Among the Poets, ed. George Bornstein (University of
Chicago Press, 1985); Inquiry; Book World; Los
Angeles Times; The Alternative; Washington Times;
National Review; Philadelphia Inquirer; Yale Review;
Paideuma; New Republic; Harper's; Washington Post;
Parnassus; Ironwood; Johns Hopkins Magazine;
Delos; Literary Theory and Structure, Essays in Honor
of William K. Wimsatt, ed. Frank Brady, John Palmer,
and Martin Price (Yale University Press, 1973);
Conjunctions; New York Times Book Review; English
Satire and the Tradition, ed. Claude Rawson
(Blackwell, 1984); Irish Times; Saturday Review;
English Literary History; New York.
Louis Zukofsky, "A foin lass bodders," © Paul
Zukofsky. Reprinted by permission. All rights
reserved. May not be reprinted
without written permission.

LIBRARY OF CONGRESS
CATALOGING-IN-PUBLICATION DATA
Kenner, Hugh.
Historical fictions : essays on literature /
by Hugh Kenner.
p.   cm.
ISBN 0-86547-424-9
1. Literature—History and criticism.   I. Title.
PN510.K4   1990
809—dc20   89-70919

Contents

HISTORICAL
FICTIONS

The Hiddenmost Wonder

"Rimini is not an attractive town," wrote Adrian Stokes in 1934. Nor was it attractive in 1964, the year I first visited. It sits four hours south of Venice, on the Adriatic flats, confronting the grey sea with bleak high-rise hotels. What you can do with the grey sea if you're so minded is wade out into it, and its floor slopes so gently you can wade out a long way. Next you wade back in, and that's the use of the sea. (If you're a child you can also tumble into two feet of water from a swing erected maybe fifty feet offshore, and be the first member of your family to fall into the Adriatic.)

Droves of black-clad old ladies from the hills totter out of buses to marvel at the sea. They even cork up gollups of the sea in bottles, which I'm told carabinieri later confiscate. Sea water after all abounds in salt, a state monopoly mere crones aren't to meddle with.

As an industrial suburb, Rimini has been utilized by Fellini, I forget in which movie. I seem to remember street walls painted garish colors, to enforce a Fellini statement of unfitness for human presence. Driving from Venice to Rimini, like Caesar you cross the Rubicon: a forgettable bridge, an unmemorable stream, a blank sign: RUBI-CON. "Alea jacta est," wrote Caesar of the moment of his crossing: the die is cast. Still true: long after his era, something final that even Caesar couldn't have foreseen attaches to my visits to Rimini.

For since 1964 I've gone back, unless I've lost count, five times. The sole disappointment of my last stay in Venice (1988) was a conference schedule that left no loophole for a sixth trip to Rimini: to the sole and ample goal there: to the world's hiddenmost wonder: the Tempio Malatestiano.

"Non e un tempio, e un ecclesia," screamed a priest at a friend of mine who'd incautiously asked when they'd be unlocking the Tempio. Thereby hangs a principle that got its builder literally excommunicated. "Tempio" (meaning something pagan) was a term of contempt, meant to indicate that (though they still say mass there daily) it was utterly devoid of Christian icons. In 1450 Italy was rediscovering its Roman heritage, its Greek. And Sigismundo Malatesta had the luck to employ the greatest master of the bas-relief who ever lived. And Agostino di Duccio crammed what would get derided as a "Tempio" with stone reliefs of Diana, and Flora, and *putti* riding dolphins, and Mars, and a Muse of the Dance, and an occasional "Angel" that might be a Grace, and an "Influxion caused by the Moon" amid which a naked man in a rowboat confronts a sea that has almost whelmed an islanded elephant, a thoughtful lion. . . . On and on. Dozens. You can take in perhaps three or four at one visit. You'd best be spacing out visits through a lifetime. Pope Pius II did not like the effect at all.

"A jumble and a junk-shop," Ezra Pound called it; yet "it registers one man's concept," Sigismundo's. Yes. It's all detail. And God, we've been hearing lately, is in the details.

It mattered to Sigismundo to believe he was descended from Hannibal, who'd crossed the Alps with elephants; hence more than a dozen stone elephants. On entering you pass four, paired in green "bardiglio" marble, holding up columns that hold up an arch. Their foreheads are perfectly shiny, no one for 500-odd years ever having been able to omit patting them. ("Aren't they lovable?" said the three-year-old who came with my wife and me in 1969. Then he patted all four.)

A document survives from 1454: "We have not begun putting new stone into the martyr chapel; first because the heavy frosts wd. certainly spoil the job; secondly, because the aliofants aren't here yet and one can't get the measurements for the cornice to the columns that are to rest on the aliofants."

You'd get the measurements after you got the aliofants; detail rested on detail. Such a notion would give Skidmore Owings & Merrill the fits. For the "Three Blind Mies," whatever else they do, keep a project coordinated, homogenized. Whereas Sigismundo had simultaneously at least three supervising architects, each with a different notion of what was going on.

There'd been since the 1330's a Gothic church on the site, dedicated to St. Francis of Assisi, and that was to be respected. (It's said to have contained Giottos that got trashed. But who, in 1450, knew that Giotto *mattered*?)

So we'll leave the Gothic brick standing, and hire two masters to install inside it something Gothic-Romanesque, in marble. (Matteo di' Pasti, from Verona, framed the side chapels in pointed "Gothic" arches; but his co-designer, Agostino di Duccio, that master carver, had another style entirely.) Next, we'll summon the foremost architect of our age, Leon Battista Alberti, to encase the *out*side of the Gothic church with a fine marble statement. As he did, until money ran out. When you glance through Tempio windows the Gothic obtrudes, imperfectly aligned between inner and outer shells.

And when you approach the Tempio from the street it does look, yes, unfinished. (From the left side it looks even worse. Seven arches arrayed like a Roman aqueduct; then abject surrender to the brick.)

The facade, though, yes, the facade: a magnificent recessed and polychromed entry, flanked by two arches that were to have sheltered tombs but never got finished; and up above, an asymmetrical gesture toward a crowning arch that was hardly so much as started. Also Alberti had envisaged a decisive dome, but 29 years after his death a brick belltower got improvised instead. I rehearse all this to show why the Tempio doesn't earn stars in the likes of the *Guide Michelin*, where they go by unities.

Walk in, though. All is now detail. Pass (and pat) those elephants. Then take in, till you're saturated, wonder after wonder, engulfed by the genius of Agostino di Duccio.

If you look up "Duccio" you'll be distracted by Duccio di Buoninsegna, a 13th century Sienese painter. Turn to the A's for "Agostino di Duccio," Augustine of the Duccio lineage, and you'll be little the wiser. Born in Florence about 1418, he had small luck any time he got hired to carve in, as they say, "the round" (though the round, even when carved by Michelangelo, was generally meant for viewing from in front). But give him a slab of marble perhaps two by three feet; have him cut back from its surface no deeper than maybe two inches; then human eyes will never have beheld the like. His great work was done in the decade he worked for Sigismundo. (No one seems to know when he died. 1481 is a guess.)

He was almost instantly eclipsed, subsumed by the sheer impossibility of what he'd accomplished. Far down toward the left of the Tempio, a so-called Chapel of the Liberal Arts contains figures of Philosophy, of Botany, that before long were being acclaimed as actually Greek. (Sigismundo, who'd been to Greece, was a notorious plunderer. He'd even plundered the corpse of a Neoplatonic philosopher, for entombment in a wall of the Tempio. Surely these too were plunder!) Then in the 18th century some letters were spotted along the hem of a stone garment, but no one could read them. Coptic? Ancient Arabic? An unknown oriental language?—so speculation boiled as late as 1813. It seemed to matter, affording doubtless a clue to the provenance of such evidently ancient miracles. Who could credit "the return of classical forms in the work of Renaissance artists"? Who could credit, what's more, a transcension of "Renaissance artists"? So "the name of Agostino di Duccio was completely forgotten." My *Encyclopaedia Britannica* doesn't know he existed.

Wave falls and the hand falls. Gowns swirl. Fabric is transparent above flesh. Children are half-seen through translucent water. . . . It is all illusion: dead stone, incised with such cunning as has not been known ever before or again.

Dead stone? Not really. Adrian Stokes in his 1934 *Stones of Rimini* devoted many pages to that stone: not igneous (fire-born) stone, no, sedimentary stone: stone formed when dissolved minerals are deposited out of water. Water "fed those organisms whose remains fed the nucleus of limestones: it was the waters that carried the calcium carbonate that cemented those remains into rock." Such rock is still alive. So—responsive to stroking—a stone elephant's forehead can shine.

And "limestone is petrified organism. We may see hundreds of shell fossils on the surface of some blocks. Nor are the animal fossils rare. The skeletons of the coral are common, so too of the crinoid, a kind of starfish."

So—marble being limestone—it's no wonder the Mediterranean imagination got obsessed with shells and coral forms the marble brought with it. Thus Sandro Botticelli's painted Venus stands on a huge tilted shell.

Which is only to say that the material helped prompt Agostino to his fluency with fluid forms. There's water in maybe half of his reliefs. I've mentioned the Flood, and there are *putti* gambolling under a fountain, and others gleefully waist-deep in water, or riding on bladders amid merry ducks. And Diana atop her moon-barge wields a great crescent to command the waters, her "pale eyes as if without fire." (That wonderful phrase is Pound's.)

Agostino does water with fluent incised scalpel-strokes, wavy. You seem to be seeing *through* the "dead" stone surface.

But once more, no, the stone is not dead but crystalline; and crystals (think of diamonds) receive light only to re-radiate it. "Although light penetrates most limestones readily"—Stokes speaking—"it becomes scattered and diffused in passing from one grain to another . . . causing the otherwise opaque rock to have a certain quality of glow."

And Duccio conceived his carvings where they were meant to be seen, by diffuse light filtered through those Gothic windows. One time, on what I'll hazard is the most beautiful piece of stone in the world, he made the whole face of his Flora ("Botany") luminous, to celebrate all the growth that thrives on light. She shines amid a dimness in the third chapel down on the left, shines in midsummer, shines on a late winter afternoon, shines especially when smokestack haze unguessed by him or his patron occludes the air over Rimini.

He was clumsy and uncomfortable carving "statues." The man who, with two inches' depth at his disposal, could persuade us that a brash goat with bulging udders is clinging to a steep grade for a nibble at forbidden leaves—that's his "Capricorn"—crammed 3-D "Virtues" into narrow spaces from which an elbow, a hand, five toes, will poke out as if seeking more room. It's just there that we perceive an awkwardness of interaction between him and the interior's supervisor, Matteo di' Pasti, who seems to have asked for some full-bodied Statements to precede Agostino's endless subtlety of the near-flat.

Intrinsic to that subtlety is a medley of vanishing-points. Many of the reliefs come in stacked threes—top, middle, bottom, near the base of a squared column. That ensemble is repeated on three sides of the column, so a column will offer nine, of which, from most approaches, you're aware of six. And Diana on her moon-barge is the bottommost of her set of three (Mars and Venus are top and middle). Yet we view her and her chariot as if from below, and the horses—lower than the chariot—as if at eye-level. So we're looking *down* at something orthodox perspective would have us squat near the floor to see aright. Then the horses: the left-hand one we see nearly from the side, in defiance of the lines of the chariot just above him. And Diana: into the great oval of her cape we're looking from the left, yet we're viewing *her* much more frontally. And (what splendor!) it all coheres.

For relief's solicitation of the eye is different from that of flat painting, of 3-D sculpture. Italian mainstream painting said, This is where your eye goes: about opposite the center, a comfortable distance back; then you'll seem to be looking into a tidied stage set. Sculpture says, Look from where you like, within reasonable limits, but for preference stay near the front. Low relief, though, says Move to and fro; accept, even, virtual viewpoints you need not occupy You'll see a face from in front; the top of the head, though, as if from partly above; then one leg frontally, another sideways; and these will all blend so you'll not notice (unless you're a postulant of Donatello's, ready with cries of "Naive!"; for Donatello does force a view from head-on, as if the carving were a slightly raised painting; whereas Agostino can arrest a cater-cornered eye).

He's not a part of "Art History" because he led nowhere. That means, no one had adequate mind to succeed him. Thus historians have no process to fit him into.

And his patron? Sigismundo Pandolfo Malatesta appears as an orthodox villain in trifles like the *Horizon Book of the Renaissance*, treacherous, bloodthirsty; whereas his nemesis Federico of Urbino features as an enlightened patron who etc. etc. But whereas Feddy bought existing, accredited paintings, Sigismundo fed living artists while they did their thing. One he fed for a time was Piero della Francesca, who is, yes, part of "Art History," and whose fresco—long since badly restored—of Sigismundo kneeling before his patron saint is on view in the Reliquary Cell (second on the right). Another he fed for a decade was Agostino. How he picked his winners is something I'd like to hear about.

No one in Shakespeare's lifetime was living in the Age of Shakespeare, that age not having been invented till long afterward. Likewise no one in the Renaissance lived in the Renaissance, a word coined in 1820's France and first spotted in English two decades after that. Previously, a man in 1450's Italy simply shared the messy breakup of the Dark Ages, very likely deserving blame for some of the messiness. And with the Pope himself for an enemy Sigismundo had as bad press then as ever since.

His marital affairs were likewise untidy. (What did happen to his second wife, a Sforza? Whispers haven't yet stopped.) One thing sure, his passion for Isotta degli Atti—mistress, later spouse—underlies the fanaticism that built the Tempio, breasting the fierce currents of the time, scrounging cash by leading loyal bowmen in crazy campaigns for half-intelligible objectives. Also, cash or no, Romagna is poor in stone. Sigismundo got it where he could. Some of the slabs that clothe the exterior were filched from graveyards, their inscriptions decipherable still. He even managed to hijack some Istrian stone that orderly folks with manifests and receipt-books had thought they were shipping to the builders of a bridge at Fano. And he stole other stones from San Apollinare in Classe near Ravenna. . . .

The intertwined S and I that accost you at the entry portal are manifest inside everywhere. (SI-gismundo? Or his initial and Isotta's?) If the elephants are surely his bullish emblem, the persistent stylized roses keep proclaiming her. And she may underlie Flora of the luminous face, also Diana, mover of the seas. On the gentle coastal slope of Rimini, a slight tide moves the sea in or out a long way. Something less slight can seem apocalyptic; in 1442 a tidal wave pitched a ship in the harbor up onto a warehouse roof, and people were killed by blocks of falling hail. Water and the moon are live conditions there, and a live woman's presence was what magnetized the Tempio.

Work commenced about 1447; the facade assigns itself an ideal date, MCCCCL, 1450; chronic underfunding was idling Duccio's chisels by 1457; by 1461 Sigismundo was ruined, by seven more years dead. Isotta survived him another seven years. In December 1943 and January 1944 allied bombers did their (luckily) incompetent best to demolish the Tempio. Their damage has been expertly repaired.

After 1461 Agostino wandered off to the only place he could find work, Florence, and what the Florentines wanted was *big* things. They commissioned a marble giant. On a huge block, fetched down from Carrara, he chiseled half-heartedly, till he noticed he'd gotten one shoulder lower than the other, and gave up. It stood around, "ruined," so one story goes, till Michelangelo saw possibilities in its asymmetrical pose and extricated a "David" from Duccio's listless mess.

Everywhere, the Tempio seems to touch on unfinished projects. Adrian Stokes, who'd planned a trilogy on the Quattrocento, abandoned it after two volumes. By the evening of my one meeting with Stokes, in 1965, the man who'd written *The Stones of Rimini* 31 years earlier, propelled by enthusiasm for Pound's Malatesta Cantos, had evolved into a Freudian crank anxious about rumors of his onetime involvement with the likes of Pound. We sat in huge immovable chairs, placed back to back. Was he playing shrink? Though his affect was courteous, I followed little of the conversation and remember less.

Pound, of course, abandoned the Cantos. And by the last time I saw him, a few years after that evening with Stokes, he was saying virtually nothing, a habit into which he'd been sinking since about 1960.

His companion thought to remind me of mottos Matteo di' Pasti had incised high in the third chapel on the right side of the Tempio.

Up on a wall of that chapel, stone elephants support what was meant for Isotta's tomb. (Was she ever placed in it? No one's saying.) "D. Isottae . . ." commences a Latin inscription on the sepulcher's face. (Does "D." conceal "Divae," Goddess? That's how an enraged Pope read it.) And above the tomb, paired elephant heads in profile, trunks downcurving, tusks erect, support twinned mottos: "Tempus Tacendi"; "Tempus Loquendi." As Speech has its time, so has Silence. The elephant is taciturn when he's not trumpeting.

Meanwhile at Rimini stone, alike silent and alive, is eloquent with Sigismundo's passion, with Matteo di' Pasti's and Leon Battista Alberti's design, with Agostino di Duccio's miraculous craft.

1989

Ezra Pound and Homer

No exertion spent upon any of the great classics of the world, and
attended with any amount of real result, is really thrown away. It
is better to write one word upon the rock, than a thousand on the
water or the sand.   W. E. GLADSTONE, 1858

Homer is the West's six trillion dollar man. For two millennia and a
half at least we have kept him alive and vigorous with an increasingly
complex and costly life-support system that from earliest times has
drawn on all the technology around. To make papyrus in Egypt, then
construct and navigate a ship to take it to Athens, entailed most of the
chemistry, the metallurgy, the carpentry, and the mathematics accessible to Mediterranean men of the fifth century B.C. What Athenians
did with papyrus was, of course, write out the two big books of Homer.

Parchment Homers were precious spoils from Byzantium, 1453.
Renaissance architects designed libraries that housed hand-made
copies; blacksmiths forged chains to keep them where they belonged.
As soon as there were printing presses in Italy, there was a folio Homer, two volumes, printed in Florence about 1480. Pound's Canto
XXX shows us Francesco da Balogna incising dies with the Greek letters they'd need for the pocket Aldine Homer. To aid comprehension
scholars made Latin versions, their printings embellished by the
newly designed Italic characters. Readers of Canto I will remember

one such version of the *Odyssey*, Divus's, dated 1538. And all over Europe lens-grinders were enabling presbyopic and myopic eyes to scan Homer's lines.

Our own silicon technology stores Homer and retrieves him, catalogues his words and cross-references them, relying on magnetic disks, on air conditioners, on central processing units, central generating stations; also on toil and ingenuity in California and Japan, to keep alive an old poet whose very existence has been repeatedly questioned. We have no such continuous record of commitment to any other part of our heritage save the Bible. The six trillion dollars I mentioned was rhetorical; what eighty generations have invested in Homer, directly and indirectly, eludes computation and nearly defies comprehension.

For we aren't even sure what the Homeric poems *are*; something more than bronze-age entertainments, surely? Our efforts to assure ourselves that we know what we're valuing have constituted much of the history of our thought. At one time the *Iliad* and *Odyssey* were esteemed as a comprehensive curriculum in grammar, rhetoric, history, geography, navigation, strategy, even medicine. But by the mid-nineteenth century A.D. they no longer seemed to contain real information of any kind at all. Had there ever been a Trojan War? Scholars inclined to think not, much as connoisseurs of the West's other main book were doubting that there had been a Garden of Eden with an apple tree, or that planks of an Ark might have rotted atop Mount Ararat. Both books got rescued by identical stratagems; the Bible was turned into Literature, and so was Homer. That entailed redefining Literature, as something that's good for us however unfactual. That in turn meant Nobility, and also Style. It also required Longinus to supplant Aristotle as the prince of ancient critics, and Matthew Arnold to become the Longinus of Christian England. He said that Homer was rapid and plain and noble: by Longinian standards, Sublime. Those were the qualities a translator should reach for, in part to sweep us past mere awkward nonfact. The Bible in the same way was edifying if you knew how to go about not believing it.

In 1861, while British ink was drying on printed copies of Arnold's three lectures On Translating Homer, Heinrich Schliemann, broker in furs, was amassing wealth in Hamburg to finance a dream. He was going to find Troy! By 1870 he'd found it, yes he had, at a place the maps called Hissarlik, found traces too of the great burning; and he photographed his wife Sophie wearing what he thought were Helen's jewels. (A photograph, no light undertaking in 1870, was merely the most recent of the technologies mankind's Homeric enterprise keeps conscripting.)

The story, as so often, now slips out of synch. Andrew Lang, the folklorist, published with one collaborator an English *Odyssey* in 1879, with two others an English *Iliad* in '83. These, for various reasons not excluding the fine print of copyright law, remained the standard English versions as late as the mid-20th century—the Modern Library, even, used to offer them—and they were already obsolete when they appeared. For Lang and Butcher, Lang and Leaf and Myers, had fetched their working principle from pre-Schliemann times. The way to translate Homer, they thought, was to make him sound like the King James Bible, the idiom of which has great power to ward off questions about what details mean. But what details mean—in particular what many nouns meant—was being settled year by year as men with spades ransacked Troy and Mycenae for such cups and golden safety-pins as Helen and Hector knew.

Ezra Pound was born in 1885, just two years after the Butcher and Lang *Odyssey*. One unforgotten day when he was twelve or so, enrolled at the Cheltenham Military Academy in Pennsylvania, a teacher chanted some Homer for his special benefit. After four dozen years, from amid the wreckage of Europe, the man's name merited preserving:

> and it was old Spencer (,H.) who first declaimed me the Odyssey
> with a head built like Bill Shepard's
> on the quais of what Siracusa?
> or what tennis court
> near what pine trees?
>
> [LXXX/512]

It was from "Bill Shepard" at Hamilton that he'd picked up his first Provençal enthusiasm, so it was a fit rhyme the heads of these two instigators made. And hearing Homer declaimed, he testified, was "worth more than grammar." Though all his life a great connoisseur of detail, he was never easy with schoolmasters' grammar. It screened out what we'll be finding a need for, the tang of voices.

That would have been about 1897, when it was just beginning to look as though the wanderings of Odysseus too might mirror an order of factuality analogous to that of the new historic Troy. In 1902, Schliemann's architectural adviser, Wilhelm Dörpfeld, explained the topography of Ithaka; in the same year, Victor Bérard published the book Joyce was to use so copiously, about the origins of the *Odyssey* in Phoenician *periploi*, a noun Pound was to gloss:

> periplum, not as land looks on a map
> but as sea bord seen by men sailing.
>   [LIX/324]

Those are arguably the two most important lines in the *Cantos*. It's characteristic of the poem's way of working that we find them embedded in a narrative about 17th century China. And the word on which they turn came from the edges of the new Homeric scholarship.

The *periplous* (a Greek noun Pound transmuted into an unrecorded Latin form, *periplum*) registers the lay of the land the way it looks now, from here.

> Olive grey in the near,
>   far, smoke-grey of the rock-slide, . . .
> The tower like a one-eyed great goose
>   cranes up out of the olive-grove, . . .
>   [II/10]

That's an Imagist detail, also "sea bord seen by men sailing": a detail from some imagined *periplous*. If you were sailing in the track of that skipper you might not find the color useful—light shifts day by day— but "the tower like a one-eyed great goose" would help you be sure of your position: such an apparition is not easy to mistake for some other tower. Likewise the Homer we encounter in the first Canto is not to be taken for Pope's or Lattimore's. Homer mutates down the centuries; we can only begin to savor the mutations when translators begin to record what they can of them.

And translators only began their notes on the *periplous* past Homeric capes and shoals when they had Homer's text to translate, some time after Byzantine scholars had carried the precious manuscripts to Italy. The first Canto reminds us just what Andreas Divus did: he mapped the words in blind fidelity. The Canto's resonant "And then went down to the ship" follows Divus's "At postquam ad navem descendimus," which in turn follows Homer's "Autar epei hr' epi nea katelthomen": *Autar*, and; *epei*, then; *epi nea*, to the ship; *katelthomen*, we went down. In placing "descendimus" where he did, Divus even kept the order of Homer's words, putting the Greek into Latin, as he says, *ad verbum*, the way one inflected language can map another. With his page-by-page, line-by-line, often word-by-word fidelity, Divus was making a crib a student in the 16th century could lay open beside the Aldine Greek, to get guidance you and I might seek in a dictionary. When Ezra Pound thought his Latin "even singable" he was suggesting what much later he would suggest of a fiddle rendition of Clement Jenequin's *Canzone de li ucelli*, that sheer note-by-note fidelity had kept the song audible.

Can sheer blind fidelity be faithful to so much? We have come to something fundamental. A while ago we were talking of fact, the order of Homeric fact archaeologists were producing, to supplant the circumlocutions of the lexicons. Pound yielded to no one in his respect for fact, but for him the "fact" was apt to be whatever he could find right there on the page: whatever Dante might have meant by "the literal sense": mere letters, queer sounds, or even just lexicon entries. Letters, sounds, tagmemes: from the 1930's till he died he would love the Chinese character out of conviction that alone among the scripts of civilized men it collapsed all of these, shape, sound, and reference, into a sole inscrutable polysemous sign. The Chinese ideogram for "man" is a picture of a man; the Chinese spoken word for "cat" is what all cats say, "mao." If you say that "with a Greek inflection," you are saying the Greek for a catly thing, "I am eager." That's a detail we find in Canto 98 (New Directions, 1970, p. 686); in the late Cantos especially we see words *exhibited*: isolated words including a few of Homer's words, set off on the page by white space. Such words, though no taller than a printed line, are aspiring to the status of the ideogram. They are centers of radiance. We may think of them as opportunisms, like Shakespeare's when he rhymed "dust," mortality, with "must," necessity.

Such opportunisms irradiate the "Seafarer" of 1911. "Blaed is genaeged" says, word by word, "glory is humbled." Pound looked at "blaed," saw a sword-blade, and wrote "The blade is laid low." There's no arguing with that, and no justifying either. Nor can we argue when, in Canto I, by a triumph of the literal, English words map Divus's words which map Homer's words and the whole goes to "Seafarer" cadences. He is following Divus because for one thing, he wants to celebrate the occasion when, thanks partly to Aldus and Divus, Homer was recovered for the West; for another because he was himself a man of the Renaissance in having been well taught his Latin and ill-taught his Greek. Latin, even Latin verse, Pound could read at sight. Greek, even Homer's, he'd pick at, with a crib. Divus might have labored with Ezra Pound in mind. No one in 400 years has owed him so much.

Now though Divus intended a drudge-like fidelity, still he too invented a Homer: whether by sheer human exuberance, or by inadvertence, or via textual error we can't always say. Now and then his Homer is not the Greek scholars' Homer. For listen:

> And then went down to the ship,
> Set keel to breakers, forth on the godly sea and
> We set up mast and sail on that swart ship, . . .

"On the godly sea"? Yes, it's alive with gods. But any modern crib, for instance the Loeb, says "on the *bright* sea," and for the good reason that the Greek word is "dian," a form of "dios," one of Homer's favorite epithets, especially for the sea you push a ship into. "Eis hala dian," reads *Odyssey* XI, 2: "into the bright sea." It's a formulaic phrase at the *Odyssey*'s numerous launchings.

But what does Divus have? He has "in mare divum," as if he were distracting us by a play on his own name. *Divus*, says the lexicon, "of or belonging to a divinity; divine." A contracted neuter form would be *dium*, perhaps close enough to *dian* to have caused confusion in a shaky time for classical understanding. How did someone, in those days before lexicons, collect equivalences between Greek and Latin

words? About Divus we seem to know nothing save that he may have
come from East Asia Minor, a better place for Greek than for Latin. But
however *divum* arrived on Divus's page, Pound followed him faith-
fully, and wrote "the godly sea."

> . . . periplum, not as land looks on a map
> but as sea bord seen by men sailing . . .

—here, as seen by a man who sailed four centuries agone, and whose
compass was not wholly reliable. It's an interesting rule, that in the
presence of a textual crux Ezra Pound is apt to be utterly literal. Those
are just the places where credentialled scholars guess. But Pound
would only guess when the text was foolproof. When he didn't understand the words, or when they diverged from convention, then
he'd presuppose someone else who'd known better than he; as Divus
had, in prompting him to write "godly."

"Of Homer," Pound wrote as long ago as 1918, "two qualities remain untranslated: the magnificent onomatopoeia, as of the rush of
the waves on the sea-beach and their recession in

> *para thina poluphloisboio thalasses*
> [*Iliad* 1:34]

untranslated and untranslatable; and, secondly, the authentic cadence of speech; the absolute conviction that the words used, let us
say by Achilles to the 'dog-faced' chicken-hearted Agamemnon, are
in the actual swing of words spoken." When men speak, not by the
book but as they're moved to, uncounterfeitable rhythm asserts itself—what we've just heard Pound call "the actual swing." It eludes
the dictionary, eludes mappings of "meaning": the translator has to
leap for it, with his own time's live speech in his ears. It's only if he
makes that leap that he makes us hear.

Hughes Salel, 1545, called Odysseus "ce rusé personnage": that's
one French way to look at *polytropos*, the *Odyssey*'s first epithet, and
from our own century we might use "that tricky bastard" as a sight-
line on Salel. (Yes, "bastard" is extreme, but it's part of an idiom.) Andreas Divus, 1538, has "multiscium," much-knowing, as it were
"savvy." Thereafter the reality fades, and the renderings decline.

Butcher and Lang, 1879, offer "so ready at need," like a detail from a hymn. A. T. Murray in the 1919 Loeb tries "man of many devices," and Liddell and Scott in their lexicon make a stereophonic mumble, "of many counsels *or* expedients." "That man skilled in all ways of contending," says the often admirable Robert Fitzgerald, here smothering perception with poetic dignity. Nobody speaks phrases like those.

You can't cut such a knot with a trick of idiom, not even one as stolidly idiomatic as W. H. D. Rouse's "never at a loss." The problem goes far too deep. It has been hard for many centuries to imagine what Odysseus was really being commended for. We have all inherited the Roman distrust for quick Greek intelligence—we associate it with huckstering—and translators, being men of literary cultivation, have additionally been infected with the changed attitude to our hero that set in when his name became Ulysses and he got tarred with the brush of fatal deviousness. Dante did much to propagate the tricky Ulysses. We need not blame him. Though he placed Ulysses in the hell of the false counselors, he had the excuse of never having read Homer. He'd read Dictys and Dares, second-century popularizers who turned the designer of the wooden horse and vanquisher of the Cyclops into (says W. B. Stanford) "an anti-hero."

Pound read Homer's Greek slowly, Dante's Italian fluently, and it's unsurprising that the way he conceives Odysseus owes as much to Dante as it does to Homer. Luckily, he was also misreading Dante, to the extent that he was thrilling to the eloquent speech and disregarding the great flame in which the evil counselor is imprisoned. So he stressed what the speech stresses, an urgent thirst after novelty, and read it back into Homer where it's not to be found. It is Dante, not Homer, whose Ulysses grows bored in Ithaca, where no amenity, no, not the bed of Penelope,

> Could conquer the inward hunger that I had
> To master earth's experience, and to attain
> Knowledge of man's mind, both the good and bad.
> [*Inferno* XXVI, BINYON'S TRANSLATION]

That was where Tennyson had found a Ulysses

> . . . yearning in desire
> To follow knowledge like a sinking star
> Beyond the utmost bound of human thought,

and that is what Pound is echoing in his own way:

> Knowledge the shade of a shade,
> Yet must thou sail after knowledge.
> [XLVII/236]

In its place in the *Cantos*, that is a doom laid on Odysseus, spoken in the regretful voice of Circe. In making it a doom Pound is faithful to one aspect of Homer, whose Odysseus thought nothing was worse for mortal man than wandering [*Odyssey*, 15:343], and for whom no place was sweeter than home [*Odyssey*, 9:28]. That is his way of compromising Homer as little as possible, all the while he is weaving the hero's need to sail after knowledge right back into a scene in Homer's tenth book, where the Greek is innocent of any such motif. Odysseus is pleading with Circe in her bedroom to be let go to continue his voyage home, and in Canto XXXIX (p. 194) the crucial six lines of her response [*Odyssey* 10:490–495] are reproduced in the Greek word for word and accent for accent (a printer lost one line, but Pound gives the line numbers, and they show what he intended). No other passage of Homer gets transcribed in full anywhere in the long poem.

Possible English for what her Greek says might run: "But first you must complete another journey, to the house of Hades and dread Persephone, to seek the shade of Tiresias of Thebes, the blind seer, whose mind stays firm. To him in death Persephone has given mind, he alone unimpaired while the rest flit about as shades." That is exactly all, and in Canto XXXIX we see it on the page in Homer's very words. But eight Cantos later we encounter it again, memorably paraphrased and amplified:

> Who even dead, yet hath his mind entire!
>   This sound came in the dark
>   First must thou go the road
>   to hell
> And to the bower of Ceres' daughter Proserpine,
> Through overhanging dark, to see Tiresias,
> Eyeless that was, a shade, that is in hell

So full of knowing that the beefy men know less than he,
Ere thou come to thy road's end.
        Knowledge the shade of a shade,
Yet must thou sail after knowledge
Knowing less than drugged beasts. . . .

[XLVII/236]

That seems to make sailing after knowledge a theme of the *Odyssey*, as it was certainly a theme for Ezra Pound. It has been recognizably a theme for Americans, in a country whose Enlightenment heritage sets knowing anything at all above not knowing it. (Never mind knowing what; our schools teach Driver Education, and there is even an American book on how to win at Pac Man.) Quoting, in another connection, "Who even dead, yet hath his mind entire!" Pound hoped he had done sufficient homage to the Greek veneration of intelligence above brute force.

Let us concede, though, that there is intelligence and intelligence, and credit Pound with having intended more than bric-à-brac knowingness. "Who even dead, yet hath his mind entire!" That resonant line is drawn from five words of Homer's, where "mind" is *phrenes*, the whole central part of the body, where you sense that you are yourself and not a shade, and "entire" is *empedoi*, meaning firm on the foot, not slipping. Both are body-words: the midriff, the foot. The intelligence is in the body the way the meaning is in the ideogram: intrinsic and manifested, independent of lexicons, not deconstructible. To have one's mere "mind" entire is a later and less substantial concept. Pound embodies it as best he can with a weight of monosyllables and a stark contrast with the way it is to be dead. Homer's word for how the dead flit about, *aissousin*, held his attention; it is a word he places on show twice in the *Thrones* Cantos [XCVII/675, CII/730]. Disembodied, they have no minds, and flutter. If intelligence is in them, it's the way it's in dictionaries. ("The trouble with the dictionary," Louis Zukofsky liked to say, "is that it keeps changing the subject.") A flitting, a fluttering: that was the Greek sense of disembodiment, and it fascinated Pound, and it was not intelligence. ("Butterflying around all the time," he said once, of aimless speculation. He was speaking of Richard of St. Victor's *cogitatio*, to be distinguished from *meditatio* and the highest thing, *contemplatio*.)

So we are learning how to take the stark physicality of the rites in the first Canto, in particular how to take the need of the shades for blood. They need blood to get what is peculiar to the body, hence to the *phrenes*, the totally embodied intelligence. Without blood, the shades cannot so much as speak. Canto I draws on the part of the *Odyssey* Pound judged *"older* than the rest": Ronald Bush suggests he may have been following Cambridge anthropology here: the tradition of studies that, following on *The Golden Bough*, made Greek intuitions seem so much less cerebral than they had been for Flaxman and Arnold. Or—since there's no knowing whether he so much as read such a book as Jane Harrison's *Themis*—it's conceivable that in ascribing the underworld journey to "fore-time" he was trusting sheer intuition. It implies, anyhow, the Homeric sense of "intelligence," of "knowledge," something so remote from "ideas"—a word whose Greek credentials are post-Homeric—as to have drawn the snort, "Damn ideas, anyhow"; ". . . poor two-dimensional stuff, a scant, scratch covering."

To sail after knowledge, then, is to seek what cannot be found in libraries, no, a wholeness of experience, and I hope I've suggested that, in weaving that phrase back from Dante into Homer, Pound was embellishing less than we may have thought. And it brought him to the superbly colloquial words of Zeus, who, admiring Odysseus, says (in Ezra Pound's English), "With a mind like that he is one of us" [LXXX/512]. That consorts with a fact that has given scandal but need not, that Homer's gods are superbly physical, embodied. Odysseus, for such a god, is "one of us," precisely in having not a Ph.D. but *phrenes*: "the embodiment," said Pound's classmate Bill Williams, "of knowledge."

Having sailed one long circuit after the colloquial, we'll not need a second voyage for the other thing Pound wanted, "the magnificent onomatopoeia." Though "untranslated and untranslatable,"

para thina poluphloisboio thalasses

may serve as our terminal emblem: not boom, rattle and buzz but the rare identity of words with whatever they signify, achieved with the

signifying sound the way Chinese calligraphers achieved it with signifying outline. Pound listened and heard the wave break, and in the
sibilants of *thalasses* "the scutter of receding pebbles": that whole
mighty recurrent phenomenon incarnated in a few syllables represented by a few marks. The way into understanding this is like the
way into understanding Homeric intelligence, something only there
when it is embodied. So meanings are only there when the words em-
body them; otherwise, like the dead, they flutter, *aissousin*. So we're
back, in a circle, to "the actual swing of words spoken," the other
stamp that can authenticate language. Pound first encountered Homer through a man speaking: Mr. Spencer, at the Cheltenham Military Academy, the man "who first declaimed me the *Odyssey*," and
was remembered for it after forty years.

Scholars now imagine an "oral-formulaic" Homer, a poet continually speaking, but speaking with the aid of formulae to fill out the
meter. When Pound, aged 84, heard an exposition of that, he responded that it did not explain "why Homer is so much better than
everybody else." That was very nearly all that he said that day. Why
Homer is so much better than everybody else is a thing there's no way
to explain; nor why, having sailed after knowledge and turned astray,
Ezra Pound should have fulfilled Dante's image with such precision:
transmuted after so much eloquence into a tongue of flame, and a
tongue that went silent.

1984

Poetic Closure

POETIC CLOSURE: A STUDY OF HOW POEMS END,
by Barbara Herrnstein Smith.
University of Chicago Press, 1971.

The British polymath Michael Ayrton informs me that "Shall I compare thee to a summer's day . . ." is the only one of Shakespeare's sonnets that makes sense read bottom upward, beginning with the last line and ending with the first. He has checked all 154. He explained that one needed researches with which to pass the long winter evenings. It is doubtful if even an Essex drizzle could propel such pertinacity without near-successes whose numerousness is the really interesting discovery.

Yet that so many of the sonnets will almost run in reverse, if we neglect some trifling medial snafu: that the Renaissance sonnet in fact is a jungle-gym in which the mind may climb either up or down: these are really, come to think of it, unsurprising discoveries. Symmetry is built into the form. True, the terminal couplet says "This End Down" or "Sonnet Closing Here," and says so whether or not any particular finality of argument has been achieved. (If any has, so much the better.) But with no such formal stoplight a poem can still seem to square things off:

> Clouds and eclipses stain both moon and sun,
> Roses have thorns and silver fountains mud:
> No more be griev'd at that which thou hast done.

—a grave and reconciling homiletic closure, which of course I've contrived from lines 1, 2, 3 of Sonnet xxv, by arranging them in the order 3, 2, 1. And as to why the line Shakespeare designed for an opening makes so plausible a closing, that raises the general question, what constitutes poetic closure?

Mere cessation does not; for instance Swinburne's "When the hounds of spring . . ." stops but doesn't close. I read it to a class the other day and after line 56 no one could tell me whether it was over or not. It was: Swinburne omitted, evidently, to supply a terminating ritual. Such as what? What is it, in the absence of a story concluded or a demonstration completed, that persuades us a poem has come to a proper ending?

Barbara Herrnstein Smith is not quite the first modern critic to have asked this question (the indefatigable I. A. Richards wondered in an essay "How Does a Poem Know When It Is Finished?"), but she is certainly the first to examine it at any leisure. *Poetic Closure* is a quietly original book: graceful, concise, page by page a pleasure to read, but above all persuasive in its calm preoccupation, as though to say, there is much here to find out.

As there is. We know a great deal more about the cellular tissue of poems than we do about their structural ceremonies. Years of critical concentration on images and their interaction have promoted adeptness at distinguishing live from dead tissue; but what is the end of a poem, and how are we satisfied that it has gotten there? The Blimpish reader is likely to respond that, gad, Sir, when poets wrote regular verse one didn't have all this damned nonsense about whether the poem was finished or not; to which Mrs. Smith's reply might run, agreed, Sir, some forms have built-in closure; but (1) this turns out to be an unimportant aspect of the question, and (2) what about poems like Pope's Epistles, that measure themselves out in couplets? Do they merely stop? Or close? And if they close, how?

That expectations of a complex order are aroused and fulfilled, that they take many specifiable forms corresponding to modes of closure equally diverse: these are themes whose realization by Mrs. Smith the reviewer has no need to paraphrase, since the interested reader will be sensible enough to acquire the book. One topic deserves touching on. Modern closure turns out to be the special topic one would expect, but for unexpected reasons.

The modern poem does not, as one might suppose, resemble that generic non-objective painting that has been hung upside down somewhere at least annually since about 1910. It is, oddly enough, the Renaissance poem one can hang upside down, or read backwards. The modern poem—Mrs. Smith puts this differently though not incompatibly—is a curiously one-way affair, its beginning and its end very sharply distinct.

"Let us go then, you and I." "Till human voices wake us, and we drown." Nothing formal, but everything semantic, tells us which of these lines will serve to open a poem, which to close it. And when the phrasing hasn't this inevitability the structure has: William Carlos Williams' mode of syntactic ordering is as one-way, and at the end as final, as a leap from a cliff.

The 20th century end may not claim to be an ending. It may resolve the poem's business by simply bringing to sharp phrasing what kind of undertaking an older sort of poem made from these materials would be. Shakespeare's Sonnet xviii, forwards, is a Renaissance deployment and dispersal of possibilities. Backward, it's a 20th century itemizing and discarding of comparisons not worth making, which ends, where the Renaissance began, with a line at once resigned and strangely hopeful, as though a poem were still possible: "Shall I compare thee to a summer's day?"

1971

The Trouble of Ending

THE COLLECTED STORIES OF SEÁN O'FAOLÁIN.
Atlantic–Little, Brown, 1983. 1304 pp.

Michael Frank O'Donovan of Cork made up the name "Frank O'Connor" to write under because in Ireland writing could get you a bad repute, the kind bigots would torment your relatives with. His contemporary John Whelan, also of Cork, made the name "Seán O'Faoláin" to exist under by simply putting "John Whelan" back into the native speech it had been derived from, thus setting one detail of disordered Ireland right. So those names and their motives attest to besetting themes: bigotry (mindless); patriotism (romantic).

O'Faoláin has now lived to be eighty-three and also, what he surely never envisaged, the unrivaled grand old man of Irish letters. When I visited him seven years ago I luckily knew enough to say "Shawn Oh-Fay-*Lawn*," which is as near as anyone expects of a foreign larynx. Laying phonetic snares for aliens had been part of the business of the romantic patriots. He lived in the Dublin suburb they now call Dún Laoghaire, though to ask directions you must say "Dunleary." In a simpler time it was Kingstown, but the patriots had chosen to remember the "Leary" who was High King in St. Patrick's time and never as far as I know came near the place. That way they could obliterate the authentic "King" of the Kingstown seaport, England's "Sailor-King" William IV.

His wife, Eileen, who didn't abide pipe smoke, he had met at an Irish-language summer school they went to in the fervent days, as long ago as when he'd been young enough to dip her ponytail in the inkwell. Of the Irish tongue he'd now say only, picking his words, that he was "glad to have known it." Romantic patriotism was for vanished times. And need I say that I'm glad to have known him?—erect, blue-eyed, and bracing.

The copyright dates of the stories in this book span the fifty years from 1932. There are ninety of them; that many times at least he has sat down to a new beginning, undertaking anew to place an Archimedes' lever, shift a world to where we can see it.

A man who's outraged at three buckos from Blarney Lane who've asked at his door for his six Easter lilies for the funeral of "some wan I never heard of in me life before"—a kid dead in the fever hospital— that man has "refused the dead" and ruined an evening. He yatters on, justifying his outrage. "Why did they come to *me* for *my* poor little flowers? . . . Me poor little six Easter lilies that I reared, that I looked after as if they were my own children. . . ." A boy who was there lets the memory pour over him twenty years later: "It was like hearing an old, old tune on a brass band; or the sound of church bells on a wet Sunday morning." Yes, it's that familiar: Passions so bitter, founded on no more than a fancy that the buckos were being presumptuous. Things got so tense they thought to send the boy home. "I saw the six lilies, calm as sleep, by the pale light of the hall. The dead child's face would be just as pale." It's a country where boys know the pallor of a dead child's face.

With what indirections, what silences, these people bully and blackmail one another! Benjy is forty-one and has a girl and for three months his mother assails him with tales of St. Augustine's mother, Monica, whose heart neglect had broken. " 'But,' she said cheerfully, 'he mended it again, God bless him and protect him. When he turned from his bad ways! Ah, that was a lovely scene, the two of them sitting in the window, and the sun going down over the sea. Hand in hand. Mother and son. Lovely! Ah! Lovely! Lovely!' "

Irish Men Afraid to Wed, ran a Dublin poster of 1956, hoping to shock you so you'd buy a paper. Mothers can be a component of their fear. But when Benjy's mother and the priest and a burst ulcer, all three, have recalled him to pious ways, and "she knew that mother love had triumphed at last," O'Faoláin's sinister little tale "Childy-bawn" is only half over. Benjy's devotion now smothers her. Out of edged love he humors what he's learned were her secret vices. But the brandy he pours for her proves to be but a fraction of what she once tippled on the sly, the coins he gives her to plunge on horses but a tithe of her extravagant wagers of yore. She's soon frantic for the old estrangement. " 'Go on!' she bawled. 'Go on, and get married! And torment some other misfortunate woman. The way you're tormenting me!' "

The last we see of Benjy's fiancée she's slapping his face, calling him a creeping rat, a cringing worm, then bursting into a flood of tears on his shoulder. He marries her five years later, mother finally dead. So runs a Happy Ending, Irish style: nearly as happy as when they at last established the Republic, and promptly had a Civil War about the minutiae of who it was double-crossed whom in effecting the settlement.

No, "Childybawn" is not a political parable, not at all; but all Irish epiphenomena emerge from the one tangle of passions, a reason James Joyce found it so easy to make state and family image one another (think of the Christmas Dinner scene in the *Portrait*). O'Faoláin is rather cool toward Joyce, whom he thinks overliterary, but he too would be hard put to distinguish his own domestic themes from his public ones. Here are two drunken Irishmen in Paris:

" 'You dirty little Freemason!' says Golden, baring his two teeth, and his lips glistening in the moonlight.

" 'You rotten little Puritan!' says Georgie with the hate of hell in his voice.

"At that the two of them stopped dead as if they were a pair of waxworks out of the Musée Grevin, horrifed by the sight of the hate in one another's faces. They were so horrified that they burst into a wild fit of laughing. They rocked there in one another's arms, falling over one another with the bitterness of the laughing and the hatred and the shame."

One thing the short story in English can't quite shake off is its magazine provenance. It is the commercial form par excellence, and the more accomplishment you bring to it the more you court slickness, contrivance, the neat nail driven home, the quick paraphrase to assist the dentist's office browser. "An Enduring Friendship" ought to end with what I've just quoted, or perhaps a paragraph later. It ends instead with some wordy wisdom: "For, of course, the truth of the whole matter is that once you go on a drunk with a fellow you're stuck with him for life; and in Ireland every bitter word we say has to be paid for sooner or later in shame, in pity, in kindness, and perhaps even in some queer sort of perverted love."

Alas; and too many of the *Collected Stories* trail off into some such blur, or else (like the otherwise admirable "Charlie's Greek") get a neat ending by exploiting a mannerism. ("We had completed the medallion of our love," is Charlie's way to explain why he's through with an affair, and its third repetition is our author's mechanical way to signal that he's through with the story.)

It's a desperately difficult form, and has had few masters. Coming to an end as though there were exactly no more to say: that is the special difficulty, one O'Faoláin in ninety stories has vanquished a good deal fewer than ninety times. He never begins less than well, and his middles have substance. But where then? Irish truths are bitter, their protagonists often fanatical. The fanaticism is rhetorical, tragicomic. Joyce had a way with final sentences that draw back in cold detachment from the blather. He had a way too of rejoining last page to first: nothing concluded, also nothing accomplished. O'Faoláin's temperament has rejected both these ways without hitting on a better. The trouble of ending, that's the Irish trouble. They've ended nothing yet, not even now.

1984

Dear Miss Weaver

DEAR MISS WEAVER: HARRIET SHAW WEAVER
1876–1961, *by Jane Lidderdale and Mary Nicholson.*
Viking, 1970.

Fourteen years ago I climbed the labyrinthine stairs to the lair of Wyndham Lewis, and had pointed out from a landing window the lights of a flat said to be, or to have been, Harriet Weaver's. Should I have made a point of trying to visit her? I don't know. Anyhow I didn't. It seemed as unthinkable as rapping on a Queen's door.

She had then been for forty years the mystery woman of contemporary Anglo-Saxon letters, essential portions of which she was understood to have midwifed. "To Harriet Shaw Weaver," ran the severe dedication of Eliot's *Selected Essays*, "in Gratitude, and in Recognition of her Services to English Letters." It was as though King James had dedicated the Bible to somebody.

And I had read, in John Slocum's library, dozens of the long letters James Joyce wrote to her. She had received almost every scrap of *Finnegans Wake* as he wrote it, and it was her opinion, her commendation, that he kept soliciting. Moreover, it was on remittances from Harriet Weaver that the Joyce family lived for some twenty years. And in her role as "The Egoist Press" she had published *A Portrait of the Artist as a*

Young Man when no established publisher would touch it; and she had also published *Prufrock and Other Observations*, and Lewis's *Tarr*, and Pound's *Quia Pauper Amavi* which contains his "Propertius," and Marianne Moore's first volume, the 1920 *Poems*. She had even published *Ulysses*, in an edition excessively rare because so many copies were confiscated.

And for five years she edited *The Egoist*. It ended, Pound had said, with 185 subscribers, which means that she subsidized it heavily. *The Egoist* appeared bimonthly, and like better circulated magazines—like the *Saturday Evening Post*, say—it ran a "Serial Story." But for 18 months *The Egoist*'s serial was *A Portrait of the Artist as a Young Man*. Nothing less distinguished would do. (What was the *Post* serializing in those years?)

Yet after so many decades' indispensability she remained utterly mysterious. When I wanted to put some of her Joyce correspondence into a book my letter was answered not by Harriet Weaver but by a British lawyer, who let me know that it should not have been possible for me to see the letters at all. That was the kind of wall you ran into. Joyce himself did not know for months the source of the first major benefaction she settled on him, anonymously, through solicitors.

So, nine years after her death at 85, a 500-page biography, scrupulously researched and clearly written, cannot help seeming (though its authors make no portentous claims) to be offering to unveil a mystery. Rather, it deepens the mystery. Thus we learn that the account books Harriet Weaver kept for her various publishing enterprises were elaborately doctored to hide the 3000 pounds' worth of losses she made up over nine years. It would have taken a team of CPA's, for instance, to deduce that Joyce's sales were not earning the royalties he kept receiving, or that the one *Egoist* book to get back its costs earned just two shillings ninepence for the firm and 75 times that much for T. S. Eliot, the author. But it was not from accountants or shareholders that she struggled to conceal such facts: it was from herself. (She "enjoyed doing arithmetic.")

She concealed things from her family likewise, chiefly, it seems, by imposing the convention that some matters were not discussed. The one relative, brother Alfred, who is known to have read Joyce's *Por-*

trait found it "repulsive and blasphemous," but apparently told only his diary, not Harriet. Another wall went up about 1936; it was none of the business of her literary friends that she was ringing doorbells, marching in streets, writing checks on behalf of the British Communist Party, nor were her Communist friends allowed to learn of her literary alliances. When she hid her C.P. card in a volume of the *Encyclopaedia Britannica* and went on attending meetings of the Labour Party, it was less a Bolshevik slyness she was conforming to than a habitual pattern of life.

"I shall think of her when I think of goodness," wrote Samuel Beckett at her death. Her goodness was a beneficent stillness. Everyone remarks on the calm she imposed. Pound remembered for fifty years "the stillness of the first encounter" they had. In whatever group, he recalled, her presence was "not like silence, come gradually, but like a sudden stopping of all noise." That quiet was a late Victorian quality. She was a Victorian survivor in a noisy century, bearing about her the calm of opulent lawns and elms, but racked, in the new time, by guilt for inherited means, of which all her life she scrupulously disinvested herself, to the immeasurable benefit of letters.

Which seems clear enough, but still unclear. The woman herself evades her scrupulous biographers, and when the book is closed continues to evade the most attentive reader. What is missing? Well, turn to page 64 and look at photograph 9: Harriet in 1905, aged 29, on the beach with her little niece and her brother Harold: a beautiful smiling girl, alertly happy. Then look at the subsequent photographs: the set mouth, the lowered eyelids; look for instance at the mask of frozen reserve Man Ray photographed in 1924; and try to persuade yourself that you are looking at the woman you saw on that beach. What catastrophic internal slippage banked so much warmth, transformed so much spontaneity into punctilious duty?

There is no way to tell. The authors sensibly don't try. On the other hand they don't explicitly ask. In their one brush against her psychic life they note only "a total lack of interest in the other sex, except as human beings," and call this attitude "by no means uncommon among young women of her generation, class, and interests. It was enough, for them, to be free to choose not to marry."

But Harriet seems not to have chosen; she seems to have frozen. Suffragettes, feminists, literary rebels, political rebels, finally Marxists: with all these she identified her energies, her being. Down under all that reserve, all that guarded, generous, responsible *functioning*, that mask-like calming presence, lay, one conjectures, a person, cryogenically suspended, never to waken. Perhaps only Henry James could have written an intelligible biography of Harriet Shaw Weaver, and he would have been guessing.

1971

On, Romanticism

ON, ROMANTICISM, *by Donald Sutherland*.
New York University Press, 1971.

Some years ago Donald Sutherland wrote a book about Gertrude Stein which among its other brilliances brilliantly employed an adaptation of Miss Stein's famous style. That was astute of him. Part of a writer's labor is to develop just the configurations of language that will serve a personal vision, and the critic who is going to write about that vision should have the sense to glean hints on how to do it from his writer.

There may be danger, however, when he later undertakes to write about something else. The devices he learned may have programmed themselves into his language habits, a distracting system of tics. And behold, on the opening page of his new book, having divided All Style into three parts, Mr. Sutherland drops into the purest Stein stutter:

"Though anyone is still free to like style undivided or to like all three of it or to prefer one of it over the other two or any two over the third, in a period there is bound to be a general preference of one or two over the remainder because the preferred style or styles suit the style of living which most people in the period have or wish for."

He doesn't carry on for 450 pages like that, else I should not have survived to write this review, but he does drop into the Stein manner periodically, and into manners related to the Stein manner. They may all be summarized as being just too cutesy-poo for anything, and cutesy-pooness keeps rearing its perfumed head at intervals all the way to the last chapter, which consists in its entirety of three punctuation marks: a period for Classicism (finality), a comma for Romanticism (continuity), a semicolon for the Baroque (tension).

There's much more to the book, luckily, and having served warning that to enter it is to risk environmental hazards, I can move to more interesting matters. On, Romanticism, says the title, the comma making the phrase into a cheer. On! Onward! Mr. Sutherland is highly in favor of Romanticism, and hopes to see it revive and gather its energies. This doesn't mean expecting that next year's artists will pick up the dropped stitches of 1830, because Romanticism is not by his account tied to a period in history. It's a recurrent stylistic mode.

In the same way, Mr. Sutherland's Classicism is more than an historical phenomenon to be associated with Romans in white togas. It denotes a recurrent taste for the simple, the public, the static. Nor is his third division of style, the Baroque, confined to visual goings-on in 17th century Bavaria. It's the art of the Grand Gesture, whenever and wherever found. And he sees Style, the handwriting of the mind, as tending always, at all times, in all places, to be dominated by one of these three manners, with characteristics of the other two mixed in.

This leads to strange bedfellows. Virgil, who wrote the *Aeneid* in Augustan Rome and would be listed by most of us as quintessentially Classical, turns out to be a highly Romantic writer with some Baroque touches, and Gerard Manley Hopkins, whom chronology would identify as a post-Romantic, is an almost pure case of Baroque.

And a pure case of Classicism? Oddly enough none is provided, perhaps because if they exist the author can't beat up any interest in them. Though he has been a professor of "Classics," which means nothing more than "things written in Greek and Latin," Mr. Sutherland feels no obligation to profess any interest in "Classicism."

He may even be telling us, subliminally, that creative artists have none either. From the way he talks about Classicism it sounds like a polar featurelessness, uninhabitable but of use to the literary theorist as a place to plot coordinates from. Mapmakers in the same way would be lost without the North Pole, though nobody contemplates living there.

So that's one peculiar thing about *On, Romanticism*, that in practice its threefold division shakes down to two. It's after all an idealized division. Classic, Baroque, Romantic. Finality, Tension, Continuity. With its aid, Mr. Sutherland can offer remarks about anything at all. Parties, for instance:

"Classicism is a public ceremonial, the Baroque a private orgy which disturbs the whole neighborhood, the Romantic a party given by a private person but thrown open to all and affording a great variety of entertainment." (So call the police to complain that they're being Baroque next door.)

Or gesture. The Classical gesture, we learn, is generally practical, as when a hand holds something. The Baroque gesture expresses less the action than the energy put into it, the psychic energy as well as the physical. The Romantic gesture is inconclusive and governed "by a sense of variable motion." And there you have it: Julia Child, Charles Atlas, Zsa Zsa.

This could turn into an erudite party game, and writing, for Mr. Sutherland, tends to be a kind of game. He's been classical scholar enough to know where to get rules. For any way of dividing up a topic is an aid to what Roman orators and Renaissance schoolmasters called "invention," which means the technique of finding things to say. I'm inclined to suspect that Mr. Sutherland's three categories have been useful to him chiefly as aids to invention, ways of getting a new theme started.

But I may wrong him, it may just look that way, and he may be stuck with the implications of his own campaign for Romanticism. It's Romantic to ramble about the way he does, whereas if he seemed to be taking his system seriously he'd be either very tidy, which is Classical, or pulled between systems and facts, which is Baroque.

So we come back to the things his preoccupations permit him to talk about, which are Hopkins, Shelley, "Don Giovanni," the neglected Renaissance poet Torquato Tasso, the wall-paintings of Pompeii, and Virgil. He never fails to have interesting things to say.

Nor does he fail, in his Romantic way, to be at times eccentric beyond belief, as when perhaps half his discussion of Virgil's poetry is devoted to minor poems Virgil very possibly didn't write, by way of setting up a view of the *Aeneid* that makes it float "on a leisurely kind of nihilism or in an atmosphere of the false dream."

He's best—this too is Romantic—on unexpected details, like the account of Mozart's librettist, Da Ponte, writing words for three operas at once, each evening's stint being at "Don Giovanni." "He began by settling down with plenty of Tokay and a very practiced girl of sixteen—his Muse, he says, for all three libretti." This found its way into the text when Don Giovanni was made to call for three dances going on at once, and Mozart accordingly wrote the three dances, using three small orchestras on stage to play them. The whole accords with one theme of "Don Giovanni," which is "a suicidal impulse toward the exhaustion of all the senses."

That's typical of the method. What starts out like an anecdote turns out to be a thematic key, according to an engaging theory that creative minds, especially Romantic ones, are likely to spin their webs out of anything near to hand. We are even invited to fancy Mozart brooding on his own name, and finding in it the terminal letters of the alphabet ("music from A to Z or from Z to A") surrounded by MORT, which means Death.

Or, reading about Pompeiian wall-paintings, we come to a page about the walls they were painted on—not squared stones, but a core of rubble sandwiched between plaster facings—and discover that we are pondering a view of reality. For the wall's interior is therefore mysterious, "loose and alive," and so Roman is this that Vitruvius, the Roman writer on architecture, has little to say about structure and much about wind, air, water, light, his buildings situated "less on a foundation than in a climate" and his whole intuition of materials tending "to ignore the solid in favor of mobilities and aerations." (Fine word, "aerations.")

Thus the Roman wall "is understood to be not only permeable to the elements but composed of them," and we needn't wonder if a Pompeian painter felt he was communing with a latent and living third dimension. By the time we've read this far we're no longer looking at the paintings, we've virtually become the painter.

One reads Mr. Sutherland for cadenzas like that, which illustrate his own aphorism that "if one entertains a hypothesis, it ought to entertain in turn." There's no way to be sure that any Roman, or even any Roman painter, really felt as Mr. Sutherland does about those porous walls, but it's entertaining to suppose so.

It's entertaining, also, to posit that Virgil wrote a doubtful poem about the Tomb of the Gnat, and then read the *Aeneid* in its light. A logician would aver drily that if the Gnat's Tomb is to bear that weight of insight we'd better be sure it belongs in the Virgilian pattern, but then a logician would be Classical (or Baroque, I'm not sure) and we're being Romantic here.

And a fussy person, having made his way through this long Disneyland of a book, would protest that the details he'd like to savor again would be most easily retrievable via an Index. But what could be more Classical than an Index, a Place for Everything and Everything in Its Place? Mr. Sutherland, true to his lights, has neither compiled one nor permitted his publishers to have one compiled, and the book's radiance is left to fade like that *summum* of Romantic connoisseurship, a sunset.

1971

Coleridge

COLERIDGE, THE DAMAGED ARCHANGEL,
by Norman Fruman. Braziller, 1971.

Coleridge dreaded nothing more than sleep, such were the nightmares from which he would wake screaming: ". . . a Woman whose features were blended with darkness catching hold of my right eye and attempting to pull it out—I caught hold of her arm fast—a horrid feel—. . . When I awoke my right eyelid swelled."

He beheld waking horrors as well, for instance in Germany "a most infamous dance called the Waltzen—There are perhaps 20 couple— the Man & his Partner embrace each other, arms round waists, & knees almost touching, & then whirl round & round, the whole 20 couple, 40 times round at least, to lascivious music."

Given the perils of being either conscious or unconscious, it is unsurprising that he should have become an opium addict, the most eminent one as it happens in intellectual history. What is arresting is the amount of work he got done, and the still greater amount he talked of getting done, and all the jottings as well in the copious notebooks that two centuries after his birth are still being edited.

More arresting still, it's no longer orthodox to attribute the poetic revolution of 1798 to his tame friend Wordsworth's "Lyrical Ballads," the book in which Thomas De Quincey for one found "an absolute revelation of untrodden worlds." Wordsworth, it is now routinely supposed in seminars, was but the dogged executant of Coleridge's ideas.

Not that it's easy, in producible texts, to document what those ideas were. But reconstituting them from the chaos of hints is another seminar activity. And in the fatal seminar tug toward mere ideas it's easy to suppose that English sensibility long ago was revolutionized by ideas, ideas like a professor's or a graduate student's. So the hero of the revolution has come to be not Wordsworth but his friend the idea-man par excellence, ateem with vast projects he never (alas) got around to finishing, knittings-together of all human thought; the corrector of Locke and Newton, the anticipator of Freud and—who knows—Einstein; the archetypal literary theorist, in fact the inventor of "organic" criticism and of all our modern notions of felt unity: Coleridge, of course.

Coleridge, "the Da Vinci of literature." Like Da Vinci he wrote a poem or two himself, notably "The Ancient Mariner" and "Kubla Khan." If you assemble all the commentaries on the former, you find that it symbolizes Absolutely Everything. As for the latter, it claims the distinction of not having been written in any ordinary way. Coleridge said he actually dreamed "Kubla Khan," words and all, in a narcotic haze. He was just writing the revelation down when some fool interrupted him and all but the brilliant beginning was lost forever. It's the generic Coleridgean story; everything always did get interrupted.

Nine years ago Elisabeth Schneider took leave to doubt the story of "Kubla Khan." Far from being the sole miraculous virgin birth in literature, it seemed to her a poem Coleridge was writing in the ordinary way, relying a good deal on memories of Milton's cadences. Having got stuck, he invented the story about the dream—for genius doesn't simply get stuck—and sent scholars happily ransacking cloud-cuckoo-land for clues to the working of the creative unconscious.

Miss Schneider's book, *Coleridge, Opium and "Kubla Khan,"* met an instructive reception. Though one reviewer "gloomily" predicted years of contentiousness, the issue was in fact quietly evaded. College anthologies still retail the dream-story, and the book which had after all implied Coleridge, on one famous point at least, to have lied shamelessly, went out of print without achieving even the Kleenex-resurrection of paperbackhood.

So went one potentially spectacular skirmish on a battleground the general reader tends not to be told about. For it is a restless field, a sort of DMZ, with sentries always alert. During more than a century this or that note, this or that unobtrusive article, has elaborated a scandalous possibility: that Coleridge was not above lifting sentences, passages, pages, even whole poems from obscure sources, frequently German. In fact the word "plagiarism" hovers in the vicinity of Coleridgean studies with sufficient persistence to have called forth rituals for exorcising it.

These rituals contain several plausible elements: that Coleridge was often in a hurry; that given a pervasive mental climate men writing on similar themes will often express themselves rather alike; that Coleridge's weaknesses, given his work's vast extent, should not weigh down his great strengths; that he had developed the ideas on his own before he stole the mere phraseology. And finally, what is originality anyway? What counts, we are sturdily told, is what he did with his borrowings.

Which is where Professor Fruman comes in. His very long book has some dealings with all these themes. Thus as to what Coleridge did with his borrowings, the answer is usually that he passed them off as his own: as simple and embarrassing as that.

I can't begin to summarize the evidence. Fruman can barely summarize it himself. His text runs to a quarter-million well composed words, plus half that much again in notes so diverse they imply almost another book. He has learned from Miss Schneider's misfortune, it may be, the danger of putting forth a volume tidy enough to be deprecated and then ignored. *Coleridge, The Damaged Archangel* can be envisaged tumbling into tranquil seminars with the plop of a winged elephant. No way to ignore that, nor to go on with one's soothing tasks till it's been dealt with.

More than half the book deals resolutely with the plagiarisms, and when, under Fruman's guidance, we've subtracted these from the vast Coleridge canon, surprisingly little is left. Even in the famous *Biographia Literaria* what makes show of consecutive sense is commonly cribbed, and what rises to oracular pronouncement—for instance the paragraph on the Primary and Secondary Imagination, or the one on "the poet, described in ideal perfection"—is in strict terms virtually meaningless.

Not negligible, though; Fruman would have us "value the famous passages for what they are, prose poems [in which] Coleridge condensed a very broad range of ideas from a variety of disciplines into a glorious hymn of praise to man's creativity, as he understood it, and as it was idealized by German metaphysics."

Instead they are constantly cited, for instance in courses on "Criticism," as though they explained something, or helped us understand works of art. That is the kind of procedure that bores intelligent students with "Literary Criticism."

The professors who misuse such paragraphs have the rather good excuse that it was Coleridge himself who invited us to view them as capstones of a reasoned and penetrable theory, though he had no real notion of the theory's elements nor any idea what would go into the vast expository volumes that he often asserted were on their way to the printer. His "critical theory" was, to put it shortly, a hoax, like so much else.

What was driving him? Chiefly the need to feel self-esteem, the self-esteem of the productive and omnicompetent writer. The need will arouse a humbling sympathy in anyone who reads of his deprived and terror-ridden youth. Floggings and humiliations were the daily routine in the school where he was virtually imprisoned as an orphan, and the need to excel was omnipresent and hedged round with terrors. If you didn't excel you were apt to end up a copying-clerk, or still worse, a conscripted seaman. It may have been there that Coleridge formed the habit of swiping excellence ready-made. It was certainly there that he developed the compulsion to be known for excelling, anywhere, always, by whatever means, in whatever discipline. He would be a poet, for instance.

Until the meeting with Wordsworth he wrote frigid and cliche-ridden verse. After, for a while, he wrote verse of a singular, poignant purity. Well enough, but he was unwilling for Wordsworth to get credit even for being a good example, and so muddied the story that today it is fashionable to call Coleridge the innovator of the two. And Wordsworth's very large contribution to "The Ancient Mariner" went unacknowledged. And "Kubla Khan," as we've seen, he deceived us about; and as to his third major poem, the fragmentary "Christabel". . . .

Well, as to that, and as to "Kubla Khan" also, he never faced the question why he couldn't finish them. Here Prof. Fruman breaks original ground. These poems, on his showing, far from being fabulous tales, were so personal, in ways inaccessible to Coleridge, that his inability to go on with them is bound up with his inability to resolve problems he couldn't even confide to diaries: problems of outraged sexuality, of impotence, of incestuous desires.

This part of the account draws heavily on Coleridge's records of his terrifying dreams. Yet if the themes came from deep terrors, the poems did not. Coleridge deserves, and receives, full credit for the miraculous word-joinery that, as far as it goes, is unlike anything else in the language.

He bore terrible burdens, not the least the burden of having to live up to the reputation he felt compelled to create for himself. There came to be no way he could afford to seem anything less than the supreme intellect of his time. Hence the grandiose projects, the unfinished drafts, the much-advertised unwritten books. Hence the plagiarism that became a habit like dope, answering the need to fill pages with foggy profundities.

The man who emerges from this shaking story achieved a little verse and a little prose that are irreplaceable, and managed not to go stark raving mad. Had he gone the way of Kit Smart we should be ready to understand. Since he didn't there will be an inclination to throw bricks at Prof. Fruman, who is unlikely to be thanked for the

Coleridge he has given us. He will be blamed instead for taking away a Coleridge who never existed, who would have vanquished, even temporarily, no demons, but would have been fit (but for lacking a Ph.D., and that might be rigged up) to teach a graduate seminar in Comp. Lit.

1971

Literary Biographies

Early alerts around the reviewing circuitry were jangling in May; my own repose was broken by calls from five different editors. In June Harcourt published Deirdre Bair's *Samuel Beckett: A Biography*, 640 pages of text and 83 of notes, with a heft (3 lbs.) contrived to apprise us that we finger monumentality. Like other literary biographies with which it weighs in—Mark Schorer's *Sinclair Lewis*, Carlos Baker's *Ernest Hemingway*, Joseph Blotner's *William Faulkner*, Richard Ellmann's *James Joyce*[1]—the life of Beckett makes its initial assertion by sheer physique. Here we have, ponderously, Fact. If *Waiting for Godot*, a mere fascicle, blows about in our minds, $19.95 will buy us the brick to tie it to.

And lo, the lead reviews flowered everywhere: testimony rather to Beckett than to the book, in which you'd not read past page 10 if you'd never heard of its subject. Yet attention to the story of his life is a puzzling testimony, since nothing of Beckett's own writing has ever received such a press.

Why this sudden access of caring? *Time* and the *New York Times Book Review*, *Newsweek* and the *New York Review of Books* did not spring to si-

[1] Which may have been the target book for Harcourt's designer; with 30 percent fewer words, the Bair cedes it less than 10 percent in weight. Not that her words are weightier, but her paper is.

multaneous attention and dedicate their most prominent space when *Endgame* appeared, or *How It Is*, or *Happy Days*. Hole-in-corner notices were the rule, or silence, or expressions of waning patience.

Beckett, we've gathered for years from the large-circulation papers, is a tedious minor author who buries the human race in sand and then stomps on it, and his biography would seem to belong with the Life Cycle of the Furbish Lousewort on the list of a minor university press. But no, the involvement of Harcourt Brace Jovanovich now testifies to something Lucelings and *Times*men have never had words for, his power to trigger the kind of chronic itch only a biographer seems able to scratch. If the great public has been widely tipped off that it doesn't want to read Sam Beckett, it's also been made party to a consensus that something needs to be done about him, and the biographer's is the tested American strategy for doing something about unassimilable phenomena like Howard Hughes and literary genius.

This is true even though a literary man draws his claim on our attention from hours totally hidden to scrutiny: hours spent sitting and thinking, consulting dictionaries, driving a pen, staring out the window, scratching through what was just written, anagramming, doodling. Even Dr. Johnson, whose works excluding the *Dictionary* fill 20 volumes, seems in Boswell's pages to be doing little save talk; periodically we're told that in this year he published so-and-so, having seemingly stepped off Boswell's stage to write it.

And what would you learn if you could sit for two hours watching Shakespeare write? Less than there is to be learned sitting for two hours watching Sam Beckett play billiards. I derived from that session (London, 1964) a lasting vision of his kinetic presence, released by joy in the game: a springy lope, a delight in Newtonian precision.

His tie draped itself over the cue as he lined up his shot; grey eye and bony hand drew a slow bead like a Hemingway rifleman; then the gaunt frame uncoiled in a mime of exultation when some syntax of clicks and rebounds unrolled as foreseen, to alter the table's geography as decisively as one Beckett sentence can alter that of a paragraph. Complex and lively, he lives in a different world from his narrators, who take none but a grudging and morose pleasure in anything, and for insight into his way with them I'll stake that evening against Deirdre Bair's whole *Life*, where his working time is spent disguising the confession and reminiscence he is somehow compelled to publish.

But I'm not reviewing her book (I've done that elsewhere): here I'm using it, and its probable prototype, the Ellmann *Joyce* too, for a probe of assumptions such books cater to, notably the assumption that a writer's life and his work are related as truth to fiction, truth being—surely?—the substantial quiddity, fiction its image in unstable water.

"Chapter Five: 1930–31"; "Chapter Six: 1931–32"; "Chapter Seven: 1933": dates like adjacent boxes, as place and number and citation (Bair has 1,670 numbered citations, Ellmann over 2,400) stiffen with their ankylosed vertebrae the recounting of long-ago years.

What was lived in those years a researcher who wasn't there must piece together from talk or from pieces of paper—letters, legal documents, diaries, fictions.

Letters can be a great help. Ellmann's Joyce would be a notably ghostlier figure save for more than 150 letters in which Jim made his brother Stannie his chief confidant during an anguished time (1902–12) of poverty and struggle. Beckett in his comparable period, the 1930's, confided to a man named Thomas McGreevy in letters without which Ms. Bair's account of those years would be thin indeed. But she pushes her luck.

"McGreevy," she solemnly assures us, "was the only person to whom Beckett has ever been absolutely truthful, to whom he told his innermost, deeply secret thoughts." That asserts that Beckett has been less than truthful with absolutely everybody else, and we're not told how she knows there were no other candors. I'll content myself with remarking that such a run of letters is apt to make a biographer feel temporarily omniscient, and pass on to another oddity.

"In many cases," we are next told, "these letters parallel Beckett's creative writings, for he transfers passages from them into his fiction and drama, from the briefest image and scantiest phrase to whole paragraphs."

Now. We're later to learn that Beckett's candor with McGreevy terminated in 1945, when he found his old friend back in Dublin toadying to the clergy. The great creative period began a year after that: all but two of the novels, all of the plays. So how did the letters to McGreevy seep into them?

Perhaps Beckett kept copies or drafts of the letters, in which case their status as unrestrained effusions grows suspect. Perhaps both letters and plays preserve copyings from a third source such as a diary, in which case we must imagine Beckett amassing verbal material for years before he'd any idea what to do with it. Perhaps Beckett, elsewhere represented as forgetting so much, remembered chunks of old correspondence verbatim. Perhaps . . .

But whatever we opt for, we're deprived of the simple model in which parallelism with the letters helps confirm that whole pages of the novels and plays are outpourings.

More public documents too can mislead or get miscopied. The first printing of Prof. Ellmann's *James Joyce* had the subject born in Rathmines instead of Rathgar, and the book still places Joyce's 1882 baptism in a church that was not opened until 1904.

Ellmann in turn has brought Joycean expertise to a review of Ms. Bair's book, noting that she places La Baule, on the Breton coast, in Switzerland (thus getting the Joyce family's 1939 movements into an impossible muddle) and has Nora Joyce urging Beckett to cooperate with her husband's biographer at a date when she'd been dead two years. (One may add that Bair's apt to be unlucky with Joyce, ascribing a circular form to *Ulysses* where it's not to be found, or depicting his bereaved friends playing his two recordings from *Anna Livia Plurabelle* though he made only one.)

Such slips, of a kind familiar to any grader of sophomore papers, suggest that large areas of information are being gotten up rather fast, for they go askew when the biographer lacks some knowledge more general than the errant fact.

Though more general, it may be trivial. Joyce was baptized in the small Roundtown Chapel of Ease, now demolished. Prof. Ellmann placed the event in the successor church, St. Joseph's, Terenure, because the Chapel of Ease records are now preserved there, and we'll hardly flunk him just for not knowing that.

Less trivial is the first event in Deirdre Bair's book, the confronta-
tion between a piece of paper and a repeated statement of Beckett's,
involving as it does a truly substantive generality.

Beckett alleges that he was born on Good Friday the 13th (13 April
1906), but his birth certificate specifies 13 May. However we choose to
resolve this we commit a judgment weightier than the facts we're re-
solving: of the casualness or otherwise of Irish record-keeping, of the
punctiliousness or otherwise of Beckett's parents, of the credibility of
numerous witnesses (duly invoked) who think it uncharacteristic
that the parents should not have been punctilious; finally, of the pro-
bity of Beckett himself, concerning whom, in dismissing the problem, the biographer writes:

> Whether or not [Good Friday 13] is true, he mentions the date with
> carefully feigned diffidence to scholars and critics. Should they seize
> upon it as being important, he shrugs offhandedly and dismisses it. He
> has planted the seed of symbol, correspondence, parallel—what-
> ever—and for Samuel Beckett their confusion is amusement enough.

What we're watching here, the book not two pages old, is the first
delineation of its principal character: a mischievous tease, not above
petty and needless deceptions, who moreover shares with Ms. Bair
the distaste for "scholars and critics" which is a minor *leitmotif* of her
book.[2] You'd think she'd watched him, "with carefully feigned diffi-
dence," assure a postulant he was born on a date he wasn't. But no,
this is fiction.

As biography is: biography is finally fiction, and save in the most
trustworthy hands—F. S. L. Lyons in his *Parnell*, William Murphy in
his *Prodigal Father*—it works the way imperfect fiction does, filling sag
with cellulite generalities when the data continuity requires are lacking. If unlike the novelist the biographer can't invent fact, he can invent ways to cover its absence.

He may have recourse to the transitional devices of the magazine

---

[2]Distaste also sponsors a certain fuzziness, since the only significance anyone could ra-
tionally ascribe to the more fateful date is the possibility that Beckett himself has gone
through life thinking it fateful. "Symbol, correspondence, parallel" are merely words
to goose critics with.

novelette. "The daydream of himself as Dr. Joyce, poet, epiphanist, and physician, surrounded by fair women . . ."—that is Prof. Ellmann getting past the fact that Joyce's motives, at 20, for studying medicine are in fact undocumented. Needing momentum at the opening of a new chapter, he contrived a sentence that would impart some. If it also imparts our cue to condescend, well, we're past believing, aren't we, that human impulses may ever really transcend vulgar formulae?

The attentive reader of Ms. Bair's 14th chapter may watch the same trick being played on a larger scale. It is wartime, and Beckett, his work in the Paris resistance dangerously compromised, is part of a refugee community in the unoccupied zone. There, as he starts *Watt*, a paragraph commences: "Beckett suffered a very real breakdown in Roussillon—probably his most serious—one directly related to the schizophrenic form and content of much of *Watt*. To Suzanne and his friends it seemed as if he had fallen victim to the general malaise that afflicts persons incarcerated against their will for long periods of time."

Note the planting of "schizophrenic," disingenuously sponsored by the strangeness of a book; note in the next sentence the look of documentation—"to Suzanne and his friends"—and the quiet plausibility of what they're said to have seen. (And no note indicates that Ms. Bair ever interviewed Suzanne—Mme Beckett.)

Then—too long to quote—paragraph follows paragraph, itemizing Beckett's several guilts and self-hatreds, specifying the warring selves within him, outlining his strategies for channeling his confusion as in writing *Watt* he "set up a smokescreen of obscurity and complexity behind which he carefully hid tantalizing clues for his readers." You'd think the biographer really knew all this.

But turn to the notes, and you'll find (1) that "information about Beckett's breakdown is from exiles, villagers and personal friends who have asked to remain anonymous"; (2) that the five-page analytic narrative was managed by Ms. Bair with the aid of three doctors and R. D. Laing's *The Divided Self*.

Here Beckett's fate, a character in a trendy fiction of Laing's, matters perhaps less than the naive reader's, who is apt to think one more book has been explained away—auto-therapy, boobytrapped against outsiders—and may even pass up *Watt*, a great delight.

And what did "exiles, villagers and personal friends" observe? Their contribution isn't particularized, and efforts to imagine collide with the statement that Beckett in those months, thanks to "astonishing reserves of self-control," could "force himself to act as if nothing untoward were happening." Still all manner of people have surely since chatted about the strange Irishman. He was certainly someone to tell stories about.

When people give interviews they're telling stories. If they're Irish in Ireland, their stories are especially apt to be pointed and shaped by narrative skills. Talk to six Dubliners about anything, and you'll get six different highly circumstantial versions.

This fact is of especial import for the biographer of Joyce, much of whose early life we must get at from oral testimony. Since in general Prof. Ellmann's notes record no contradictions, we must assume he's resolved them with the aid of what we're forced to trust all through *James Joyce*, his sense of what will fit his narrative. The same is true when Ms. Bair cites interviews. It's the writer we're being guided by, not the sources, who spoke words we're almost never allowed to hear.

If we could hear their voices we'd be hearing that very essential human phenomenon, gossip: the endless talk by which people assimilate one another's oddness. Gossip is oral, gossip is an unbounded sphere of speech, renewed without cease. It is never idle, also never objective; it unites those present in a sustaining fiction about someone absent. It thrives in villages, it thrives in all small communities, academic, cultural, professional, it thrives in neighborhoods, thrives wherever people subsist on each other's company, make do with each other's mysteries. It thrives in Dublin.

Contrariwise, print is a praying mantis, gossip the mate she eviscerates. From gossip the book-writer sucks a goo called information, to cement edifices of assertion with. Footnotes that cite "interviews" and "informants" have evolved with print-dominated conventions. John Aubrey's 17th century *Brief Lives*, among our earliest literary biographies, are unabashedly gossipy, and Boswell a century later is generally respectful of oral provenance even when he must work with "materials" imparted by others. There emerges from *The Life of Samuel Johnson* not only the firmly drawn protagonist whom we now tend to think of as Boswell's literary creation, but also a sense of the variousness of human testimony. When it varied unacceptably Boswell rebuked it, but he preserved it.

It was Boswell's working assumption that the world couldn't have too much of Johnson's exemplary wisdom, with which his celebrated writings formed a continuum. In the age of psychoanalysis we may doubt this continuity, and biography in the age of the tabloids tends to assume that what isn't readily apparent is probably discreditable.

The literary biographer in particular tends not to reflect on his assumptions (an exception is Leon Edel's *Literary Biography*, a suite of meditations on what he was about when he was writing the life of Henry James). The tacit assumption tends to be that the subject's work, whatever trim surfaces it may present to unwary critics, is really his effort to live with the events of his own life, systematically falsifying them out of mischief, neurosis, desperation.

This work—what we had before the biographer arrived—critics if they like may continue to twiddle at, elaborately doing next to nothing (though as Didi said to Gogo while they waited for Godot, "It's the way you do it, the way you do it"). It is for the biographer to disclose the authentic mess of misfortune, self-deception and imposture that make up a word-man's life. With more grip on things he'd be something other than a word-man. And it's for the unwary reader, like Aesop's dog, to drop the solid bone and snatch at the bone an inverted dog seems to hold beneath the stream.

1978

The Poet and the Pirate

EZRA POUND: THE LAST ROWER, *a political biography*
by C. David Heymann. Viking, 1976.

Pound comes to the reader of this book refracted through curious habits of Mr. Heymann's which we'd better inspect. Here's what he tells us about his title:

> I remembered reading some place a quotation by Jean Cocteau. He had called Pound "a rower on the river of the dead"—"un rameur sur le fleuve des morts." The Last Rower: it is the Ulysses image in its peculiarly American form—"that non-Homeric, romanticized figure out of Dante by way of Tennyson which so spectacularly haunts the imagination of Ezra Pound."

Start by casting an innocent eye. You note pure *Time*-coverese, though at *Time* a copy-editor's eye would have caught "quotation by Jean Cocteau" and emended "by" to "from"; writers don't compose quotations, they get quoted. What Cocteau may have meant doesn't matter; Pound the Rower is a luscious mortuary phrase, which Mr. Heymann proceeds to improve by contributing "Last." He then tells us it is the Ulysses image (though Ulysses the seafarer rowed no rivers); moreover, "the Ulysses image in its purely American form." (But think of some other Americans whom it fits? I can't.) Then ground is touched, a 20-word quotation which a footnote assigns to Leslie Fiedler. Fiedler has done more for the cadence of the Heymann sentence than for the articulation of a guiding sense. From the passage as a whole one gathers that Mr. Heymann intuits the magnitude of his theme. You'd be hard put to say what else you gather.

Unless, that is, you happen to have available Vittorugo Contino's *Ezra Pound in Italy*, published in Venice in 1970 and unlikely to be consulted by American promotion committees. There we find Pound's answers to the questions of a young Sicilian poet, Vanni Ronsisvalle, notably: "Cocteau called me the rower on the river of the dead: 'le rameur sur la fleuve des morts'; it is sad to look back." Though this switches the gender of "fleuve," may it still perhaps be what Mr. Heymann "remembered reading some place"? It may indeed; the reader of both books cannot but be struck by insistent similarities between the coda of *The Last Rower*, which purports to be a 1971 interview Mr. Heymann secured with Pound, and Pound's words to Ronsisvalle, published in 1970.

HEYMANN

"You ask about my London and Paris friends—Joyce, Hemingway, Brancusi, Eliot. When I was in Zurich in the winter of 1967 I saw Joyce's bare grave—Joyce's name with Nora's sat in a corner of the cemetery, the names nearly illegible on a stone hidden in the grass. . . .

"Hemingway never disappointed me. . . .

"Brancusi seemed to me a saint . . . I said as much in *Guide to Kulchur*. . . . Le Musée de l'Art Moderne in Paris contains much of his work, but I would like to see his 'Table of Silence' in Rumania. . . ."

RONSISVALLE

"When I was in Zurich in the winter of '67 I saw Joyce's bare grave—other graves had little Christmas trees and wreathes with candles as is the custom there. Joyce's name with Nora's nearly illegible on a stone hidden in the grass. . . .

"You ask about my Paris friends in the 1920s: Brancusi, Joyce, Hemingway. Stein, whom you mention, I knew very slightly.

"Brancusi seemed to me a saint, he is first in my list of values in 'Guide to Kulchur.' I want to see his Table of Silence, a venetian friend has offered to take me to Roumania to see it.

"Hemingway did not disappoint me."

Mr. Heymann also offers this dialogue:

"You still manage to do a good deal of travelling," I suggested to Pound.

"No," he answered. "I haven't really done much travelling—in fact, I have stayed put for years at a time. I don't see that restlessness is necessary."

"For artists?"

"For anyone."

With which compare:

To Ronsisvalle's supposition that he had travelled a great deal:

"I have not done much travelling, in fact I have stayed put for years at a time. I don't see that restlessness is necessary for artists or for anyone."

Add what claims to be a statement from Olga Rudge to Heymann, "Ezra might seem detached and no longer interested, but he follows everything, nothing escapes him. Think of an automobile with its engine idling—it doesn't run but all its parts are moving"; reflect on the improbability of Miss Rudge (if you've met her) saying "might" where "may" is meant, compare the more grammatical version in the Contino book: "You see, E.P. may seem detached, no longer interested, on the contrary he follows everything; think of an automobile with the motor running, it is not moving but it is functioning"; ponder what purport to be Pound's last 1971 words to Heymann, introduced with a great pother of descriptive atmospherics—"It is sad . . . very sad to look back," and their analogy with his words to Ronsisvalle just after the Cocteau citation, "It is sad to look back"; note finally the virtual identity between what Heymann says Pound said about Eliot and what Pound wrote in the Eliot Memorial Issue of the *Sewanee Review*, even to a phrase he wouldn't have *spoken* ("instead: Westminster Abbey"): and confront your awakened doubts about how much of the Heymann "interview" with Ezra Pound (by 1970 a virtual non-speaker) ever occurred.

Your doubts are accentuated in the narrative portion of the book, especially if you've written on the subject yourself and find your own sentences coming back refracted as though by deep water. William Chace in *Contemporary Literature* (Autumn '76) has exemplified with parallel passages Mr. Heymann's habit of lifting, slightly modified, the words and the rhetorical patterns of the people who did the work. I'll bypass the issue of quasi-plagiarism and concentrate on the pattern of modification, which is after all what exerts pressure on a naive reader.

Nothing in Mr. Heymann's sensibility prompts him to retouch a sentence that has acquired a little blurred patch. You even suspect that he rather fancies those blurs, so freely does he impart them to the sentences of others.

The poet "was to spend much of the next two decades putting the facts he had been taught in school together again" in a chronometrical pattern of his own design. . . .

"Chronometrical," evoking the chronometer: what does *that* mean? Some ultra-fussiness about dates? No, it's just a fancy substitute for "historical," as you may learn by checking back to the source to which Mr. Heymann duly credits the quoted part of his sentence. If there's a difference between "chronometrical" and "historical," we may guess that our author doesn't much care about it.

And what does "cloying" mean here? "He had $80 in his pocket, a manuscript of poems, the cloying desire to see those poems in print. . . ." *Cloy*, says Merriam-Webster, "to satisfy or fill to capacity or to excess, as the appetite." The one thing that cloys a desire is its excessive gratification, but since at the moment in question the young Pound wasn't seeing his poems in print at all, that can't be what is meant.

Again: "And at San Zeno (Verona), looming in the semidarkness, the coveted signed column, luminous in its detail. . . ." The *coveted* signed column: are we to imagine Pound wishing he could chop that stone shaft out of San Zeno and take it home? No, the word is just

wrong. The column was admired, yes; meditated on, yes; its existence was repeatedly cited, yes; but coveted it was not. And the context in which Pound cited it—Canto 45, for instance—will generally
imply a rebuke of covetousness. Here as so often a vaguely apposite
word has been thrown in the general direction of a sentence judged in
need of some intensification.

A tiny point, one word, but Ezra Pound taught three generations to
watch single words.

Watching Mr. Heymann's way with them, one grows aware of the
need he feels to be vivid, to intensify, to lend something personal to
accounts of events that were after all before his time (he is 31) and have
had to be reconstructed from the narratives of others. In the little
modifications that Heymannize a borrowing, facts sometimes go
wrong as well as epithets; T. E. Lawrence (of Arabia) for instance is
converted into D. H. Lawrence (of Nottingham and Taos). Or errors
creep in when borrowing isn't in question, as when Heymann complains of Pound's "desultory examination of Socrates' *Ethics*" (read
"Aristotle's"; Socrates wrote no book), or evokes "gondolas in dry-
dock in the vast Piazza San Marco," which is akin to finding skiffs dry-
docked in Times Square.

To say that there are Poundian lessons Mr. Heymann hasn't ab-
sorbed—about watching single words, about leaving blanks for what
you don't know—is also, alas, to say that the book's usefulness is impaired. For in addition to what he reprocessed from the books of others, Mr. Heymann had a rich lode of material which he was the first
writer to see, the FBI files on the "Pound case," and his hold on this is
impaired by a certain vagueness about his man. The material is laid
before us, many pages of it, wholly new information about the dis-
tressing frenzies of those years: Pound's involvement with hierarchies of Italian officials, his broadcasts over Rome radio, his efforts to
play economic advisor to the short-lived Salò Republic, his rantings
about bankers and race, his arrest, detention at Genoa, imprison-
ment near Pisa, ambiguous incarceration in Washington.

It is this new material, Mr. Heymann well understands, that justi-
fies his writing about Pound at all, and it all pertains to Pound at less
than his best, sometimes at a worst we can barely comprehend. To un-

derstand it at all, the reader needs a more accurate sense of Pound at his best than Mr. Heymann's reader is likely to take away. The Good Pound of *The Last Rower*—Pound the poet—is blurry and at his best a nature mystic. The Bad Pound by contrast is merely mad.

But the poet's mind entertained an intricate dance of sharply perceived and discriminated identities, and only when you're comfortable with that fact can you accept what Mr. Heymann intermittently recognizes but finds baffling—the survival of Pound's best through his worst period, its near-total availability to his talents whenever he collected his attention properly. The man who wrote the *Pisan Cantos* was the same who had been delivering the broadcasts, and the *Cantos* were possible, including their finest pages, not because he could cut his aesthetics loose from his morals but because they were always continuous.

The story begins with Douglasite economics, which unluckily enters Mr. Heymann's narrative on one of those pages where inattention to words is contaminating substance. I'll need a long excerpt:

> Preparing an autobiographical sketch for the 1949 edition of the *Selected Poems of Ezra Pound*, the author expostulated: "1918 began investigation of causes of war, to oppose same."
>
> Soon after his initial inquiry, he discovered a root cause—or so he thought. Late in 1918, in the offices of A. R. Orage's *The New Age*, Pound encountered Major Clifford Hugh Douglas, formerly chief construction engineer of the British Westinghouse Company in India, and the "inventor" of a new system of economics, called Social Credit. To Douglas's mind, both war and lack of money had been caused by financiers' manipulations—usury—and his mathematically drawn panacea, or at least the main one, called for the distribution through central banks of national dividends. Pound was easily convinced.

Setting aside the inaccuracy of "expostulated," one discovers more innocent wrongness here than is compatible with the establishment of a base to triangulate from. Douglas in 1918 had not "invented" a "system," he was offering a diagnosis. He was trying to explain why systems of production never seemed to distribute enough purchasing power to buy back the product, a fact that was highlighted by the widespread prosperity discernible during wartime, when a considerable fraction of the product didn't need buying back because it got destroyed. (This was pertinent to the *causes* of wars because it seemed evident that Britain and Germany had gotten onto a collision course out of competition for foreign markets, and the question to be answered was why foreign markets were needed: why the home market was always underfinanced.)

His diagnosis did not indict "financiers' manipulations," but rather what he took to be a fallacy that inhered in the accounting system, and would have caused chronic shortages of money no matter who operated the system. Nor were "central banks" the mainspring of his remedy; "Centralized financial credit-control," he wrote in *Credit-Power and Democracy*, "will break up this civilization, since no man, or body of men, however elected, can represent the detailed desires of any other man, or body of men."

In fact the proposals of Douglas entail such a degree of decentralization, such a maximizing of personal freedom, that believing he means what he says can seem almost insuperably difficult. We are simply unaccustomed to problem-solving that doesn't entail centralization of power. Thus Earle Davis in his *Vision Fugitive: Ezra Pound and Economics* (1968) muddles himself through supposing that Douglas must have meant something like the New Deal (which makes Pound's opposition to Roosevelt an insoluble problem). Charles Norman, Pound's first biographer, likewise couldn't believe that Douglas, so far as he made sense, wasn't just Marx in different language, Marx being the only kind of economic radical Norman could conceive of.

Nor, ironically, was Pound himself more lucky. Douglas, he perceived, had formulated a principle, a description of how money seemed to operate inside an economic system. If true, this principle resembled Clerk Maxwell's electromagnetic equations, the theory on which something practical could be constructed, to the great liberation of mankind. It was in quest of that practical implementation that he turned his eyes toward Mussolini, ignoring Douglas's warnings about centralized power. ("Politics," he wrote in 1933, "might mean: capacity for getting action on Douglas's ideas.")

I'll linger briefly with the Maxwell analogy. Maxwell's equations, we may say, made radio possible. For millennia, before Marconi, the range of the human voice had been restricted to the circle a man could fill by shouting. Afterwards, a whisper in London could be heard in Seattle. But the laws Maxwell formulated were active in the universe before he formulated them, and studies of acoustics in free air remained valid after Marconi had liberated the carrying-power of the voice from their domain.

Similarly, there was no intrinsic naiveté in supposing, as Pound did, that Douglas had reduced to law, in his "A + B Theorem," something that had always been the case but had gone unnoticed. And it was no affront to the competence of Adam Smith, let alone of traditional wisdom, to suppose that, given this new understanding, the system of production and exchange need no longer be damped down by the scarcity whose working Smith analyzed. New technology follows new principles, and Douglas seemed to have made a new principle available in showing why the operative scarcity is apt to be a scarcity of money, not of goods.*

At any rate, Pound was impatient. Douglas was trying to guide a political party in England, and Pound had a radical suspicion of British institutions, adapted as they were to defusing anything novel. That was one reason he thought that Mussolini's Italy offered more hope. Another was his reading of Mussolini himself: Mussolini seemed in many ways a 19th-century American type: the man who got things accomplished. And Pound's understanding of the Italian Renaissance had been shaped in his young manhood by the Swiss historian Burckhardt, the first chapter of whose key book was entitled "The State as Work of Art." Mussolini seemed to fit the artist's role.

By the 1930s another of Pound's American vectors was operative: his Puritanism, which coupled the generous assumption that by paying attention anyone of good will could understand anything important, with the corollary suspicion that failure to understand might connote something worse than inattention: might connote impurity of will. Hence two complementary extremes: his diatribes against statesmen who showed no sign of understanding, and his increasing

*I've tried to sketch an exposition of Douglasite principles in *The Pound Era* (1971), pp. 301–317. The serious student also needs to master evidence presented by Dennis R. Klinck in *Paideuma*, V-2 (Fall 1976), pp. 227–240, authoritative on Pound's misapplication of Douglas. If your college library hasn't *Paideuma* ask it why not.

susceptibility to the notion that by holding their attention during a quarter-hour audience he could put Social Credit across. His quixotic trip to America in 1939, hoping to get Roosevelt's ear and prevent the coming war, is the subject of one of *The Last Rower*'s most touching chapters.

The lure of false clarities, not to mention the Puritan susceptibility to devil-theories, helps explain his vulnerability to anti-Semitism. Some defects in Mr. Heymann's exposition of this tricky topic stem from his not having known that remarkable woman Dorothy Shakespear Pound, who exercised with no malice whatever the methods that used to be normal in the British professional classes for restricting the number of people one needed to bother about. (Dorothy's father was a London solicitor; her mother wrote novels and kept a salon.) One began by excluding whole groups: Catholics, Jews, Americans, the uneducated, tradespeople, provincials. One then readmitted individuals one by one; Dorothy even began by *marrying* an American, Ezra Pound. You can call this procedure British snobbery, or you can call it a strategy for survival on an overcrowded island. Though the naturally gregarious Ezra resisted its assumptions, and though the Pounds had many Catholic and Jewish friends— more, probably, than most Protestant gentiles in Europe in their generation—the proximity of so intensely English a woman had certain long-term effects. When Jews began to enter his field of attention, it was easier than it should have been for him to think of them *en bloc*.

They began to enter his field of attention in the 1930s, not because he was listening to Hitler but because his attention had turned to the mechanisms of *international* credit, and he'd decided that the failure of its masters to identify themselves with national interests stemmed from the fact that many of them belonged to a group most nations tended to exclude from positions of influence.

This was not, so far as it went, a notion that necessarily led to hating anyone. The imperatives it postulates are social, not biological, and Stephen Birmingham raised no one's blood pressure when he explained in *Our Crowd* how the affluent Jewish families of New York looked out for one another, in part because no one else was going to look out for them. But once the race of the banker had been admitted to the field of relevant forces, Pound's defense against conspiracy-theories had become perilously thin. All manner of unpleasing phenomena can be explained by this pattern if you can identify enough Jews, and during the frenzy and exasperation of the war years Pound was scenting crypto-Jews everywhere. The name of John Calvin, even, might conceal Cohen!

Here as so often—I've merely sketched a couple of examples—the theme to grasp is that every idea that went wrong had entailed a set of distinctions: in fact had been engendered in the act of making one more distinction, one of the minute verbal distinctions that were the central habit of his mind. That is why one must proceed so slowly and carefully in stating the elements of his main ideas. And though he was to caricature all his own perceptions and descend into frenzied demagogic rant, the governing system of distinctions was always available whenever he could manage to recall himself to its plane, and the econo-political ideas could straighten themselves out again and give off their original light.

That is why we find blocks of sense embedded in the frenzy; it was true, and deplorable, as he told an audience on an otherwise disgraceful occasion, that John Adams' works were (1939) unobtainable, "whereas the works of Marx, Engels and Trotsky were readily available in selections costing mere pennies." More important, he recalled himself to order in the *Cantos*. Mr. Heymann states accurately that in the Infernal years—in Pisa and in St. Elizabeths Hospital—it was work on the *Cantos* that saved him. Their most cryptic pages record his struggle with himself, his struggle to keep his attention on what he knew for sure, the temptation to seek underpinnings for his errors (and the discovery that underpinnings matching his criteria were seldom to be found). Generally the *Cantos* give us the sane version, speeches and letters the demented.

This gets blurred by reflex response to things in the *Cantos*. Mr. Heymann quotes a sequence of passages that mention Jewish themes, and thinks it evident that they are "full of hate." It seems more accurate to say that they tacitly acknowledge the hate, and try to cut it back to some factual kernel. "The tale of the perfect schnorrer" is told in Canto 35 the way Pound heard someone Jewish tell it, in what his phonetic spelling means to record as a Jewish accent (no more caricatured, by the way, than he elsewhere caricatures the American intonations he cared about so deeply). Part of its point, told that way, is that the Jewish community knows its schnorrers, and speaks of them sharply; Pound had great trust in the wisdom of such communities.

As for the notorious detail from Canto 74, which begins,

> the yidd is a stimulant, and the goyim are cattle
> in gt proportion and go to saleable slaughter
> with the maximum of
>   docility . . .

—one would think it evident that the group who ought to feel insulted are the goyim. In St. Elizabeths after receiving Jewish visitors Pound once remarked—I was there—that they had, as expected, been "stimulating." No enterprise—he was always sponsoring enterprises—seemed capable, he said, of getting under way without at least some Jewish personnel, whose role in the world, so he thought, was to counter the "Xtn" penchant for inaction.

And there is the moving moment in Canto 91 when the most continuously sustained paradisaic vision so far in the poem—not a mere dozen lines but nine consecutive pages—is suddenly brought to nothing by some angry lines about "kikery," and he has to consult a good many luminous memories to get it going again. Since the poem is not automatic writing but elaborately worked over, and since he had everything to gain by not interrupting that astonishing passage (and it does resume again), the conclusion seems inescapable that he meant to record the manner in which vision is dispelled by upwelling frenzy. It is a moving, humiliating confession, and he could have made himself look just great by omitting it.

The real problem presented by such details is not ethical but poetic. The intention is one thing, the realization another. Paradoxically, they are part of a willed effort to be fair about things he might easily have omitted. And an un-Poundian stridency, betraying the fact that will is doing the work of ease, makes it all but inevitable that most readers will get the intention of the detail precisely backwards.

I speak with a confidence based upon the fact that during perhaps 50 hours spent in Ezra Pound's presence over a total span of 20 years I never heard him make an anti-Semitic remark, and not because the subject never came up. It is perfectly evident that other acquaintances were less fortunate, that some on some days heard little but rant. I can only conclude that there were in his psyche simultaneous levels of integration, that I was wholly fortunate in my sampling, and that the Pound I knew was closer to the poet of the *Cantos* than the Pound of some other accounts. There were long spells when he was *not* obsessed, moreover knew that his obsessions existed. If indeed he was mad, he wrote to me once, ought not intention be directed to what drove him that way? And Mr. Heymann quotes a letter to the firm of London solicitors of which Dorothy's father had been a member. The date is October 1945; he had undergone the horrors of the Pisan cage, six feet by six, three weeks of sun by day and floodlights by night, under omnipresent guard; he was indicted on a capital charge; he was without legal counsel; and having outlined various public facts he wrote, "You will see that there are elements in the case far more interesting than my personal welfare."

Mr. Heymann, who lets us know that he is himself Jewish, seems exemplary in his fairness of intention. Given what I think is his radical misunderstanding of a number of the things he quotes, it is the more remarkable that he quotes them so calmly. One more of his quotations—not from Pound—deserves special pondering.

Harvard's Harry Levin, speaking for the committee that had attempted to award the 1972 Emerson-Thoreau medal of the American Academy of Arts and Sciences to Ezra Pound, only to find itself overruled by the Academy's council, dissented tartly from the council's implication that the committee had been in some way naive. The committee, he asserted, did not need to be told that "art cannot be isolated from morality." Its members were not "irresponsible aesthetes," nor was Pound. "Members of the committee never questioned the assumption that art is grounded in ethics. Pound, like his master Dante, is not only an artist but an impassioned moralist."

Pound's long life was to end just a few months later, but not before word of Professor Levin's stand had reached him. He sent back, through an intermediary, two words of gratitude: "It matters." A weary old man's three syllables, still they contain the substance of what he'd been saying all his life.

1977

King Crank

ROBERT GRAVES: THE ASSAULT HEROIC,
1895–1926, *by Richard Perceval Graves.*
Illustrated. Viking, 1986. 387 pp.

A fearful crank, yes; his theme for fifty years was how all opinion current in England was Wrong; in particular, all learned opinion.

They revered the Classics, and Homer? Well, in 1959 a Robert Graves version of the *Iliad* casts Homer not as celebrant but as satirist, his Agamemnon no valiant leader but just such a Colonel Blimp as Graves had suffered under in the trenches.

They venerated the New Testament? *The Nazarene Gospel Restored* has it encoding an utterly subversive text, passed along for centuries by the unsuspecting. Having risen from the dead himself ("died of wounds" at the Somme, 1916, an official telegram said), Graves knew how Jesus had done it, to survive as The Wandering Jew.

They deemed English Prose the Englishman's natural gift? In *The Reader Over Your Shoulder* Graves detects a national aversion to ever putting plain things plainly. By preference avenues were explored and stones not left unturned.

And their literary values! They thought T. S. Eliot was a poet, who'd put nightingales in the wood where Agamemnon died, though he died in a bath-house, not a "bloody wood"; moreover since his fleet ran into winter storms he'd have died in January when there are no nightingales. The poet's job is getting things straight and Eliot couldn't.

And so on, not in squibs but in substantial volumes, emitted with unsettling frequency from his stronghold on the Spanish island of Majorca: parcel-post-bombs in a long campaign to subvert the English social structure while getting English publishers to pay the bomber. The idea was to lower, if possible to zero, the general reader's faith in a class that drifted from public schools through Oxbridge to cultural authority: Bible-readers, Homer-readers, frauds.

Himself an Oxford B. Litt. and a public school alumnus (Charterhouse), Robert Graves might have been explained away as half Irish had his other half not been German. His middle name was von Ranke, the historian Leopold von Ranke was his great-great uncle, and he could claim a way with the footnote by birthright. (The two volumes of *The Greek Myths* overwhelm with some 2,000 source notes, many of them relevant.)

As for the Irish Graveses, Robert's grandfather Charles, the Protestant Bishop of Limerick, "had once conversed in Latin with one of the brothers Grimm . . . spoke six or seven modern languages, and had a European reputation as a mathematician." The medical Graves of Graves' Disease fits in somewhere. The bishop's brother could claim friendship with Wordsworth. And Robert's father, Alfred Perceval Graves, was a versifier whom Tennyson encouraged. His "Father O'Flynn" is still sung:

> . . . Don't talk of your Provost and Fellows of Trinity,
> Famous forever at Greek and Latinity,
> Faix and the divels and all at Divinity,
>   Father O'Flynn'd make hares of them all!
>   Come, I vinture to give ye my word,
>   Never the likes of his logic was heard,
>   Down from mythology
>   Into thayology,
>   Troth! and conchology if he'd the call. . . .

A hit in the 1890s, that made thousands for the publisher, hundreds for the composer, and one pound twelve shillings for hapless A. P.

Graves, who'd incautiously accepted a batch price of 80 pounds for 50 songs. The Graveses had a way of not faring in the world. (Still—"Never the likes of his logic was heard"—isn't Father O'Flynn a possible paradigm for Robert?)

Luckily, Alfred's wife Amy Ranke had come into money: a godsend because each of their five children—and notably Robert von Ranke Graves, born 1895—got off to a wobbly start. Though after 1934 novels like *I, Claudius* raked in cash, it was frequent small remittances, mostly from home, that had bought off the wolf at the door during seven grim years of trying to live as a poet. We can understand if the activity of his middle years seems governed by a certain look of calculation.

And Gravesian years were apt to be many. Longevity was one thing that ran in the blood; Robert's father lived to be 85, his mother into her nineties; he himself breathed his last at 91. They were prolific too; Robert, who raised eight children, was himself one of five, and from his father's first marriage he had five half-siblings. The intertwined Graves–von Ranke family trees spread across six pages of this new biography. In the first World War ten of them were fighting on each side.

Wherever he turned, a Graves of Robert's generation was apt to bump into colorful relatives: half-brother "Bones" who chummed with young P. G. Wodehouse and maybe modelled for rascally Stanley Featherstonehaugh Ukridge; half-brother Philip whose *Times* articles had exposed *The Protocols of the Elders of Zion*; brother John who'd played tennis with Ezra Pound in Rapallo; not to mention sisters Clarissa and Rosaleen, who shared rooms while pursuing incompatible vocations, a Christian Science Practitioner, a medical student.

The biographer himself is the son of Robert's brother John, from whom he had a huge pile of family papers that haphazardly document five generations clear back to the 1760s. So he knows the effervescent family from the inside—as a child was even taken to see Robert's formidable mother—and displays, like any Graves, an array of enviable skills which include, this time, refreshing common sense. A proper respect for his erratically gifted uncle doesn't keep him from observing weaknesses, notably a way Robert had of yielding up his mind to his hero(ine) of the moment ("Peter" Johnstone, Siegfried

Sassoon, Lawrence of Arabia, a charismatic named Besanta Mallik, the first wife Nancy Nicolson, the poet Laura Riding).

He has also rejected the usual biographical format, long chapters whose seamless unscrolling gives the look of accounting for every mortal day. Those tempt a biographer to seem to know more than he does, and our author prefers exactness about what's known and what's not. (His endnotes delight; for schoolboy Robert's slug of cherry-whisky before a boxing match he cites two sources, then takes stock of another biographer's "cherry-brandy," based on "a remark made by Robert in 1943, which he later retracted." "Of such trivia," he adds drily, "are scholarly footnotes sometimes composed.")

Thus he opts for the Poundian prescription, "Leave blanks for what you don't know." His chapters average five pages. Some run less than two. Each has a title and a focussed theme, without "must have" and "would have" sentences to blur the vividness. His book, despite one's possible first impressions, is no family-album reverie.

This first volume, moreover, with its 1926 cutoff date, must acknowledge a formidable competitor, his uncle's own 1927 *Goodbye to All That*. A book by which Robert Graves hoped to get the War out of his system, moreover an autobiographical classic with a title so brilliant it became a catchphrase, *Goodbye to All That* fictionalizes freely almost from page one, partly out of deficient recollection (shell-shock), partly out of belief that "literal truth is relatively unimportant," partly because of British libel laws, and partly, perhaps, out of sheer boredom with the unmilitary episodes. (It lets you think that the chief accomplishment of Robert's first 30 years was just getting through the war.) So despite a plethora of testimony, our author says his chief problem was "to find precise answers to questions beginning what, where, how, when, and why."

Let it next be stated that intelligence and family genes have triumphed; *The Assault Heroic* is fully as readable as *Goodbye to All That*, and a good deal more informative. A knack with character is another thing it displays. If Robert's first wife Nancy, who left with their children after 11 years, was perhaps an impossible bride from the first, yet on these pages her interest never palls.

Feminism in those years meant chiefly securing the Vote, but

Nancy was ahead of her time. Even now she'd be a feminist's feminist. On the wedding morning—she 18, he 22—she read the marriage service for the first time and was furious all through it. "I'll get something out of this wedding at any rate" said she afterward, grabbing a bottle of champagne. That did wound her groom, and her going-away outfit was the "land-girl's" uniform, breeches and smock. She wouldn't wear a ring, nor cease being "Miss Nicolson." Soon she wished they could be "dismarried" and live together without obligation. She made Robert's sister Rosaleen wear trousers, smock, and red tie. It was likely Nancy's adherence to so many oddities that kept Robert from accepting the Oxford Professorship he'd been offered to free them from need of windfalls and donations. (How careless Oxford once was with professorships! Robert Graves never finished the B.A., and his B. Litt. had been rigged by a friendly don.)

Yet her crazy vitality redeems her. They'd farm! She hacked at mangel-wurzels. She could draw—they'd make a mint from illustrated books! (They didn't.) She'd be independent and open a shop! She opened it and the initial cash-flow was good, but for reasons unclear it soon proved "an expensive mistake." Meanwhile chipper Nancy bore and reared four children. Her husband continued to have episodes of depression and shell-shock. That war was second only to Vietnam in its long-term effect on survivors.

Robert had seen a dead German in Mametz wood, and exorcised the horror in a poem:

> . . . propped against a shattered trunk
>   In a great mess of things unclean
> Sat a dead Boche: he scowled and stunk
>   With clothes and face a sodden green:
> Big-bellied, spectacled, crop-haired,
> Dribbling black blood from nose and beard.

If that horror didn't haunt his dreams (we don't know) it was because finding language had distanced it. And before long his verses were addressing Nancy:

> Give then a thought for me
> Walking so miserably,

Wanting relief in the friendship of flower or tree:
  Do but remember, we
  Once could in love agree.
Swallow your pride, let us be as we used to be.

Still, he could cite Shakespeare's "Phoenix and the Turtle": "So they lov'd, as love in twain / Had the essence but in one." Married since 1916, they stuck it out till '29. *Goodbye to All That* is tightlipped on the long episode.

Meanwhile a poem published in 1920 gives a glimpse of the odd nowhere that was to become his poetry's "emotional landscape":

Time has never journeyed to this lost land,
  Crakeberries and heather bloom out of date,
The rocks jut, the streams flow singing on either hand,
  Careless is the season be early or late.
The skies wander overhead, now blue, now slate . . .

A wavering, a "Celtic" rhythm. Wales, our author conjectures; yet, if based on Wales, some place of the starsmit mind. Graves was growing convinced that poetry descended from primitive magic: not a skewed belief at all when we reflect on the power of verbal taboos, on "Knock wood!" and the concept of "unprintable" words. (In 1927 Robert Graves wrote a small book called *Lars Porsena, or, The Future of Swearing*. "Lars Porsena of Clusium / By the nine gods he swore": so commenced a poem everyone used to know. Poetry's energies ebb as great oaths lose force.)

Unfolding in magic places, magic events won't roll over to be explained: as "Welsh Incident" would put it, "Things never seen or heard or written about, / Very strange, unWelsh, utterly peculiar / Things."

Then in 1924, in an issue of John Crowe Ransom's *The Fugitive*, he and Nancy came upon poems by a forceful American woman, Laura Riding Gottschalk. By the next year she was divorced from Mr. Gottschalk, and Robert was writing to her, "and Nancy, seeing the good effect upon Robert of someone in whose work and outlook he found intellectual stimulation of a high order, had suggested that Laura should be given an open invitation to come to England so that the two poets could work together more closely."

Whatever Nancy's faults, jealousy was not then one of them.

Next Nancy's health faltered, and a hot climate was prescribed. They got an academic appointment in Egypt, and with them, newly arrived for just that purpose, sailed Laura Riding.

End of Volume I, with the fireworks all in the future: collaboration with Laura; Laura throwing herself from an upstairs window, it's been said to make a point; Robert charged with attempted murder; Nancy leaving for good; divorce and Robert's remarriage (not to Laura); the long spate of eccentric books. Robert swashbuckled always; one reviewer (me) of *The Nazarene Gospel Restored* received threats of maybe a lawsuit.

Having taken the great risk of making his first volume exactly overlap *Goodbye to All That*, Richard Perceval Graves has shown he can satisfy on his own. His book in most ways supersedes the famous predecessor, while whetting an appetite for its own sequel. What may survive of Robert Graves is perhaps a dozen poems and the distinction of central place in a model biography.

1987

A Torch in the Labyrinth

ROMAN CULTURE: WEAPONS AND THE MAN, *edited*
with introductions by Garry Wills. Braziller, 1966.

We invent the past, from what is at hand, and have invented Greece
after Greece. Each time it grows strange, as did Swinburne's within
living memory, we restructure it. The Greece currently in favor is by
Heisenberg out of Camus: *vide infra.*

We have been less prodigal with Romes, because for many centuries no one in Europe felt remote enough from a Roman world to see
it as strange. The language, paid out like a spaceman's umbilical cord,
kept connections intact as late as Dr. Johnson's time. Latin was food
for schoolboys; it transmitted, it *was* the past on which their minds
fed. The great benefit of rendering the acquisition of Latin unspeak-
ably arduous was that the grown boy could be trusted to read it no
more as soon as he had gotten clear of the schoolmaster. Thus his notion of what Latin literature contained was bounded by the curriculum excerpts—Caesar, Cicero, Horace, Vergil—and for centuries a
synthetic but very stable Rome served as model for ideals of duty,
public service, civic responsibility.

But no more; the tradition of teaching the language is almost gone;
and we have entered the time of Invented Romes. It is a less cata-

strophic time than deplorers like to suppose, since the people who do read Latin are likely to read very widely, unencumbered by any distinction between curricular classics, good for forming the minds of boys, and all those words the Romans had better (the anxious pedagogue used to think) have left unwritten.

The standard authors, moreover, are no longer translated with an eye to convincing a phantasmal Dr. Busby that the ablative absolute has indeed been correctly construed. Thus we have Dr. Copley's *Catullus 105*:

> Dickie-boy Trill
> climbed Helicon hill
> to fetch a pail of poesy
> the muses saw
> and (being quick on the draw)
> they knocked him arsover noesy

—of which an approved version would run, "Mentula [proper name coined from colloq. epithet, usu. thought to denote Caesar's chief engineer Mamurra: cf. xxix.13] tried [lit. tries] to climb the Piplean Mount [lit. Pipleus mountain, in the Pierian district, hence sacred to the Muses]; the Muses with little forks [*furcillis*: cf. Aristophanes, *Pax* 637, and the familiar conception of the devil's pitchfork] precipitately thrust him out": amid which neurotic nonsense the would-be poet vanishes as absolutely as though Catullus [Gaius Valerius Catullus, c.84–c.54 B.C.] had never conceived him.

Seizing these twin opportunities—a bad tradition lapsed, and an abundance of readable translations—Garry Wills has assembled for us a Rome *de nos jours* ("an airless world—*à huis clos*: a modern world") whose Seneca's "dark comedies" are "closer to Genêt and Beckett than to Sophocles," and whose portrait busts, "faces impervious to what lies just before them, masks that proclaim an exceeding inner busyness," anticipate "the features of Dostoevsky, Joyce, Thomas Mann, Eugene O'Neill, Robert Oppenheimer." If this isn't the Rome *Life* was confecting last spring, with its vastness and its monuments and picturesque emperors, the reason is that by Professor Wills' reading of the evidence the visual grandeurs were not central concerns of the Roman mind but compensations for its inability to do what it would have liked. "They could not deal easily with the cosmos, like Plato; so they settled for policing the Mediterranean. The famous boast of Vergil [*excudent alii spirantia mollius aera . . .*] has an odd air of regret about it, a resigned triumphalism."

It is a persuasive reading, reinforced by 33 haunting illustrations: a statue of Augustus with flaccidly gesturing arm, captioned ". . . political choreography . . . ," or two views of the Colosseum, without and within, linked to a simile in the Introduction: "Like it, Roman culture had a large external simplicity, a labyrinthine internal life, and subterranean passages prowled by animals."

Most of the book—some 300 pages of it—takes us by torchlight through that labyrinth: not surveying "major figures" but lighting up, glimpse after glimpse, a succession of Roman themes, in poems, epigrams, excerpts from letters, scraps of orations, handbooks, plays, Christian tracts. Item:

> I see Dolabella has been left a ninth of Livia's estate on condition he changes his name. Good essay-question in social ethics: "Should a young noble change his name in order to benefit under a lady's will?" We shall be able to answer it with more scientific accuracy when we know how much a ninth amounts to.

Item:

> Bits of me, many bits, will dodge all funeral,
> O Libitina-Persephone and, after that,
> Sprout new praise. As long as
> Pontifex and the quiet girl pace the Capitol
> I shall be spoken where the wild flood Aufidus
> Lashes, and Daunus ruled the parched farmland . . .

Item:

> Nothing could save me—not our love, our marriage,
> ancestral glory, our children who mourn today:
> they could not keep Cornelia from her dying.
> What am I now but dust that a hand could hold?
> Black doom and shallow pools of stagnant water
> and the streams I walk through, silent and icy-cold.

Item:

> In the very act of generation, the male [serpent] thrusteth his head into
> the mouth of the female; which she (for the pleasure and delectation
> that she taketh) gnaweth and biteth off.

Item:

> Dim shapes, they travel'd the dark way
> through waste night, Death's ringing palaces,
> an emptiness inhabited—
> travel'd as men go through woods
> foiled of light by an elusive moon
> while Jove darkens heaven, and heaven's dark
> erases many-colored earth.

Respectively, L. P. Wilkinson, Ezra Pound, Constance Carrier, Phile-
mon Holland, Garry Wills, lending tongue to five Romans who no
longer have their classroom sound: Cicero, Horace, Propertius, the
elder Pliny, Vergil: "a troubled people who can profitably trouble us."

At present we hear little of them, much of the Greeks, notably of
the *Iliad*, which is achieving a cult status among the more serious campus *literati*. It is arguable that the cult of the *Iliad* is of a piece with a
sheer evasiveness at the nerve of our century. In the nineteenth century, as Professor Wills points out, "classical" for the first time came to
denote Hellenic, not Latin; Homer, not Dante's Vergil; romanticism
had reached back toward the primitive, and subsequently Victorian
progress and optimism managed an elaborate condescension toward
Rome's "agglutinative, encrusted" sensibility. Today a time that has
seen through progress and optimism gropes toward the past again,
and Rome eludes its hands.

Making contact with its romantic heritage, it encounters in the conclusion of the *Iliad* "Nietzsche's 'metaphysical solace'": D. S. Carne-
Ross thus invokes Nietzsche's name in the course of explaining
(*Arion*, Spring 1965) why T. S. Eliot's invocation of Vergil will not do
for "our own sense of reality." It is against the *Iliad* that we are to lean,
for that poem "has shown that man can live with 'the certainty of a
crushing fate, without the resignation that ought to accompany it.'

. . . It has shown, what Camus' *homme absurde* was looking for, that it is possible to live 'without appeal.' "

If the Roman was unwilling to live "without appeal," and if he had not the unencumbered intellect for "a linear undeviating epic, arrowy lyrics, a philosophy that asks and answers to the point": if he had not, in short, the advantage of being Greek, he was able to muster nevertheless a suspicion that the Greek directness had something illusory about it. Greece never had, we may say, a civilization; never had the responsibility of sustaining, in anxiety and compromise, the lives of others distant in space and time. It is a service to make a start at showing us—for Professor Wills' anthology is after all no more than a start—that the Rome that bore that burden and was gnawed by metaphysical untidiness already inhabited (as Swift and Johnson understood) the world we know.

1966

Kid Lit

THE OXFORD COMPANION TO CHILDREN'S
LITERATURE, *by Humphrey Carpenter and Mari Prichard.*
Illustrated. Oxford University Press, 1984. xiv + 588 pp.

Hilaire Belloc might have composed his all-purpose blurb expressly
for this new Oxford Companion: "a book which those who pick it up
will not readily lay down, and those who lay it down will not readily
pick up." You'll either lose track of time in euphoric browsing, or else
slam the thing shut in exasperation. An entry is something of arbitrary length and relevance, to contain whatever lore the authors had
handy, and what kind of book of reference is that?

The short answer is that it's not a reference book, no, a plum pud-
ding displayed like a reference book. From the entry on *Huckleberry
Finn*: "Unfortunately a malicious engraver tampered with one of the
plates of E. W. Kemble's illustrations, adding a male sex organ to the
figure of Silas Phelps in a picture showing him talking to his wife. The
page had to be cut out and a substitute stuck in by hand, which de-
layed American publication (originally intended to be in time for
Christmas 1884) until February 1885."

When you see eight percent of the *Huckleberry Finn* entry expended
on that incident, you may guess that literally anything may pop up

anywhere. You guess right. Things you'd never have thought to look
up include "Markoosie (1942–), the only Eskimo author to have published in English," Chile, China, Czechoslovakia, Problem Fiction,
Puppets, Puritans, Racism, Sexism, South Africa (where "the general
quality of books is poor"), Stein (Gertrude), Switzerland, even Yan-
kee Doodle.

Some connection, however tenuous, with children's literature is
enough to warrant inclusion. Stein (Gertrude)? She "wrote one children's book, *The World Is Round* (1937), in which her highly idiosyn-
cratic narrative technique is applied to the experiences of a child
named Rose," and that's all there is to that entry. Chile, which has produced "only a very small body of children's literature," also harbored
"the celebrated Gabriela Mistral," who wrote some children's poems.
In China, despite 3,000 years of literacy, "nothing was written especially for children until the 20th cent.," and today's Chinese kid-books
"at their worst seem like political tracts."

Such entries on the whole waste space, being too sketchy to sound
authoritative and too brief to tell you anything interesting. You taste
the joys of the book in its more leisurely pieces, especially its more
British ones. There all manner of oddments turn up. I don't know
where else you'd read that the Victorian poet W. E. Henley ("I am the
master of my fate; I am the captain of my soul") was the original of his
friend R. L. Stevenson's Long John Silver, or that Bernard Shaw wrote
Androcles and the Lion out of contempt for *Peter Pan*—he wanted to
show J. M. Barrie "how a play for children should be handled," or
that, because Tenniel the illustrator went through a spell of thinking
Lewis Carroll "too fussy" to work with again, the second *Alice* book
nearly had its pictures drawn by Arthur Sullivan's librettist W. S. Gilbert.

The *Peter Pan* entry is especially rich. Henley makes another appearance: the name "Wendy" records his little daughter's baby-talk
attempt at "friend." In "the heyday of trickwork on the London stage"
no expense was spared on special effects of which some never got
used; the play seems to have been the *Star Wars* of its era. At the first
night in 1904 the author of *The Prisoner of Zenda* was among the few
spectators not to be enchanted; his comment on this orgy of childish-

ness was, "Oh, for an hour of Herod!" *Peter Pan* would nevertheless become "a permanent piece of children's mythology," a process no doubt hastened by the installation in 1912 of a statue of pixie Peter in Kensington Gardens. It's a little startling to be told that it was put there "at Barrie's expense." Sir James M. Barrie was childlike—Max Beerbohm called him "a child, as it were in its bath, splashing and crowing as it splashes"—but no one ever called him impractical.

And here is the art-dictator John Ruskin (1819–1900) writing to the artist Kate Greenaway, whose specialty, "sunlit and flower-surrounded children clothed in imaginary 18th-cent. costume," seemed to Ruskin's eye altogether over-dressed:

"As we've got so far as taking off hats, I trust we may in time get to take off just a little more—say mittens—and then—perhaps—even shoes! and—(for fairies) even . . . stockings—and then—."

There was no "and then"; Kate Greenaway stuck to her costume-pieces, which inspired among other things "a persistent fashion in children's dress."

"Children's Literature," for heaven's sakes; not only is that under-taking impossibly grandiose, it also blandly ignores any culture where interaction between the adult's world and the child's proceeds without paper-and-ink mediation. What the authors are at home with has been spewed from printing presses, chiefly British ones, and most especially British presses of the time when Ruskin and Kate Greenaway thrived. That was toward the end of a long tradition of books meant to get children both literate and fantasizing innocuously.

As early as 1658, Jan Komensky, later known as Comenius, had found Hungarian pupils "so ignorant that he began to devise the PICTURE BOOK which even the most unlettered child could learn and read from," and in England a *Pretty Book of Pictures for Little Masters and Misses* had been published by 1752. In another forty years there were American editions of that, wherein little Colonial Masters and Misses could be regaled by "Tommy Trip, a Tom-Thumb-like character with bookish tastes who rides on his dog" and takes on "the giant Woglog."

There was much agonizing about taste and bad example; Edward

Lear's 1846 limerick about the old man of New York who "murdered himself with a fork" got deleted from *The Book of Nonsense* after 15 years by Lear himself, and the first book to record "Peter Piper picked a peck of pickled pepper" got denounced in 1820 as "vile trash" even in the absence of the word "pickled."

By a decade after John Ruskin's death, though, the children's market was being redefined by mass-producers of "reading matter" (what a phrase!), whose weekly papers—*Gem, Magnet, Boy's Friend*—consumed derring-do by the ream and sponsored a new breed of wholesome hack. The chief of these, Charles Hamilton (1876–1961), was an educated man who had published a Latin version of "Waltzing Matilda," and also a tireless impersonator of specialized yarn-spinners who existed only as pseudonymns of his. As "Frank Richards" he wrote the "Billy Bunter" stories for *Magnet*, as "Martin Clifford" the Tom Merry stories for *Gem*, as "Owen Conquest" the Rookwood stories for *Boy's Friend*. "It was roughly the equivalent of writing an average-length novel (70,000 words) each week," and his 7,000 stories, totalling 72 million words, earned him a place in the *Guinness Book of Records*. If you were to believe items in the daily press, Frank Richards, Martin Clifford and Owen Conquest even met one another occasionally, presumably to discuss their common profession. This information grows less mysterious when we learn from the article on "Harmsworth, Alfred" (1865–1922) that the *Daily Mail*, the *Daily Mirror* and *The Times* were all controlled by the proprietor of *Gem, Magnet*, and *Boy's Friend*.

We're told far less about what went on in America, a pity since a Companion to Children's Literature *in English* would have made a far more manageable assignment. Time and space wasted on perfunctory nods toward Chile and Czechoslovakia and China might then have been expended on some real research into non-British parts of the English-speaking world.

As it is, though one of the editors claims to be "currently writing a biography of Ezra Pound," the Companion is notably less reliable on American topics than on British. Anyone who describes Al Capp's *L'il Abner* as "a tough hillbilly folk-hero" can never have looked at Capp's transcendent creation. Perhaps Mammy Yokum ("Pansy") was tough, but Abner Yokum was a hillbilly Candide. (Trivia question: what was Pappy—"Lucifer"—Yokum's middle name? Answer: "Ornamental." No, the Oxford Companion does not tell us that.)

Victor Appleton, the pseudonymous creator of Tom Swift, receives no entry, nor does Tom himself (though the Bobbsey Twins do make it). Popeye's creator, E. C. Segar, is omitted too, notwithstanding that he gave "Jeep," "Goon," and "Wimpy" to the language. Popeye himself does squeeze by, in a brief item disfigured both by the non-mention of his creator and by the statement that "A Disney 'live-action' film based on the cartoons was released in 1981, but did not enjoy much success." The film, starring Robin Williams and Shelley Duvall, was the work of Robert Altman, whose fans, and Disney's too, have reason to complain.

Not that the inaccuracies that plague books of reference are confined to American materials; in the "Flashman" entry I found *Tom Brown's Schooldays* ascribed to Arthur Hughes the illustrator, instead of to Thomas Hughes, barrister and founder of Rugby, Tennessee.

But in cross-checking that, I was ensnared once more by the richness of a typical British entry. Thomas Hughes, what of Thomas Hughes (1822–96)? He went to Rugby School when Matthew Arnold's father was headmaster. "His lack of intellectual attainment kept him from Arnold's inner circle of favorites," and that may have been a good thing, since it exempted him from "pressure" toward "spiritual drives that were almost morbidly intense." He became a political radical, a vocation he expressed by founding the Working Men's College in London, where he held classes in boxing and took on all comers.

Having become a member of Parliament and visited America several times, he began in 1879 "a model community for young Englishmen for the 'Tom Brown' type, who were to lead the outdoor life and keep themselves by farming the land." He bought land in eastern Tennessee and named it "Rugby," but the scheme failed thanks to the laziness of his colonists. Back in England he died, aged 74, a judge.

And across the page, my eye is caught by the statement that "during the 19th cent. girls in America were recorded playing a game called 'Humpty Dumpty' which involved throwing themselves back-

wards and then trying to regain their balance," and then by a mad exegesis of the Humpty Dumpty rhyme someone published in 1906; it
begins by observing that to sit on a wall is impossible for an egg. On
the very next page Martin Gardner is explaining Lewis Carroll's *Hunt-
ing of the Snark* as "a poem of existential agony," and on the page after
that . . . but there is no end to this paper-chase.

1984

A Thousand
Lost Golf Balls

"What gets you," wrote Irving Layton, "is their unbewilderment"; he
was pointing to golfers.

> . . . you see at a glance
> among sportsmen they are the metaphysicians,
> intent, untalkative, pursuing Unity.

He adds that

> . . . no theory of pessimism is complete
> which altogether ignores them.

Also T. S. Eliot in his best mock-declamatory manner had the choric
voices of *The Rock* lament like Isaiah over the future desolation of such
a landscape as these metaphysicians traverse.

> In the land of lobelias and tennis flannels
> The rabbit shall burrow and the thorn revisit,
> The nettle shall flourish on the gravel court,
> And the wind shall say: 'Here were decent godless people:
> 'Their only monument the asphalt road
> 'And a thousand lost golf balls.'

The golf ball, the Unity they pursue, is spherical and white and compact and in every way Platonic, with this complication, that whereas the ideal golf ball is laid up in heaven, what is pursued in suburbia is a rubberoid imitation which gets lost. We are to imagine archaeologists some day puzzling over these small pocked spheres, yielded in large numbers by the deserted land, though only by certain tracts of it. It will occur to someone that objects so numerous and so strangely localized must have figured in a religious observance, windswept like whatever happened at Stonehenge, since (except at Notre Dame) they are not to be found adjacent to temples.

Writing for us, though, and not for posterity's analysts, Eliot chose, it would seem, an object of nearly ideal triviality, to emblematize "decent godless people": people, that is to say, unpersuaded not only by the Christian God but by any god: in one very general terminology, people lacking myths. Such people are given over to obsessive patterns of action they have no way to justify. One use of myth is to furnish reasons for a ritual act. A myth is a story, and we can see that a scorecard lacks plot.

In demotic usage a myth is an *untrue* story, by extension a non-existent entity, as when columnists wrote of President Carter's mythical energy policy. It is more useful to think of a myth as an invisible plan beneath the visible one, enhancing its value like oil under the back yard. Myth in the 20th century became the *sine qua non* of viable fiction, lacking which, we had merely incidents concatenated. Interest in myth was partly a way of permitting fictions to be serious when they were no longer Christian. Once a common fabric of belief had disintegrated, only myth lent seriousness. This usage is now so much conventionalized that critical ecumenism speaks of "the Christian myth," paying it the compliment of having once conferred significance on mere events almost as the myth of the Lone Avenger now has power to do.

(Parenthetically, I find it interesting that no novel of pretension occupies itself with golf; something there is about the golf ball that does not love myth.)

Myth entered 20th century literary consciousness by way of the Irish Revival, a movement originally brewed up by nominal Protes-

tants who found the scheme of redemption subscribed to by the majority of their compatriots unusable by artists in that time and place
for good reasons we need not go into. Yeats and AE embraced theos-
ophy, partly as a substitute religion, partly as an armature for imaginative constructs. About 1910 Yeats paid his old idol Maud Gonne a
handsome mythological compliment in a poem called "No Second
Troy."

It consists of four rhetorical questions: (1) Why should I blame her
for her turbulence? (2) How could she have been peaceful

> . . . with a mind
> That nobleness made simple as a fire,
> With beauty like a tightened bow, a kind
> That is not natural in an age like this,
> Being high and solitary and most stern?

(3) Being such a woman, what could she have done? and (4), spectac-
ularly, "Was there another Troy for her to burn?"

It is unnecessary to explain how the myth of Helen of Troy is being
used to enhance this haranguer of mobs whom Yeats later saw as "an
old bellows full of angry wind." It is important, though, to realize that
for Yeats the employment of the myth of Helen turns on an active belief in reincarnation. When a 17th century London poet referred to
Queen Elizabeth I as Diana—"Queen of Heaven, chaste and fair"—
no structure of belief is implied except belief in the superior rhetorical
leverage of classical terms. Such an address implies no more than this,
that England's Queen merits that maximum of praise to which the un-
assisted vernacular cannot aspire. Our rude tongue expends itself be-
lauding dairy-maids, and for queenly encomia we must invoke the
terms of the ancients.

But Yeats did believe that the great dead return, hence his unsettling rhetorical power. *We* are not required to believe it, but we need to
acknowledge that he does; and that, surveying his woman's possible
pre-carnations, he judges Helen the only possible one. Here she is,
then, reenacting her old part on Dublin's makeshift stage.

That *we* need not believe it is an interesting proviso. Since she has
no option, tragic compulsion lurks beneath the poem's surface of

compliment. A literary convention of graceful compliment is consequently unsuitable. To receive what it implies, we must somehow manage to take the myth seriously, if necessary in some way short of actual belief, and Yeats is aware that his readers will be able to manage this. For he wrote at a time when there were several alternative ways to entertain a myth seriously without yielding it ultimate assent.

One of these stemmed from *The Golden Bough* and the general prestige of Comparative Religion. People all over the world, such studies showed, had shaped their lives, indeed given their lives, at the behest of stories, held "true," which turned out to be variants of a few kernel stories. These were the great myths, and Max Müller was famous for reducing them to the Solar Myth: stories which involve a dying and reviving god but are really about that central concern of agricultural people, the sun going away in the fall, to return in the spring. No Comparative Religionist failed to observe the bond between the date of Easter and the spring equinox, when the sun is clearly back.

Any reincarnate being is a solar myth. Even Maud Gonne may qualify as a solar myth; was it not said that men might thresh a barn of corn by the light from one strand of her hair?

Another approach to the myth of Return was maintained by, of all disciplines, physics, which by late in the nineteenth century was satisfied that one event caused another with perfect predictability. Laplace had written:

> An intellect which at a given moment knew all the forces acting in nature, and the position of all things of which the world consists—supposing the said intellect were vast enough to subject these data to analysis—would embrace in the same formula the motions of the greatest bodies in the universe and those of the slightest atoms; nothing would be uncertain for it, and the future like the past would be present to its eyes.

Such a universe is a closed plenum, embracing a finite inventory of states. Day after day of ceaseless change is its norm, until one day it exhausts its repertoire and assumes a state it has occupied before. That state must necessarily be followed by the state that followed it last time, and the cycle of Eternal Return has begun anew:

Another Troy must rise and set,
Another lineage feed the crow,
Another Argo's painted prow
Drive to a flashier bauble yet.

Though literary people did not read the physicists, they could receive this doctrine of historical recurrence from Nietzsche, who found it inexpressibly exciting. It allows you to believe in, for instance, reincarnation or something like it, while not being especially crowded by that belief, so enormous are the time-spans involved. Also if your Golden Age lay in the past it will some day be back, which may be a comfort in deflationary times, while if your Golden Age lies in the future, be sure that the future is guaranteed to come.

It was into this curious amalgam of believabilities and things that had been fervently believed that Yeats launched his poems and plays: celebrations of the present when it could impersonate the past, of the past when like the story of Cuchulain it might be expected to animate the present or perhaps the near future. For a Fenian revolutionary like Yeats the use of myth is like the use of brandy, to put spirit into the troops.

T. S. Eliot, however, did not come to myth through Yeats, whom he was orthodox enough to hold always at arm's length. (His praise of Yeats came very late indeed. It commenced with the 1938 play called *Purgatory*: oddly enough, a play about Eternal Return.) No, Eliot was impressed by the "mythological method," as he called it, when the method was used by James Joyce, who simply *used* it without asking that its assumptions be for a moment believed.

The myth in *Ulysses* adheres to the definition of myth we suggested earlier: an invisible plan beneath the visible. So invisible is it that the book nowhere spells it out. The myth is hinted at only, and only by the book's title.

Joyce may have discovered this way of working in the course of hearing many homilies, which transposed the text of the week into Dublin terms. Every day we may wash Christ's feet; every day we may crucify Him anew; each day presents us with such an opportunity as the Rich Young Man sought out and then refused. The very first story in *Dubliners* takes its text from the Gospels. It is called "The Sisters," and presents us with two women whose brother has died. If we observe the women carefully we may notice that one of them, like the scriptural Martha, keeps constantly busy while the other, like the scriptural Mary, prefers talk. In the very last sentences there is an eerie hint that the dead man may have come to life again; but no, that was an effect produced by overwrought nerves. There is no Messiah present of any description.

The next story to be written, "Eveline," is a variation on the Gospel theme, "Follow Me." The next one, "After the Race," pertains to a rich young man. Though the 22-year-old Joyce had an informal contract to deliver ten stories to *The Irish Homestead*, the paper apparently decided their view of life was exceptionally bleak, and after those three it published no more. There is no indication that anyone at the *Homestead* guessed where the plots were coming from.

Joyce knew when he entered into the agreement that he would need ten story ideas in a relatively short time, and he may have reasoned that the Gospels, abounding as they do in brief narratives, make a splendid quarry for plots. As we have seen too, the reenactment of Gospel narratives by daily lives was underwritten by homiletic convention. From this it was an easy step to Leopold Bloom's reenactment of the *Odyssey*. Bloom's story was at one time to have been a *Dubliners* story, to be called "Ulysses," which means that by 1906 Joyce was seeking plots in sacred books other than the one they expounded in the pro-cathedral.

When *Ulysses* appeared T. S. Eliot was excited by the possibilities of what he called "the mythological method," an improvement, so he said, on the narrative method. He perceived in the mythological method a way of shaping the anarchy and futility of modern life, and at one time he seems to have meant his long poem, *The Waste Land*, to be shaped by a systematic parallel with the *Aeneid*. The hero-observer was to move across the sea, bearing his tribal totems from Cambridge (Mass.) to London, the Unreal City. Mme Sosostris was the Sibyl of Cumae; the woman at the dressing-table (in a passage where we encounter the Virgilian word "lacquearia") was Dido. In the end, like Aeneas, he would leave her to her grief and keep journeying, if not to found Rome then to "set his lands in order" at the behest of something said by the thunder (*Jupiter tonans*).

Though this scheme was abandoned, its traces are on the poem as we have it, and as we know from the 1925 essay "Ulysses, Order and Myth," Eliot's interest in "the mythological method" outlasted his work on *The Waste Land* by at least three years. That is the essay in which he speaks of myth as a way for the poet to shape modern futility. Modern life, for Eliot, was always something that needed shaping; it had no substantial forms of its own save a futile quest for lost golf balls.

Nor did "Ulysses, Order and Myth" exhaust the subject. When Eliot commenced writing plays he turned again to myth for his plots. *Murder in the Cathedral* takes its events from history but its shape from the *Agamemnon*, a play in which the hero returns from abroad amid shrieking premonitions of doom. And it is well known that the later plays derive from Euripides; Eliot himself divulged the source of *The Cocktail Party* in the *Alcestis*, the play about Herakles bringing back a lost wife. Eliot's Herakles was Sir Henry Harcourt-Reilly, psychiatrist, whose taste for strong drink was modelled on that of Herakles in the spirit in which Joyce modelled Bloom's "knockmedown cigar" on the firebrand with which Ulysses blinded the Cyclops.

Such a detail verges on the farcical, and the mythological method is always in danger of turning into an elaborate joke the author and the reader share. Modern anarchy and futility can trivialize the myth, and trivialization had better be protected by a climate of fun. If Joyce does not trivialize the *Odyssey* it is because his estimate of urban life is not as low as Eliot's, whose nostalgia was for ancient rural villages.

Eliot takes it for granted that what a myth may do, besides help you invent a plot, is give access to an old story's power. If Yeats (born 1865) could assume readers whose sense of myth was shaped by Max Müller, Eliot (born 1888) belonged to the generation of Carl Jung, whose Collective Unconscious is itself a fascinating myth about myth. When Jungian Man hears versions of old stories something stirs, deep down; he need not even consciously acknowledge the pattern of the story he is hearing. Unlike the myth in "No Second Troy," which energizes the poem only in being explicitly evoked, the myth beneath an Eliot play seems credited with an efficacy that does not depend on our identifying it. The spoken rhetoric, even, may offer to do no more than juggle with golf balls, putting forth none of the portentousness that makes things so difficult for the actors in *The Family Reunion*. In the theater, where we have no page to look at, we may not even be aware that it is verse. As for the people who speak the words of *The Cocktail Party*, they seem trivial stick-figures of drawing-room comedy. It is clear that Eliot expected a great deal of the plot he'd taken from Euripides: nothing less than the ballast of seriousness, subliminally acknowledged.

Eliot's theater, we may say, died without having been born. It has certainly inaugurated no tradition. Myth, correspondingly, has withdrawn into the interstices of language itself, incarnate in grammatical forms, as when we say that the moon pulls the tides and attend not to a goddess and her toils but to the shape of the sentence, to what Ernest Fenollosa called the transfer of force, subject-verb-object, none of them static. The moon is a process, the tides are a process, the pull is a mystery, the sentence is an ordering. In Einstein's world things regularly happen with neither agents nor forces, in a ballet that maps the configurations of space-time but neither causes those configurations nor is caused by them. No one believes any longer in the closed world of physical determinism, and Nietzsche is dead. In such a world as we now inhabit, the mythological method is an archaic one for literature.

Its hegemony extended from Yeats's generation to Eliot's. Looking back, we may note that its career began in belief and ended in skepticism. Yeats wrote out of a belief in reincarnation which made his poetic statements potentially *true*; people had lived out the same passions in a less scruffy setting, and were condemned now to live them out anew. Eliot wrote out of an acceptance of anarchy and futility, the myth present by virtue of the poet's will, to give a poem shape where human actions were shapeless. We are now apt to attribute the power of Eliot's poems to their oracular language, and find him least persuasive precisely where, as in the late plays, he depends on myth and not eloquence.

If we are left with what Eliot dismissed, undeniable empirical golf balls by the thousand, we are not thereby left with unmeaning. What is no longer active, having become part of literary history, is one order of poetic meaning, whereby "meaning" was a palpable *enhancement* of the given, and either left aside what it could not enhance, such as golf balls, or else pointed to them as instances of anarchy and futility, unburied skulls in a domain surrounding the space where the poet performed his rites.

Yeats and Eliot, we may come to decide, had an unsuspected thing in common: both of them possessed gnostic sensibilities, avid to discard the mere given and pursue poetry amid the mind's arcana. The mythological method, as pursued by them, was a kind of trivializing of religion because a trivializing of this present world, the world scorned by the Irishman and humorously shunned by the American. It was Joyce of all writers, neither believing in myth nor disbelieving in it but finding it a convenience, who was centrally orthodox in devoting his attention to whatever was in front of him. He enters his second century growing in stature.

Great issues, said Sherlock Holmes, may hang upon a bootlace. One thing studies of myth in literature should never tempt us to do is suppose that literature grows impossible when bootlaces and golf balls prove to occupy, as they do, an unromantic amount of human attention.

1984

The Fourth Policeman

Like the man with no name I was born a long time ago—I am older than the Free State itself—and like Myles in the Scotch House I have the impression of having been here a long time yet do not seem to be growing old enough. "I have no corns or ulcers and am still encountering things which are *quite new* to me."[1] When the man in *The Third Policeman* encountered such things it was with the sensation of having dropped into an altered universe, a sensation I can still experience some time after arriving in Ireland. Just the other afternoon in my favorite corner of the Georgian Bar in Buswell's, I was minding my drink and my business, which was doing desultory research in a copy of *The Third Policeman*, when a man walked over whom I'd better describe.

He was seventyish maybe and rubicund and short and sturdy—as wide as he was tall more or less, with white hair falling every which way from under a black hat. There was no need of the hat since we were indoors but he kept it on because that was the way to keep track of it. He had been down at the far corner of the counter talking with

This essay is a talk I gave in Dublin at a Flann O'Brien Symposium in April 1986. Every word of the opening anecdote is true.
[1]Flann O'Brien, *The Hair of the Dogma*, London, 1986, 65.

two other men, he standing and they sitting on barstools, and now that he made his way in my direction I could see how his black gabardine was slipping down off his shoulders. Beneath it the usual compilation of tweeds and sweaters had been improvised against what Bord Fáilte calls "spring." His left hand held a pint and from his right a canvas knapsack dangled toward the floor. It was small and contained something fairly heavy—the world supply of Omnium, perhaps.

What had drawn him in my direction was the sight of me reading. He took up his stance, the knapsack not dangling but hanging straight and heavy like a stalled pendulum, and he said "Print."

"Print," he repeated. "That is the most dangerous stuff ever invented. Tell me what it is."

I held up the book. Flann O'Brien. *The Third Policeman.*

"Ah," he said, "not for me. I was once a professor of History. History is science. That is . . . art." "Art" underwent the dropping inflection of dismissal. And he turned and walked away, and out of the room.

When I made to go out myself, past that far corner of the bar, one of the two men on the stools stopped me to say, "And so do you know the poet?"

(The poet!) I said I did not, and wanted to know what had been his name. So my man asked the other man, "What is the name of our friend the poet?" and the second man furrowed his face and could not recall. I thought to prompt them: "He said he had been a professor of History." The first man emended crisply: "And a poet." That seemed to be as far as we were going with that. Then said my first man, "Show me what were you reading?" Once again accordingly I displayed *The Third Policeman.* "Flann O'Brien," said he. "You are aware that was not his real name?" And with barely a pause he went on to inform me. "His real name is O Fay o lan." "O Fay o lan?" I asked; "O Fay loin?" "That is it," he confirmed. "O'Faoláin. That is his real name."

I need not specify the one certainty I have salvaged from all this bewilderment, that the professor-scientist-poet, the one who was aphoristic about the dangers of print, can only have been de Selby, the same who held that sleep was a succession of fainting-fits and who as recently as ten years ago had himself listed in the telephone book under the guise of a stone-quarrying firm in Tallaght. That would have been in his scientific period, back when hammering was inseparable from the de Selby dialectic.[2] Since then he has clearly passed over into a poetic incarnation. You can tell that from the fact that he is no longer listed. Tom Moore was never in the telephone book, and neither was Father Prout. That, de Selby would confirm, settles the matter.

I hope I need not impress on you that every word of the foregoing is true. I have chosen to wind my way into my part of the Symposium in this leisurely fashion because there can be no doubt that the world of *The Third Policeman* is a very queer one. That is how it differs from *At Swim-Two-Birds*, a very queer book but not a very queer world, and I need some plausible analogy for the ease with which we glide into that queerness. As a foreigner I liken it to the queerness that can ensue shortly after Aer Lingus has glided me into Dublin: the queerness amid which my encounter with de Selby seemed perfectly natural.

Let me dwell on those differing varieties of queerness. When a cow takes the witness-stand in *At Swim-Two-Birds*, or when a horde of cowboys comes pounding out of Ringsend—

> So when the moon had raised her lamp o'er the prairie grasses, out flies the bunch of us, Slug, Shorty and myself on a buckboard making like hell for Irishtown with our ears back and the butts of our six-guns streaming behind us in the wind. . . . Be damned to the lot of us, I roared, flaying the nags and bashing the buckboard across the prairie, passing out lorries and trams and sending poor so-and-so's on bicycles scuttling down lanes with nothing showing but the whites of their eyes.

—at such times we know that games are being played with literary conventions. "When the moon had raised her lamp o'er the prairie grasses"—that's a giveaway: that is not something *seen*, it is the hack's prefab elegance, no different from the "rosyfinger'd dawn" of every

[2] *The Third Policeman*, London, 1967, 144. Subsequent references will be abbreviated TP and will be given parenthetically in the text.

hack's example, Homer. "With ears back," with a "streaming in the wind"—those are the obligatory formulae for a Western writer's horse; "with *our* ears back," is a mite careless, since it loses the distinction between us and our horses (a distinction, however, that could also elude Swift). It's all literary, though: all an exhibition of conventions adopted, dropped, shifted, mingled. And any character immersed in a convention finds its every inflection fully natural. Distress only occurs when the author behind the convention is careless of its exactions, as when the cow on the witness-stand complains of not being milked regularly.

But *this* is something different from a word-game however stylized:

> About a hundred yards away on the left-hand side was a house which astonished me. It looked as if it were painted like an advertisement on a board on the roadside and indeed very poorly painted. It looked completely false and unconvincing. It did not seem to have any depth or breadth and looked as if it would not deceive a child. . . . As I approached, the house seemed to change its appearance. At first, it did nothing to reconcile itself with the shape of an ordinary house but it became uncertain in outline like a thing glimpsed under ruffled water. Then it became clear again and I saw that it began to have some back to it. . . . I gathered this from the fact that I seemed to see the front and the back of the "building" simultaneously. . . . Then I found myself almost in the shadow of the structure, dry-throated and timorous from wonder and anxiety. (TP, 52–3)

That is different entirely from anything to be found in the Dermot Trellis saga, or anything else with "Flann O'Brien" signed to it. Words are not generating matter by their promiscuities; no, a man who has seen something outside the pale of anyone's experience is taking lengthy pains to find the words for it. He is in a place as queer as Ireland, and undergoing assault from its queerness.

Before he was assaulted by the queerness of a police station that evaded the normal dimensionalities of space, he was exulting in the amenities of what he'd come to take for normal because it was so pleasant:

> It was a new and a bright day, the day of the world. Birds piped without
> limitation and incomparable stripe-coloured bees passed above me on
> their missions and hardly ever came back the same way home. My eyes
> were shuttered and my head was buzzing with the spinning of the uni-
> verse. (TP, 42)

There are many such passages in *The Third Policeman*, and if you
read them in a hurry they can resemble in their monotony the Finn
passages in *At Swim*, if you read *those* in a hurry. They have irritated
even Tony Cronin, who once complained of the book that it was "full
of oddly generalised and amorphous description, that of landscape,
which occupies such a large part of it, being composed in the most la-
bourious way out of mere landscape-elements, like a child's picture."[3]
But that is like complaining that Gerty McDowell's reveries are composed of mere adolescent clichés, like a women's novelette. Exactly
what they bespeak is infantile salubriousness, the narrator being a
monomaniac who has spent his life mostly among his books and papers (TP, 39), and has never before had to ignore the onus of killing
someone. Later, when he must ignore the prospect of being hanged,
we can see the mechanism with especial plainness:

> All my senses, relieved from the agony of dealing with the existence of
> the Sergeant, became supernaturally alert at the work of interpreting
> the genial day for my benefit. Men who were notable for the whiteness
> of their shirts worked diminutively in the distant bog, toiling in the
> brown turf and heather. Patient horses stood near with their useful
> carts. Birds were audible in the secrecy of the bigger trees, changing
> branches and conversing not tumultuously. (TP, 125)

Such is the, so to speak, "normal" world of much of the book, and
we'll do well to notice that it too, on first encounter, strikes our man as
queer:

> My surroundings had a strangeness of a peculiar kind, entirely sepa-
> rate from the mere strangeness of a country where one has never been

[3]From *Irish Times*, 12 December 1975, as reprinted in Rüdiger Imhof, ed., *Alive-Alive O!*,
115. Let it be recorded that by 1986 Mr. Cronin was explicitly repudiating this early
view. If, here and elsewhere, I cite him for the sake of disagreement, it's because he's
nearly unique in having gone on record about *The Third Policeman* in any detailed way.

before. Everything seemed almost too pleasant, too perfect, too finely made. Each thing the eye could see was unmistakeable and unambiguous, incapable of merging with any other thing or of being confused with it. (TP, 39)

We are at liberty to extend his remarks on the queerness of this. If we are in Ireland it is a peculiar Ireland indeed. For eleven consecutive chapters—clear to the end of the book—there is no wind, no chill, and (save for a surly downpour on Execution Morning) no mention of rain falling. Ornamental clouds move in an otherwise flawless sky. Apart from those toilers "notable for the whiteness of their shirts" (surreal detail!) the landscape is strikingly unpopulated. The turf-cutters resemble details in a Flemish painting. Oaths are not sworn. Invective is not launched. Not a church is anywhere to be seen, nor a priest. Despite all the talk of bicycles, no cyclists pass.

Moreover, in what part of what century are we situated? Mankind having entered the bicycle era, we are somewhere, say, post-1895. (Mr. Dunlop's pneumatic invention is ubiquitous.) There seem to be no motorcars, at least they do not happen to be mentioned. Sergeant Pluck does allude to the possibility of a motor-cycle "with overhead valves and a dynamo for light" (TP, 55), and de Selby, whose distance from present time is never specified, once examined some "old" cinematograph films in which he found "a strong repetitive element," never having seen any projected (TP, 50). The time-table of the Age of Technology (before or after electric light, before or after electric trams, before or after petrol engines) seems not to be marking off eras in its familiar inexorable way. That may reflect merely the irregular percolation of technological awareness into rural Ireland, though more likely our author is exploiting that irregularity to make plausible a dream-universe defined chiefly by omissions.

And among the striking omissions are the linguistic ones. Apart from proper names, I do not recall one Irish word in the book anywhere. It is particularly noteworthy, in a book so full of policemen, that the word to designate them is always and only "policeman." The word "Garda" never appears. It is as if there had been no Gaelic League, as if the Republic had never been proclaimed, as if there were no Treaty, no 1925. An "Act of Parliament," of all things, is what it will take to secure the regulation of rat-trap pedals (TP, 77). That is pre-1919 talk, and no one remarks on it. An Ireland from which politics and political awareness have simply been subtracted, that is an unsettling place indeed.

The policemen, moreover, are not cogs in some larger machinery of justice, a-clatter with courts and magistrates, lawyers and jailers. No, they *are* the machinery of justice, in a cosmos that has regard for only two things, bicycles and documented identities. "Why should anyone steal a watch when they can steal a bicycle?" (TP, 61) is one of the working maxims, and another is that "If you have no name you possess nothing and you do not exist and even your trousers are not on you. . . . On the other separate hand you can do what you like and the law cannot touch you (TP, 61–2). This account does need to be slightly modified. Just outside and above the tidy system there exists an Inspector O'Corky who is irascible about other irregularities such as murder, but Inspector O'Corky is easily placated by the simple act of taking into custody the nearest adjacent party, for summary hanging on the following dawn.

I spell out these presuppositions in detail because I have never seen them spelled out before. They get passed over, I think, thanks to our author's insidious success in insinuating us into the world of his book without awakening any challenge to its salient strangeness. (I can think of no parallel save "A Modest Proposal," in which bourgeois values—the sheer nuisance, e.g., of beggars—have settled in unquestioned by the time Swift springs his trap.) In its very simplicity it is an extremely sturdy world. We are even willing to believe that securing money to publish a commentary on de Selby is sufficient reason for the murder of old Mathers, and that is the more plausible because old Mathers, like everyone else in the book, is seemingly not going to be mourned by anyone. The only social relationships that obtain are defraudment and persecution; those suffice, it seems, to propel a plausible cosmos. De Selby himself underwent "a long series of prosecutions for water-wastage" (TP, 146), and his commentators seem united less by devotion to his memory than by a passion for accusing one another of fraud.

"Great hatred," wrote Yeats, "little room."

Flann O'Brien seems confident that he has created a plausible cartoon of Ireland, or of some country resembling it. He evidently has, since no one complains about the likeness. Such complaint as I have seen is confined to matters of descriptive style. It has also been hinted that *At Swim*'s "fun" comes to us in this book somewhat impaired. Yes.

No, unlike the world of *At Swim*, explicitly and by definition arbitrary, the world of *The Third Policeman* is nearly naturalistic. Its premises do not shift. It is intense to the point of claustrophobia. And it creates and contains its own language. That does seem the way to put it. In speaking of *At Swim* we'd say by contrast that the language creates the world.

And if our book's world is a cartoon of Ireland, achieved by ruthless reduction, its language too is a cartoon, achieved by ruthless selection and iteration of devices that characterize the Middle and Early Modern Irish, where so proud a heritage lies. We've long known of the author's minute and extensive acquaintance with the Irish language and literature in its chronological layers; also of the fun he has in *At Swim* with the Finn saga, and his derivation of unexpected themes like the cowboy stampede from such Irish themes as the cattle-raid. Likewise much of *The Third Policeman* enshrines the motif of the miraculous journey. But more intimately, most of its (highly peculiar) language derives from Irish-language mannerisms of a kind familiar to even a casual reader who has had to rely on translations: such a reader for instance as myself.

Friends who know Irish assure me that in this respect an annotated edition would surprise by its bulk. Let me neither destroy my own credibility nor offend the author's shade by attempting even a beginning. Let me only enforce my present argument by remarking a few obvious headings. There are the riddles:

> "That is a fine day," I said. "What are you doing with a lamp in the white morning?"
>
> "I can give you a question as good as that," he responded. "Can you notify me of the meaning of a bulbul?"
>
> "A bulbul?"

"What would you say a bulbul is?" . . .

"Not one of those ladies who take money?" I said.

"No."

"Not the brass knobs on a German steam organ?"

"Not the knobs."

"Nothing to do with the independence of America or such like?"

"No."

"A tumour, or the lather in a cow's mouth, or those elastic articles that ladies wear?"

"Not them by a long chalk."

"Not an eastern musical instrument played by Arabs?"

He clapped his hands.

"Not that but very near it," he smiled, "something next door to it. You are a cordial intelligent man. A bulbul is a Persian nightingale. What do you think of that now?" (TP, 65–6)

Here the riddle intersects another Mylesian theme, the slipperiness of Gaelic lexicography. Time and again Myles would have a little fun with Dr. Dinneen, whose Sisyphean task had been to reduce to alphabetic lists a language unsuited to that by nature and structure. "Suppose," Myles once asked, "one looked up in an English dictionary to find the exact meaning of 'chair' and found it was 'a yellow worm which infests sandy soil in arid regions; a type of eastern footwear; ale made from gooseberries. . . .'[4] But such was the kind of variety he was delighted to produce, listed under one word, in Dinneen's *Irish-English Dictionary*.

But I digress. Riddles. Lists, long lists, little lists: a tricycle, a patent tandem, a velocipede, a penny-farthing. "Bereavement, old age, love, sin, death and other saliencies of existence" (TP, 55, 93). (And among the things the narrator hopes to take out of eternity are "a bottle of whiskey, precious stones to the value of £200,000, some bananas, a fountain-pen and writing materials, and finally a serge suit of blue with silk linings" [TP, 137].) Riddles, lists, elegant unforeseeable similes ("My knees opened up like a rosebud in the rich sunlight, pushing my shins two inches further to the bottom of the bed" [TP, 115]), finally, a repeated reliance on constructions that foreground

[4]*The Hair of the Dogma*, 48.

the adjective and the noun. "The sun was in the neighbourhood also, distributing his enchantment unobtrusively, colouring the sides of things that were unalive and livening the hearts of living things"; or still better, ". . . a gentle day, mild, magical and innocent with great sailings of white cloud serene and impregnable in the high sky, moving along like kingly swans on quiet water" (TP, 151).

The book's verbal mannerisms, in short, seem contrived to demonstrate a pressure of Irish usage, notably *learned* Irish usage—middle Irish, early-modern Irish—upon the English that furnishes its dictionary. This is to be carefully differentiated from the stage-Irish of Boucicault or Somerville and Ross or even Synge, where characters, unlearned and but newly arrived into bilinguality, achieve marketable charm by inadvertence. " 'Tis destroyed I am surely"—in such expressions we behold Irish syntax taking charge of English words. But there is nothing of that class anywhere in our book. O'Brien's delectable pedantries are beyond the reach of any Christy Mahon or Pegeen Mike.

Nor is there any trace of big grinning feckless charm. The verbal surface is stretched over an abyss, criss-crossed by taut chains of logic, very thin ones. The logic commences, of course, with de Selby, and most readers have found themselves feeling, now and again, that de Selby nearly makes sense. "It is difficult," as the narrator notes, "to get to grips with his process of reasoning or to refute his curious conclusions" (TP, 117).

The speed of light being finite, it is perfectly true that the image you see in the mirror, formed as it is from rays that left your face an infinitesimal fraction of a second ago, is that of someone infinitesimally younger than you (TP, 64). From this de Selby deduced that one's early youth should be perceptible at the end of a near-infinity of reflections set up between parallel mirrors, an argument one tends to reject before quite being sure what is wrong with it (TP, 65). De Selby, and not de Valera, might have been founding father of the Institute of Advanced Studies, sometime host of Schrödinger, the cat in whose famous thought-experiment was simultaneously both dead and alive. Certainly de Selby is kin to other celebrated Irishmen: notably, to William Rowan Hamilton, who produced circumstances under which 2×3 and 3×2 need not yield identical products,[5] and to George Francis Fitzgerald who argued that a rapidly moving body gets smaller along its axis of travel. Fitzgerald also resembles de Selby in his pursuit of vain goals, as, about 1895, his repeated efforts to fly, on the back lawn of Trinity, beneath a top hat, on huge canvas wings. He achieved a maximum altitude of six inches. Yet the Fitzgerald Contraction, which sounds less likely than flight, survives, unassailable, embedded in the universe described by Relativity. De Selby too may be right about something equally improbable.[6]

Yes, logic pervades the book. It's unnecessary to adduce Sergeant Pluck's account (TP, 84-5) of the molecular interchange between rider and bicycle. Logic, logic, not sentiment, is a salient Irish tradition. (It was Matthew Arnold who told the Celts they were "emotional." They made as if to believe him, that being what English consumers seemed to want.) The Synge family treated John Millington as its black sheep, his plays extrinsic to the family tradition of mathematicians including one Nobel Laureate. (I was in college with one mathematical Synge; she's now at the famous place in Princeton.) De Valera was the only modern head of state to earn an obituary in the Transactions of the Royal Society, on account of his mathematical attainments. It was written by J. L. Synge, F.R.S., mathematician and nephew of the playwright. Even Yeats of the Celtic Twilight was a great counter, a connoisseur of diagrams (interpenetrating cones, recursive cycles). And Joyce—there was a time when *Ulysses* seemed nothing but a crabbed diagram.

As the British pass for literary people and are at heart literary philistines but avid technologists and even train-watchers, as Americans pass for technologists but fear technology and are at heart connoisseurs of abstraction, so the Irish have for a century suffered the world to misperceive them as the dreamers of the smile and the tear, knowing themselves to be implacable with logic, aware too that logic does nothing to a people save divide them, devoid as it is of criteria for agreeing on premises. But though logic's consequences divide its

[5]See Seán O'Donnell, *William Rowan Hamilton*, Dublin, 1984, 145.
[6]See Liam Byrne, *History of Aviation in Ireland*, Dublin, 1980, 28–9.

possession can unite. Of the three peoples mentioned, the Irish alone have the singular strength of knowing what their true tradition is.

To find Ireland in *The Third Policeman*, you may well be thinking, is like identifying a skeleton from its dental records. Or better, *The Third Policeman* is like an X-ray negative of Ireland: black and white interchanged, no trace of smile and soft skin kissed by sunlight, all skull and ossature and articulation. And if this is X-rayed Ireland, a most salient Irish saliency is not absent. The world of *The Third Policeman* is ruled by fiat, and by a Trinity, of policemen. They hold the keys to the upper world and the nether; they are themselves a great mystery, especially the third; people in difficulty come to them in supplication; all difficulties pertain to one entity, the bicycle, which resembles the soul in the mystery of its relation to the body; they are severe about the sexual improprieties on which a commingling of bodies and bicycles can open.

Policeman MacCruiskeen, he is a creator: of curious boxes in infinite regress, of a mangle which wrings screams out of light, of a card of no known color, the color of which drives men mad.

Policeman Pluck, he is the beneficent one of the trio: implacable if need be and willing to hang you if it will balance books, but also a saver of people from themselves by losing their bicycles but finding them again on petition.

Policeman Fox, though, he is the great mystery: trickster, illusionist, compressor and expander of time, more than once alluded to by the others though in such bizarre terms we'd place no hopes in seeing him were it not for the book's title. Christian discourse has likewise found that the Holy Spirit presents obstacles to visualization. To painters who presented Creator and Redeemer explicitly, the dove always seemed an expedient.

I've said enough now to be thoroughly misunderstood. I am far from asking anyone to suppose that such hints sketch a "meaning" for the book. *The Third Policeman* is after all far from deliberate enough to bear any great weight of interpretation. I trust I have done a service if by sketching an interpretation I've displayed the absurdity of any attempt to interpret. The book is a black joke, a comic turn; it is not a *Divina Commedia* and never dreamed of being one. In particular, it is not what Mr. Cronin once suspected it aspired to be, an allegory; he was right to say that as allegory it fails. And I'd be surprised to learn that when its author specified his policemen's functions any such scheme as I've hinted at—Creator, Redeemer, uniting Mystery—occurred to him at all. If it had, and if I judge him aright, he'd have forthwith banished the book from his mind unwritten.

What I've tried to hint at is an order of feeling he drew on as he elaborated his comedy. Jokes draw on stable orders of shared feeling. Vivian Mercier in *The Irish Comic Tradition* has shown how Irish jokes about marriage form around an unstated core that can seldom have been consciously present to their inventors: the pagan tradition of the Sheela-na-gig, that monstrous grinning hag. Flann O'Brien likewise, setting out to write a funny book where we'd learn on the last page that the man in the story was dead all the time, elaborated what he called "a sort of hell" for a character he called "a heel and a killer," and in the process came closer than he ever did again to inventing something not just brilliant but disturbingly coherent. For into that carefully defined intention flowed powerful feelings with which the Church in Ireland can affect the scoffer and the devout alike: feelings concerning a hidden order you can view as malign or beneficent but certainly as arbitrary, indeed machine-like; with a sort of bureaucracy, a loose division of functions, a mysterious busy-ness, a tradition of arcane logic, and an odd way of spoiling itself on human contact.

Whether life itself be a gift or an imposition, whether God's grace might not have been more generously exercised in not calling us into existence to experience its workings, is a question the Irish Catholic sensibility seems never to have been able to resolve to its own satisfaction. The one-legged man remarks of life that there is nothing so dangerous. "You can't smoke it, nobody will give you tuppence-halfpenny for the half of it and it kills you in the wind-up. It is a queer contraption, very dangerous, a certain death-trap. Life?" (TP, 45).

That's akin to the sustained perversity Myles exploited in *Cruiskeen Lawn* year in, year out; different, though, in voicing a coherent feeling, one sustained by a national tradition. It hints at how a Catholic Swift might have sounded, had he known Middle Irish rhetoric.

The three policemen draw their substantiality from the robust Irish custom that portrays policemen as both enormous and comic. But, drawing as well on concentrated mythic power secreted in deeper and more solemn recesses, they break from the funny-policeman stereotype the way their police station breaks from the dimensionalities of normal space. They resemble at times men as trees walking. Far from being a text that welcomes exegesis, *The Third Policeman* has the primitive clinging power a work little premeditated can sometimes acquire. Think of Nashe's lines—

> . . . Brightness falls from the air,
> Queens have died young and fair,
> Dust hath closed Helen's eye . . .

No one forgets that, though no one is even sure what the first line means. Nashe dashed it off in plague-time, surely not thinking he was destining something for the ages. Or take the story of Scrooge, one of Dickens's hurried entertainments. Or the raven that says "Nevermore" and won't let you forget it. *The Third Policeman* belongs in such company. Long after we've forgotten the plot's intricacies, a dark weight and sense stays lodged in memory. O'Brien wrote it rapidly, and seems to have had fun writing it.

Then after he was distanced from it by the time it took a publisher or two to miss the point—an exercise at which publishers are nigh infallible—he suddenly stopped sending it out. Into a drawer it went, for 25 years. For he seems to have re-read it, and been unsettled: the first of thousands of readers it has unsettled. He liked his effects under rational control. And this book grimaced at him, from expressive levels he was careful never to monkey with again. The dark secret of Myles na Gopaleen was this: that he alone knew about *The Third Policeman*, that radioactive sheaf of typescript. I imagine a Fourth Policeman coming to life, a Policeman the book had managed to keep offstage by its pretense that when the Third appeared there would be no more. And unlike the Three Policemen of Flann O'Brien's invention, the Fourth was Brian O'Nolan's explicitly formed and highly orthodox conscience, and he raised a huge whitegloved hand and boomed out "No!"

For despite even such orthodox—not to say "literary"—touches as a path to Eternity that led through a *selva oscura*, a dark wood, and a gate to Eternity that resembles a church porch and is surely the entrance to a tomb, the book's vision of Eternity was subversive and devoid of hope. The book's hope consisted in pantheistic yearnings, for an eternity of being a person no more but, say, "the chill of an April wind" (TP, 159) or the agony of the sea when it bursts upon a lonely shore in despair, or "a big wave in mid-ocean . . . a very lonely and spiritual thing" (TP, 162). Those are the most deeply felt passages in all his writing. Like much else in the book, they have pagan Irish antecedents. And the Fourth Policeman reminded him they were wrong. Wrong.

Today he would be almost 75. The only consolation we can take from his early death is to reflect that an O'Nolan of 70 might have nerved himself to destroy that typescript for good.

At Swim-Two-Birds, where the puzzles and sources lie on the surface, will always attract exegetical attention. Just now it converges neatly with our present interest in metafictions, autonomous texts, intertextuality. In gloomy moments I predict a time of eclipse for *The Third Policeman*. We seem to be moving into a critical period with no vocabulary for getting a grip on it. But I next predict that it will be rediscovered, and again, and again. There's no killing a piece of mythic power like that. It will survive while Ireland is Ireland and the English-speaking world's uneasy conscience, and the Fourth Policeman that failed to kill it in the cradle will have no power over it.

1986

Poets at the Blackboard

Russell Baker has remarked on the proclivity of Americans for combining a good time with something improving: he instanced people who went to the seashore and sang hymns. Today's program, however improving, cannot offer, save to special tastes, an explicit good time; otherwise it would start with the showing of a motion picture which unfortunately has not been produced. *With Bill and Ez at College* would be a marvelous silent film.

The mind's eye can screen many bits: the medium long shot for instance in which Williams is standing with a billiard cue in his right hand, its butt resting upon the floor: when suddenly the fat lady beside him is knocked flat by a bolt of lightning. Yes, that happened.

And we might build a long sequence out of Williams's efforts to attend an outdoor performance of *As You Like It*. The opening close-up is cued by his own statement that he was wearing a derby hat. The face he wore under the hat he describes as "a round smooth face," though photographs show something blander and blanker. A bland blank face: the classic Keatonian face for such a hat. We are next to imagine Bill Williams, topped by that hat, climbing the ten-foot fence between the cemetery and the Botanical Gardens. "I climbed," runs his narrative, "straightened myself and jumped inside." Reenacting this for screening, we need to recall that anybody jumping ten feet in such a hat has one hand on top of the hat. He had next to get from the place where he had landed around to the greenhouse embankment where the play would be. Of course the heavies promptly threw him out.

The director must now idealize the plot. Such deeds in movies are attempted in threes, whereas life here afforded merely twos. Our hero ought to have tried again, been thrown out again, and succeeded on the third try. Anticlimactically, he succeeded on the second. This he did by a simple merge with the crowd that was having its tickets taken at the turnstile. It was after Bill Williams had gotten inside that the number of tickets and the number of people was noticed to differ by one. They yelled after the invader, but couldn't find him.

None of that was undertaken to rescue the heroine: simply to crash *As You Like It*. Imagine any Penn undergraduate going to such ludicrous trouble for that purpose at this end of the twentieth century! Bill Williams was determined to see *As You Like It* because he meant to see any play that came by. Nothing better characterizes American undergraduate culture at the turn of the century than its combination of what Guy Davenport calls "impossible idealism" with an utter and simple passion for theatergoing.

Drama was not even thought of as "culture." Williams, who is our chief witness in such matters because Pound wrote very little about student days, recalled that you could see any play you liked for a quarter. That was what it cost to be at the very top in the back of the theater, the vantage-point from which he saw plays aplenty. He kept climbing up there because, he says, he wanted to *write* plays: moreover, plays in verse. The attraction of *As You Like It* is apparent, a pretty good verse-man having set his hand to it.

Every eminent writer of that generation seems not only to have been a habitual playgoer, but, in his schooldays, to have appeared in a play. Joyce played a schoolteacher in *Vice Versa* at Belvedere, T. S. Eliot a Lord in *Fanny and the Servant Problem* at Harvard (where the second footman was played by e. e. cummings). Pound's and Williams's adventures in greasepaint we shall come to. They all went on to write plays. Joyce has left us one play, each of the others more.

Ezra Pound's way of writing plays was to transpose them from foreign languages, but *Kakitsubata* and *The Women of Trachis* are neverthe-less *his* plays. And his preparation for translating Sophocles' *Trachi-niae* in the 1950s included appearing in the fifteen-man chorus of a production of Euripides' *Iphigeneia* at the University of Pennsylvania five decades before.

When we think about that production today what most arrests us is the plausibility of Williams's recollection that the teen-aged actors spoke entirely in Greek (though they didn't). The *lexis* and *melos* moreover entailed a long-range collaboration between Euripides and Professor Hugh Archibald Clarke of the Penn faculty, the disappear-ance of the Euripidean music having obliged Professor Clarke to un-dertake a conjectural restoration. And of this Greek play we may note with wonder that while it was being rehearsed the college paper gave progress reports at two-week intervals over perhaps six months, treating *Iphigeneia* as one of the great events of the Philadelphia sea-son. It would even "have a great influence upon the general univer-sity world of the East." "Impossible idealism," indeed!

How many performances there were I do not know, though public demand was presumably less than insatiable; but on April 28, 1903, an audience which included William Carlos Williams was gathered at the Academy of Music for a Greek play whose *Choros* of Captive Women included seventeen-year-old Ezra Pound. Williams was watching Ezra more than anyone else, though he would also remem-ber how the Messenger brought down the house by delivering his lines "with startling intensity." Ezra was unforgettable, "dressed in a Grecian robe, as I remember it, a toga-like ensemble topped by a great blond wig at which he tore as he waved his arms about and heaved his massive breasts in ecstasies of extreme emotion." That was what Wil-liams wrote several decades later. At the time the college paper had been more restrained. It said that the dances of the chorus were gone through "with care and some grace," and went on to mention the ap-preciation of the audience. And there was no doubt someone some-where to point out that Euripides himself directed an all-male chorus, women on stage being unthinkable till Roman times.

On another first night it was Williams who trod the Penn boards, in something called *Mr. Hamlet of Denmark*. This was not written by William Shakespeare; it was written by someone who had looked at something of William Shakespeare's, and it appears to have been a musical comedy. William Carlos Williams played Polonius. From between a huge white beard and a huge white mane of hair his bland blank face peered forth. *Mr. Hamlet* was more popular than the *Iphigeneia* had been. It played a week in Philadelphia; it played in Atlantic City, New Jersey, in Wilmington, Delaware, in Baltimore, Maryland, even in Washington, D.C. Medical studies in those days could seemingly sustain such interruption.

As poetic comparatists, we cannot but observe the justice of the casting: Pound immersed in an effort to simulate a classical occasion, Williams in—well, the classical analogy will have to be the New Comedy: Menander to Pound's Euripides. Subsequent work of the two of them, and especially subsequent dramatic work, is epitomized by this particular contrast.

Such stories are quaint, as though someone had contrived them to sustain the analogy of silent film. The cast photographs—you can see them in Noel Stock's *Ezra Pound's Pennsylvania*—are quainter, and tempt acquiescence in Pound's and Williams's later half-dismissal of the University as a genteel museum. One thing, though, that decades have not turned wholly quaint is the Penn curriculum, particularly as it looks on a piece of paper, the way an incoming freshman first sees it. By the time Ezra Pound had completed the freshman registration process what he had signed up for included the following:

· English Composition;
· Public Speaking;
· Algebra;
· German Grammar;
· American Colonial History;
· The Principles of Government in the United States; and
· Latin. And people have called *The Cantos* heterogeneous.

There is no place you could find such a list save in the curriculum of an American university; I mean that as a sober historical statement. In America you do not "read" a subject the way they do in England, nor undergo formal lectures the way they do in Germany. No, you *take courses* in a sort of checkerboard pattern controlled by the clock, much as in high school. You have been attending to Principles of Government in the United States; a clock strikes; another clock strikes; you are attending to Latin. Such discontinuities were introduced at Harvard by a relative of T. S. Eliot's, President Eliot of Harvard, he of the five-foot shelf, a man by whom T. S. E. seems to have been a little embarrassed: the black sheep, as it were, of the family. President Eliot had destroyed the old rationale of the Harvard curriculum by introducing a smorgasbord of electives, of which T. S. was quick however to avail himself, as was Ezra Pound of the equivalent freedoms at Penn. (Algebra and German Grammar; what are *those* doing side by side?)

A kind of functional mapping is feasible between such curricula and the poetry Pound and Eliot wrote: curricula and poetry in which no transition need be justified, in which everything has been somehow lifted to a plane removed from the plane of historical process, everything is of equal importance, and everything is laid out in an order seemingly arbitrary within which the mind may trace webs.

Classrooms enclose a kind of contemporaneity into which every subject is brought, with always some skeptic at hand to ground talk in the real. A class may comprise every shade in the spectrum from ultra-intensity to infra-Philistia, and though the class Philistine sometimes falls asleep and sometimes makes irreverent remarks, the one who does these things may not be the class Philistine. Sextus P. Pound and Apeneck Sweeney Eliot could regard the classics with a somewhat less than perfectly Victorian decorum they'd acquired not from their teachers but from classrooms.

> The primitive ages sang Venus,
>   the last sings of a tumult . . .

"Tumult" is somehow the wrong word for the hallowed intensity with which something classical is supposed to come through. It is exactly the right word for Pound's purposes, and the sort of word, oddly enough, that an inattentive student might come up with on being suddenly challenged by the professor. (The Latin is *tumultus*.) "Tumult" not only looks like but in fact *is* a Latin word. It just doesn't look like what "poetry" looked like at Penn.

Pound's professor in the Penn Latin class remembered him at the back of the room, characteristically at the back of the room where he could evade the scrutiny that bombards the front rows. He was also reported by someone—Williams passes this on—as exhibiting a certain aloofness, which he underscored by taking out and winding with deliberation "an immense tin watch." Something was going on in his mind, all the same, because he kept attending class. In his eighties, Peter Whigham has testified, Pound could read unfamiliar Latin verse at sight. (Unlike how many of his classmates? It does not do to discount the fellow at the back of the room.)

To return to that wonderful list.

- English Composition. That was his lifelong subject. At the Ezuversity in Rapallo you majored, James Laughlin will confirm, in English Composition.
- Public Speaking: the voice, the role, the persona. Homer, Odysseus, Sigismundo, Kung, the knack of becoming any of them.
- Algebra: recall the famous cadenza of 1914 (reprinted in Chap. XI of his *Gaudier-Brzeska*) which relates Dante's four levels of understanding to four levels of mathematical abstraction, moving upward to analytic geometry. That was only one heritage of Pound's study of algebra at Penn. The way algebra satisfied his aesthetic sense will have sponsored his lust to make arcane manipulation of symbols (see the *Thrones* Cantos) yield satisfaction and symmetry. He used to say that he passed his last mathematics exam by simply knowing how the solution should look. No mathematician will reprove a statement like that.
- German Grammar. German grammar was never an obsession of Pound's, but substitute Chinese and you get the idea. There had to be at any time in his mind some language of which he was interested in the inner workings.
- American Colonial History. Familiar, isn't it?
- Principles of Government in the United States: equally familiar, including their decline all the way to Franklin Roosevelt. And
- Latin. . . . "Rome," he would say, explaining his Italian allegiance, "is where they speak Latin." The wellspring of the Spirit of Ro-

mance, it drew him lifelong no less bewitchingly than the Fountain drew Ponce.

If that seems a scenario for large stretches of *The Cantos,* it is nevertheless a Penn first-year curriculum, the one Ezra Pound happened to take. And in the time-exempt rituals of *The Cantos,* where all is always now, we may see (scourged by the urgency of Ideas into Action) the classroom rite in which all moves toward one great goal, an exam just two weeks away.

Pound remembered Professor Reithmuller on Whitman, in an exotic immigrant's accent:

> "Fvy! in Tdaenmarck efen dh' beasantz gnow him"
> (meaning Whitman, exotic, still suspect
> four miles from Camden)

He remembered the girl who used to come puffing into German class and "ended in a Baptist learnery / Somewhere near the Rio Grande." But most of all, we may guess, he remembered the curricular rite the *Cantos* reconstruct, everything synchronic, everything interrelated without apology. As the poem extends itself by block after block of knowledge—Renaissance Despots, The Rise and Fall of Venice, The History of China, Roman and Moslem Numismatics, Byzantine Edicts, Comparative Chinese & Greek Philology—we may remark on its likeness to an extended elective curriculum and reflect that there is more to college than the freshman year.

On the other hand Williams said flatly, "I never went to college," defying all effort to link his poetic cosmos to a classroom. He meant that he never took what we now call a pre-med course. The Horace Mann School had sufficed. Consequently, Williams never took a college-level course in any language or literature: in that as in so many ways Pound's and Eliot's polar opposite.

Some years ago the State University of New York at Buffalo commissioned a trial design for its new campus from Gordon Bunshaft, who proposed that they house the entire university in a single huge building, one of the trim glass elevated boxes of his predilection. A model of this immaculacy was prepared; and SUNY's responsible persons, staring bemused at the model, found themselves asking what on earth it would be like with students in it. A sardonic voice one day crystallized their misgivings: "The students will have to be *sprayed*."

Such a metaphor governs many pre-med requirements, calculated to spray the incult before they gain entrance to white-coated austerities. And noting that Bill Williams had not Ezra's knack for the minutiae of book-learning, we may judge it a very good thing that he was not forced though a sequence of courses designed to civilize him. Every reader of the *Autobiography* remembers the ruinous obsession with Keats that misused his energies for many years. Survey courses might merely have transferred the obsession to someone like Swinburne.

As it was, the writing Williams did in Penn courses consisted mostly of Case Histories, a not uninteresting discipline. The case history is dense, it is cryptic, it is crisp, and it is factual. That is not a bad way to be writing day in, day out, if God is determined to drive Keats from your mind.

And Williams fondly recalled another antidote: "the wonders of pathology, histology, and anatomy." When Pound used to assail his friend's lack of education, "I'd reply that a course in comparative anatomy wouldn't at all harm him if it came to that."

Most of Williams's work, as it happens, can be gathered under those two rubrics: the Case History (see "To Elsie"), the Comparative Anatomy. Many a Williams poem asks to be compared to some other poem that is more like classroom poetry. Compared with this other poem, the Williams poem discloses a system of structural mappings despite its refusal to use the same words: much as a bat, on dissection, proves to be not an anomaly among birds, but a regular vertebrate mammal. Consider a sequence of his best-known lines:

> . . . under the surge of the blue
> mottled clouds driven from the
> northeast—a cold wind. Beyond, the
> waste of broad, muddy fields
> brown with dried weeds, standing and fallen

patches of standing water
the scattering of tall trees

All along the road the reddish
purplish, forked, upstanding, twiggy
stuff of bushes and small trees
with dead, brown leaves under them
leafless vines—
Lifeless in appearance, sluggish
dazed spring approaches—

A later mention of "the stark dignity of / entrance" marks one of Williams's rare recourses to etymology, nudging our recognition that "stark" means "naked." Who is it that enters so? The comparative anatomist may discern the return of Persephone, even cite such a locus as Milton's

> . . . Not that faire field
> Of *Enna*, where *Proserpin* gathring flours
> Her self a fairer Floure by gloomie *Dis*
> Was gatherd, which cost *Ceres* all that pain
> To seek her through the world. . . .

No indeed, not that faire field: only

> . . . the reddish
> purplish, forked, upstanding, twiggy
> stuff of bushes and small trees

—something as remote from a fair Italianate field as only a Jersey poet can imagine. Yet the glimpse of dazed Persephone perdures.

Time and again in this way Williams compels his aggressively local diction to recapitulate such inherited themes, reminiscent of the skeletal and neural and muscular themes recapitulated everywhere among the phylae of mammals. Cherish the ape's shaggy coat; and what it covers is like what Circe's fair skin covers.

Clearly, at Penn Pound and Williams were enormously receptive, if not always to what the authorities thought they ought to be receiving. Genius never wastes time, because it will always find a use for what it is putting its time to. One thing we might think the two of them ought to have been doing was going to hear distinguished literary men when talks by these were arranged, but as far as can be ascertained their score at this kind of self-improvement was goose-egg. Yeats came and read in 1903. Williams explicitly did not go to hear Yeats. He thought Pound heard him, but misremembered; Pound was then at Hamilton. Henry James came by later. No one of any subsequent importance seems to have heard Henry James: certainly not Pound, and certainly not Williams. It is not clear, on reflection, that either of them was what Williams needed: not at any rate Yeats, who in 1903 was immersed in *The Shadowy Waters*, that disastrous obsession of his late-early years. Lines like

> I have never been golden-armed Iollan

and

> o o o o for golden-armed Iollan

would not have done Williams a particle of good. Their possible effect on Pound is another question, but it is probably as well that the Pound-Yeats acquaintance began after Yeats had gotten that particular set of noises out of his system.

So what was acting on their minds at Penn? To our list so far—curricular structures, plays, new acquaintances (most signally one another)—we may add one more item, which may be emblematized by the blackboards.

The National Endowment could (and does) do worse than pay someone to wander from college to college, simply photographing— by preference late in the day—as many blackboards as possible. In a hundred years the collection would be priceless.

Several hours into the academic day, the blackboard is confronting students with a dense overlay of symbols left over from previous classes. When their instructor in the heat of exposition is moved to chalk up something of his own, no more than his precursors is he likely to wipe his whole expanse clean, not wanting to turn his back to the class for too long (a principle of rhetoric, not of safety). Erasing just a little, he makes his additions slantwise. And as the palimpsest builds up day-long—diagrams, short lists, circles with three points marked on them, bits of math, supply and demand curves, bits of Aramaic—all superimposed, all bespeaking the day's intellectual activity in that room—you feel yourself in the presence, as Beckett put it, of something you could study all your life and not understand. The blackboard with its synchronic overlay, its tough and hieroglyphic fragments of a congeries of subjects (nothing obvious goes on the blackboard; what is obvious can merely be stated)—the blackboard is our civilization's Great Smaragdine Tablet (which said "Things below are copies," and was itself one of the things below). Absence of explicit and consecutive sense, teasing intimations of domains of order that others comprehend, that I could comprehend had I world enough and time, these are elements of its daily rhetoric, as it marshals, at random, enigmatic signs.

Minds exposed to its daily irradiations can come to prize enigmatic signs for their own sake. There are ideograms and hieroglyphics in the *Cantos*; an early poem by Williams runs the letters S O D A down its page within a twinkling border of asterisks; documents are pinned to the pages of *Paterson*; these deeds bespeak connoisseurship of the enigmatic, emblematic sign, the one that was left on the blackboard by somebody else. ("SODA," yes, is an *electric* sign; but what iconographic fervors attend its emblazonment? Provided with light bulbs, would Babylon's skies have cried "SODA"? So much depends on such questions.) In such connoisseurship we may discern a willingness to cede part of the poem to others, the way I cede much of the blackboard in my class to the day's earlier instructors. To cede expertise so, to acknowledge in hermetic signs the authority of other minds, their deeds and domains, is to inhabit the twentieth century: also to have encountered the found object, something somebody other than you has understood and shaped, like the letters in *Paterson*.

Putting letters into a poem was not a new notion—Browning did it in *The Ring and the Book*—but formerly the poet worded the letters himself, as he worded everything else that bore his signature. Nor was putting learning into a poem new. But Milton or Donne would not exhibit any learning they had not themselves wholly mastered.

The Pound of *Cathay* was content if Fenollosa and Mori and Ariga understood Chinese on his behalf. What has been jeered at as egregious parading of knowledge he didn't have (the cited symptoms include errors in spelling Greek, though many of those were committed by typesetters) is better seen as an awareness that other people know much that is worth acknowledging. By putting a Greek word on your page you indicate the blessed existence somewhere of a professor who can explain it. God be praised, one need not carry the whole of civilization in one's head. "Civ/n, not a one-man job," Pound wrote to Louis Dudek.

So to the extent that specialized learning belongs in large part to other people, its tokens can be treated as found objects, arcane, numinous, penetrable. They will lead the curious somewhere else; they will lead the curious off the blackboard, in fact *out* of my poem, which is O.K.; it is my American didactic impulse that directs the curious out of my poem, just as my Whitmanic inclusiveness points to large areas of expertise elsewhere which I can acknowledge but not hope to command.

Discussing a poetic, we circle toward the definition of a university system as understood by Americans: a system in which other people are learning things you are not, and you look daily at blackboard traces left by professors whose subjects you are never likely to study, nor need you. The break that defined modernist poetics was preceded by a tacit break with the educational theories of the Renaissance, when they claimed to understand just what combination of learnings would constitute an educated man. Though "core curricula" swish their lissome veils, that claim is no longer seriously made; it was not made at Penn, nor at Eliot's Harvard; it is not made so far as I know at any American university today save the ones whose gimmick is the Great Books Program, out of which no distinguished writer is likely to come. The worst thing that can happen to a twentieth-century writer is to be persuaded that somebody else can tell him what he ought to know. (Pound was always telling people that? Yes, he was; but telling them what they needed to know about *writing*, a specialty. It is licit to map specialties.)

It is unsurprising that Pound and Williams should have left Penn feeling they had been taught trivially, much of the time, by people they could respect only intermittently. That was a natural consequence of not becoming some teacher's apprentice, instead taking a clutch of courses taught by specialists who frequently know little save their specialty and may even be (said Williams) sometimes bastards.

Seeing what they became, though, they were well taught. It is hard to specify anything they should have been taught instead. Especially, it is doubtful that creative writing courses would have been a good idea. God help Williams if he'd been flypapered by such a course. And if Pound had been enrolled in one, God help the instructor.

1982

Loove in Brooklyn

Donna—"A foin lass"—*mi prega*—"bodders me": what proportion of the great Canzone is literary convention? And what happens if its substance be moved in the direction of *volgari eloquentia*, vernacular speech? Speech of a time and place: Brooklyn: the 1930's. Guido's *stil nuovo* was allegedly grounded on Florentine vernacular of the 1290's, a diction of which we possess no tape recordings. Zukofsky's version of c. 1938 is a comic *tour de force* and a four-way commentary: on Guido's Canzone, on Pound's 1928 and 1934 versions, on the possibility of American local speech underpinning philosophic song. Literary historians are glib in their talk of speech. To make speech course through verse means imagining, impersonating a speaker.

A FOIN LASS BODDERS

A foin lass bodders me I gotta tell her
Of a fact surely, so unrurly, often'
'r 't comes 'tcan't soften its proud neck's called love mm . . .
Even me brudders dead drunk in dare cellar
Feel it dough poorly 'n yrs. trurly rough 'n
His way ain't so tough 'n he can't speak from above mm . . .
'n' wid proper rational understandin'
Shtill standin' up on simple demonstration,
My inclination ain't all ways so hearty

Provin' its boith or the responsible parrty
Or what its vertus are to be commandin'
The landin' coincidin' with each gyration
Or if prostration makes it feel less tarty
Or 't' sumthin' to be seen by any smarty.

In that extenshun where memory's set up
Loove takes position, in condition right, till
It's light's diffusion from a penumbra
Of Mars' contention makes it stay het up
Wid such ignition, recognition, title,
The soul goes choosin' clothes, the heart longs sombre—
Once in that likeness it is cumprehended
Commended possible to the intellective
Faculties, subject ov place, and dhare abidin'
In such dimension whatev'r force betidin',
For so its quality has not descended
So splendid, perpetually effective,
Not so elective, but to thought subsidin'
Because othrewise it can't go presidin'.

No, it ain't vertue tho it is that comin'
Out as perfection, in connection righted
Not az benighted mind, you feel 't I tell you,
Beyond desert, you know it's justice—hummin'
Wid predilection worth correction blighted,
Somewut poor-sighted—its weakness, friends tell you—
Often it is such vertue 'ts death approaches
If 't poaches so its pow'rr plods and iz halted
In no wise vaulted but wid contr'ry weight you're
Surprised, not that it were opposite nature
Only a slight lack of perfection encroaches,
And such as no man can say 't's chance defaulted
Or that loove 's bolted from its lordly stature
Worth the same, forgotten all nomenclature.

Living it ranges when its will is flaunted
Far beyond measure, from born treasure turnin',
Then not adornin' itself with rest ever
Moves so it changes color, laughs till 't weeps—haunted
Its image 's seizure 'n' fear, an' leisure yearnin',
Scarcely sojournin' in one place tho ever

You'll see that he was where worthy folk throve; the
New love, the quality 't has, moves to such sighing
So that descrying the thing's place man causes
Such clamour to rise, fired his passion pauses;
No one can know its likeness who don't prove the
Fact, love won't move tho it draws t' himself, aye 'n'
It don't go flying off to beds ov roses
Nor cerrtainly to pick large or small posies.

Like his own sweetheart's is love's disposition
So that his pleasure it seems has her assurance,
Breaking with durance to stand where he surges,
Not that the fleet darts of beauty lack vision,
Rather tried measure of fear is your pure ans-
wer to man's prurience when high spirit urges:—
And no one's able to know love by its features,
Complete ewers of whiteness aim to contain it,
Whose ears retain it the same don't see 'ts figure,
Coming from it man's led eye on love's trigger
Away from colour and apart from all creatures
Where sutures in darkness take the light, plane it,
Fraud can't sustain it, say faith is love's rigour
So that kindness comes forth but from his vigour.

You may go now assuredly, my ballad,
Where you please, you are indeed so embellished
That those who've relished you more than their salad
Days 'll hold you hallowed and away from shoddy—
You can't stand making friends with everybody.

                                        LOUIS ZUKOFSKY

Zukofsky's Brooklyn philosopher, having downed a few to loosen
his tongue, rambles ingenuously through five long sentences before
dismissing what he's uttered as a "ballad." He rhymes at every few
words, the rhymes as if by accident mapping exactly the high craft of
the *Donna mi prega,* where "Each strophe," Pound wrote, "is articulated by 14 terminal and 12 inner rhyme sounds, which means that 52
out of every 154 syllables are bound into pattern."

Pound saw little for English to do with the pattern save acknowledge it. Beyond offering an impression of sonoric intricacy in the first
strophe of his 1928 version—

> I for the nonce to them that know it *call*
> Having no hope at *all*
> 　　　　that man who is base in *heart*
> Can bear his *part* of *wit*
> 　　　　into the *light* of *it*,
> And save they know't *aright* from nature's *source*
> I have no will to prove Love's *course* . . .

—he made no effort to follow Guido's rules. Zukofsky did, to the letter: every rhyme in its place. Which is a way of saying that Zukofsky welcomed difficulties, the more arbitrary the better; but a way of saying, too, that he sensed a way to make this clotted discourse speakable. Read it in short phrases, with a rising inflection on every rhyme-word:

1a	No, it ain't vertue
	tho it is that comin'
2a	Out as perfection,
	in connection
	righted
3a	Not az benighted
	mind, you feel 't I tell you,
1b	Beyond desert, you
	know it's justice—hummin'
2b	Wid predilection
	worth correction
	blighted.
3b	Somewut poor-sighted
	—its weakness, friends tell you—

Once you've dealt with your awe at the recognition of intricacy—1a and 1b, 2a and 2b, 3a and 3b using identical sounds, with internal rhyming in the 2's and a link-rhyme from 2 to mid-3—you begin to realize how the rhyming cues a colloquial phrasing. This speaker, jingling his key-chain, thinks in short takes, spinning out a copiousness no one can stem. Sensing how talk and exactness tended to diverge, Pound had avoided rhyming's claims because they interfered with exact words: he sought, in a high literary exercise, the impression of precision:

> A lady asks me
>   I speak in season
> She seeks reason for an affect, wild often
> That is so proud he hath Love for a name
> Who denys it can hear the truth now . . . (1934)

This version (from Canto 36) intends that "affect" shall carry its technical aura, and screws up "reason" to a reasoner's pitch, and throws emphasis on the monosyllables "wild" and "proud." The 1928 version [*Literary Essays*, 155–157] had opened,

> Because a lady asks me, I would tell
> Of an affect that comes often and is fell
> And is so overweening: Love by name.
> E'en its deniers can now hear the truth . . .

—abandoned, we may guess, because the iambic base tended to obligate "filler" words; "fell" depends on a rhyme, not on wildness (the Italian is *fero*, from *ferox*), and a colon doesn't make Guido's explicit connection between Pride and the name of Love. To fashion something fit for the *Cantos* Pound revised away from this idiom, toward local accuracy, and without discarding the tang of the living voice he requires us to imagine some pretty special speech, "the conversation in the Cavalcanti-Uberti family," which he guesses was "more stimulating than that in Tuscan bourgeois and ecclesiastical circles of the period."

To posit a rarified speech wasn't L. Z.'s way. "A foin lass" is one by-product of his work on "*A*"-9, a *double* Canzone which in its first half fits to Guido's schema details culled from H. Stanley Allen's *Electrons and Waves: An Introduction to Atomic Physics* (Macmillan, 1932), from the '30's proletarian bible, Marx's *Capital* in the Everyman's Library translation (1932), and from the same author's *Value, Price and Profit* (an edition dated 1935). This enterprise may well have been prompted by a suggestion of Pound's, that Guido's tone of thought in 1290 perhaps seemed as subversive "as conversation about Tom Paine, Marx, Lenin and Bucharin would to-day in a Methodist bankers' board meeting in Memphis, Tenn." The voice throughout most of the first half of "*A*"-9 is that of a chorus of *things*, embodying a fancy of

Marx's [*Capital*, Everyman edn., p. 58] that if artifacts could speak they would expound their disengagement from human use. Their diction is impacted, abstract, cumbrous:

> Hands, heart, not value made us, and of any
> Desired perfection the projection solely,
> Lives worked us slowly to delight the senses,
> Of their fire you shall find us, of the many
> Acts of direction not defection—wholly
> Dead labor, lowlier with time's offenses,
> Assumed things of labor powers extorted
> So thwarted we are together impeded—
> The labor speeded while our worth decreases—
> Naturally surplus value increases
> Being incident to the pace exhorted:
> Unsorted, indrawn, but things that time ceded
> To life exceeded—not change, the mind pieces
> The expanse of labor in us when it ceases.

This stanza, the third of the five-and-a-coda that consumed two years' work, 1938–40, afforded the following grid of rhymes:

```
-----------value------------any
-----perfection------projection solely
----------slowly----------senses
-----------you shall--------many
-----direction-------defection wholly
----------lowly-----------offenses
--------------------------extorted
-----thwarted----------impeded
------speeded------------decreases
-------------------------increases
------------------exhorted
--sorted--------------ceded
------exceeded-----------pieces
-----------------------ceases.
```

Another two years' work a decade later (1948–50) fitted into the spaces between these rhymes a new set of terms from the *Ethics* of Spinoza (also Everyman edition); hence in the second half of "*A*"-9 we read,

Virtue flames value, merriment love—any
Compassed perfection a projection solely
Power, the lowly do not tune the senses;
More apt, more salutary body moves many
Minds whose direction makes defection wholly
Vague. This sole lee is love: from it offences
To self or others die, and the extorted
Word, thwarted dream with eyes open; impeded
Not by things seeded from which strength increases;
Remindful of its deaths as loves decreases;
Happy with the dandelion unsorted,
Well-sorted by imagination speeded
To it, exceeded night lasts, the sun pieces
Its necessary nature, error ceases.

We recognize not merely the same rhyming sounds, but in most cases the identical words, and are apt to find meaning in the few substitutions; thus it seems appropriate that in a new canzone that has changed the theme from "value" to "love" the words "increases" and "decreases" should have changed places, and the sweatshop foreman's "exhorted" have given way to "the dandelion unsorted." (Every stanza in the second half of "*A*"-9 encloses a flower, but nothing grows amid the machinery of the first half.)

Though 26 key words, and "52 out of 154 syllables" in each stanza are locked down by the pattern, it has proven possible despite these constraints to turn the stanza, the whole canzone, completely around. It is like turning a horse in a stall completely around without leading it out of the stall: annihilated, reconstituted. (By analogous effort, the poem implies, it should be possible to turn human conditions around.)

Concurrent with an early stage of these labors, the "Foin lass" was virtually a *jeu d'esprit*: "a relief," Zukofsky said in a 1940 preface, and the fun he was having with it comes through the text. (Fun for this poet was like playing 4 chess games at once, as a relief from playing 20 at once.) He was also gaining practice in the difficult form, familiarizing himself with the sense of the Cavalcanti, and working himself free from what would have been intrinsic with Guido's Canzone as he received it, the idiom and rhetoric of Ezra Pound. Not that Pound is to be swept out of sight; in 1940 Zukofsky issued one of the rarest of 20th

century bibliographic items, just 55 copies of a mimeographed packet
of aids toward the comprehension of the first half of "*A*"-9, containing
a gathering of Marx and Allen citations, a page of mathematical lore
that doesn't concern us here, Guido's text, the two Pound versions,
the "Foin lass," the "*A*"-9 stanzas, and a prose "restatement" of the
latter. The intention, he said, was to have the 75 lines from "*A*"-9 "flu-
oresce as it were in the light of seven centuries of interrelated
thought." Fluorescence occurs when a substance of the proper composition is struck by invisible rays, so this metaphor tells us both that
the atomic texture of "*A*"-9 is special, much there that doesn't meet
the eye, and that what should concern us in the array of exhibits is not
the bits and scraps "*A*"-9 picked up but the radiation of forces. (Pound
had written of "magnetisms that take form, that are seen, or that border the visible," and again, "The mediaeval philosopher would probably have been unable to think the electric world, and *not* think of it as
a world of forms.")

In this array the "Foin lass" is the strangest element save a fugitive
one stranger still: two stanzas of a yet slangier Brooklynese version
done by Zukofsky's friend Jerry Riesman. Stanza 2 of this runs

> It sets up 'n dat part memory hails from
> An' pulls a quick change into a range of light
> Very like at night when Mars' shadow comes down
> An' remains. De heart gives it de flair to come
> T'rough; d'soul—oomph. Its name's a feelin', same's "a sight
> T'sore eyes". It's made: 'n'right den an' dere goes to town
> After takin' shape from a form which is seen
> In de bean only if ya foist get de drift;
> In dat case it'll shift yet for a right guy'll stay
> In place, dough it can't rest because it don't weigh
> Down but spreads out like electric light, so clean
> Is its sheen everywhere, 'cause it's got lift.
> A swell gift; but 'tain't all fun, y' figger out de lay.
> It can't show true color any udder way.

So we may compare for instance
   1. In quella parte
         dove sta memoria
      Prendo suo stato   [Guido]

2. In memory's locus taketh he his state   [Pound, '28]

3. Where memory liveth,
     it takes its state   [Pound, '34]

4. It sets up 'n dat part memory hails from   [Riesman]

and finally,

5. In that extenshun where memory's set up

     Loove takes position   [Zukofsky]

—the latter already poised for the next rhyme:

> in condition right, till
> It's light's diffusion from a penumbra
> Of Mars' contention makes it stay het up
> Wid such ignition, recognition, title . . .

Here it's suddenly an effort to stop quoting. Zukofsky has surpassed the amusingly idiomatic Riesman in one salient respect, that he keeps the sentence moving on, each phrase reaching forward for the next. This has entailed making the rhyme-words terminate phrases; Riesman put in all the rhymes too, but it's an effort to find them.

Zukofsky's colloquial games with meaning are subtler too. Thus Cavalcanti says that the shade on which luminous Love is formed comes from Mars and stays: *e fa demora*. But for Zukofsky's street-wise guy it's Loove that stays, moreover stays het up, a meaning clamped firmly in place between a preceding rhyme, "set up," and a subsequent word, "ignition," a word Mr. Wise Guy would know, on his car-filled street. This speaker won't let us forget what he's always aware of, an incandescence in the trousers.

Whether Mr. Wise Guy can be imagined to say "perpetually effective" later in this stanza, or "forgotten all nomenclature" at the end of the stanza that follows is another question; Zukofsky's mask stays in place no more firmly than a mask of Swift's. By stanza four either the speaker has mutated or he's talked himself clear up to the highfalutin:

> Scarcely sojournin' in one place tho ever
> You'll see that he was where worthy folk throve; the
> New love, the quality 't has, moves to such sighing
> So that descrying the thing's place man causes
> Such clamour to rise, fired his passion pauses . . .

It's a notable moment when this flight drops suddenly back to the demotic:

> It don't go flying off to beds ov roses
> Nor cerrtainly to pick large or small posies.

"Posies" seems to have been prompted by the sound of Guido's *pocho*, "small":

> E non si mova
>
> perch' a llui si tirj
> E non s'aggirj
>
> per trovari giocho
> E certamente gran saver nè pocho.

"And (Love) does not move, but makes all move toward it; and it does not bestir itself to look for pleasure, nor, certainly, for great knowledge nor small." Here Pound had first written,

> Love doth not move, but draweth all to him;
> Nor doth he turn
> for a whim
> to find delight
> Nor to seek out, surely, great knowledge or slight.

By 1934 Pound had reconsidered "knowledge"; in Canto 36 he wanted to align Guido firmly on the side of "proof by experiment," against the scholastic "knowledge" of "Aquinas head down in a vacuum"; and besides, the full experience of love is, ah, *physical*:

> Nor yet to seek out proving
> Be it so great or small.

This is delicately learned: "proving" in the old sense of "testing." (And it means? That Love doesn't sleep around?) Zukofsky slips in "prove" a little earlier, right where Guido has "che non prova," and lets his stanza end with a worldly-wise wink:

No one can know its likeness who don't prove the
Fact, love won't move tho it draws t' himself, aye 'n'
It don't go flying off to beds ov roses
Nor cerrtainly to pick large or small posies.

(That grotesque "aye 'n' " rhymes with "flying," also with "sighing.")

In the "Foin lass" the splendid audacities—"Provin its boith or the responsible party," with an overtone of paternity suits; "Sumthin' to be seen by any smarty"; "You can't stand making friends with everybody" (Pound: "To stand with other / hast thou no desire")—are what strike at first reading. For the rest, the version is so infolded its cheekiness emerges slowly, under prodding, aided by diligent comparison with what's to be found in two books by Ezra Pound, notably the Guido text, the homage in Canto 36, and the other Ezratical version with its dedication to the ghosts of Campion and Lawes. In this "Foin lass" resembles the normative Zukofsky poem, which contains so much more than it seems to have room for. By some miracle of fourth-dimensional topology, Zukofsky routinely folded universes into match-boxes. He was content to let the initial impression seem to fall far short of poetry's promise, the reader's disappointed eye discerning merely the cube at the core of the hypercube. Time and thought attend a slow unfolding, and we may find ourselves looking up words we thought we knew, even "a" and "the." This experience too fluoresces in the light of Guido's dismissal of all save "persone ch' anno intendimento": "You can't stand making friends with everybody."

1978

P.S. from H.D.

END OF TORMENT: A MEMOIR OF EZRA POUND,
by H.D., With Poems from "Hilda's Book," by Ezra Pound.
Edited by Norman Holmes Pearson and Michael King.
New York: New Directions, 1979.

Such French and French-Canadian De l'Hotels as ventured into English-speaking North America bowed long ago to the Anglo-Saxon assumption that foreigners don't know how to pronounce their own names. For since all tongues are at bottom mangled English, "Do little" was plainly what these people were trying to say; and Doolittle they accordingly became.

Another thing sturdy Saxons comprehend is that "poets" do very little of anything. A girl would have blundered therefore had she signed her poems with her name, "Hilda Doolittle," especially about 1912 when poems that neither rhymed nor scanned by the metronome were apt to be taken for evidence that poets these days were taking even less trouble than formerly. American, moreover, and female on top of that—after all these years the contemptuous review in *The Spectator* nearly writes itself.

It was never written, because she signed them "H.D.," identified only as an *Imagiste*, and in a period that teemed with French

"schools"—Symbolisme, Le Paroxysme, L'Impulsionnisme, Le Fu-
turisme—controversy was readily deflected to the topic, what *Les
Imagistes* might pretend to be about.

This maneuver was contrived by Ezra Pound, who in after years
frequently said that he had invented "Imagism" chiefly to get a hearing for five or six poems by "H.D.," though he had subsequently attached to the term three or four didactic emphases of his own. Pound
had known H.D. since they were classmates in Pennsylvania. At one
time they were more or less engaged, something her people wouldn't
stand for. She followed him to London, was married—not to him but
to Richard Aldington, the third Imagist—and divorced. She was bi-
sexual, she divined. There were some years with the girl who went by
the name of "Bryher" and was in fact a steamship heiress who had
been married to Robert McAlmon of Nebraska. It is all the stuff of a
novel, material Henry James would have prodded at gingerly.

In March 1958 H.D., nearing seventy, was in a Swiss *Klinik* recovering from a broken hip. Ezra Pound had been twelve years in a Washington madhouse. And H.D. commenced a journal:

> Snow on his beard. But he had no beard then. Snow blows down from
> pine branches, dry powder on the red gold. "I make five friends for my
> hair, for one for myself.". . .
> First kisses? In the woods, in the winter—what did one expect? Not
> this. Electric, magnetic, they do not so much warm, they magnetize, vi-
> talize. We need never go back. Lie down under the trees. Die here. We
> are past feeling cold; isn't that the first symptom of *rigor mortis*? . . .
> There are very few left who know what he looked like then. . . .
> "Where are you? Come back—" is shouted by the crowd above on the
> icy toboggan-run. "Shout back," I say, and he gives a parody of a rau-
> cous yodel, then "Haie! Haie! Io," (you have read this in his poems). He
> seems instinctively to have snapped back into everyday existence. He
> drags me out of the shadows.

A memory from Pennsylvania, 1905, when she was eighteen, he
twenty. And the cold is the cold she has felt all her life and can still feel
in the Swiss March, the cold of her "icy," "chiseled" verses, the suspended animation of a beauty whose prince kissed her into death-in-

life, and dragged her "out of the shadows" seven years later as "H.D., *Imagiste*."

All the key words tell three or four ways; "Haie! Haie!," shouted by Pound in 1905 up the toboggan-run, is a cry from his 1912 poem "The Return":

> . . . As if the snow should hesitate
> And murmur in the wind,
>   and half turn back; . . .
> Gods of the wingèd shoe!
> With them the silver hounds,
>   sniffing the trace of air!
> Haie! Haie! . . .

That poem envisages the return of the Greek divinities, its rhythm unmistakably Pound's but its idiom partly hers, and she, with her "Hellenic" modes of language, is part of what is returning, "With fear, as half-awakened."

It seemed to her in 1958 that what had happened to her whole life was simply Ezra Pound, who among the trees of Wyncote, Pa. used to call her "Dryad" and read to her out of Balzac (*Séraphita*, with its androgynous protagonist) and Whistler and William Morris. They had played, it seemed, at being in a novel together, the novel that became two tragic life-stories: the novel which in *End to Torment* we find her writing down, compactly, allusively, collapsing time upon time, the Imagist way.

Its convention, and substance, is that of a daily journal, its last entry dated 13 July, when she receives a letter describing the departure of Ezra and Dorothy Pound for Italy aboard the *Cristoforo Colombo* two weeks previously. He has been set free at last: an end to his torment anyhow.

The letter was from Norman Holmes Pearson, professor of American literature at Yale and her literary executor, who encouraged her to compose this memoir twenty-one years ago but did not live to prepare it for publication. It is neatly footnoted now, with for Appendix the text of *Hilda's Book*, poems Ezra Pound wrote for her more than seventy years ago and sewed into vellum covers. One still leads off his collected shorter poems, *Personae*; it is called "The Tree" and tells of the wisdom that came to him when he turned into a tree, as it were to mate with his "Dryad," tree-spirit. Another commences,

> Child of the grass
> The years pass Above us
> Shadows of air All these shall love us

and ends,

> Keep we the bond & seal
> Ne'er shall we feel
> Aught of sorrow.

He was—what?—twenty-one? twenty-two? bravely young, sure of their future, his rhythm already his own, uncounterfeitable; and not foreseeing at all a madhouse on one side of the Atlantic, and on the other a *Klinik* where the aged child of the grass would collect her bruised thoughts while a broken bone knitted.

1979

The Reader
as Wailing Wall

THE CONFESSIONS OF EDWARD DAHLBERG.
Braziller, 1971.

The Lament has been at some times, and is still in some places, an art form of the folk. Five years ago, on a Toonerville Trolley of a train, Genoa to Rapallo, I was the sole enthralled witness of a splendid gestural aria. A large determined woman extracted, standing, for five wordless minutes, the maximum of dramatic effect from the presence of dirt on her seat. Witness, ye gods! Give ear, state railway officials! Her cadenza of grimaces and handkerchief-flutterings, lente, sostenuto, appassionata, con fuoco, at last pianissimo, rivalled, without sound, a sustained stretch of opera. It was markedly better than Gian-Carlo Menotti. It approximated Verdi at least, in his *Aida* period.

If you have had such an experience it is some kind of preparation for the latest Dahlberg. Giving sudden rein to a tendency that has throbbed and surged for years beneath his most business-like sentences, he accosts the startled reader—"No matter what I do it is likely to be wrong; one bungles everything, for the brain is feeble and an intuition is a saline and marshy guess. . . . Have I not been every man's cully, especially my own?"

("Cully," says the dictionary, "One who is cheated or imposed upon; a dupe, gull; a simpleton." First recorded use, 1664.)

Dahlberg presses on: "Oh, the heavy unbearable hours and troops of minutes, and all imaginary, when the heart feels barren as the region around Lake Titicaca, where there is no fuel to warm one's imbecilic existence but the dung of llamas."

We move backward in alarm. He advances, lamenting, ululating. "This memoir," he keens, "will be gorged with putid defects." ("Putid," says the dictionary, "Foul, base, rotten, worthless." Recorded in 1580, and now rare. In short, a Dahlberg Word, especially as it is a trap for proofreaders more familiar with "putrid." For "No matter what I shall do, I am doomed," and his publishers have perhaps betrayed him in not spelling it wrong.)

The reader is now backed up against the wall. The reader *is* the wall; the Wailing Wall.

Is this the man whose unforgettable portrait of his mother (which Sir Herbert Read called "as relentless, as detailed, as loving as a late Rembrandt") made *Because I Was Flesh*, only seven years ago, as unforgettable as *Walden*? This the son of the indomitable Lizzie, the Kansas City lady barber who taught him her galvanic sense of fact? Alas, it is he, but changed; he has lost his grip on everything but language.

And when that happens the language changes too. At the start of the second chapter we encounter one peerless sentence: "Bookeless and museless, as John Milton has it, I came to Los Angeles in 1919 to drink the Pierian waters in that dump." Quintessential Dahlberg, the Dahlberg of *Because I Was Flesh* and *Do These Bones Live*. Across taut syntax and a firm narrative base runs the witty descent from Milton's diction to that of "dump." In past years he has made whole chapters out of sentences like that. Not this year. This year the acrid documentary flavor withdraws into smoke; the wailing resumes.

And the reader whose devotion to Dahlberg's unique qualities has carried him this far into the *Confessions* comes gradually to terms with the fact that this book is what the former books merely teetered on the brink of being. It is a sustained exercise in self-indulgence. One way of putting it is that he is not *telling* us anything, not as he once told us about Kansas City. Retracing, for 300 pages, the part of his life he covered in two chapters—30 pages—of *Because I Was Flesh*, he has chosen to turn it into Symbolic Narrative concerning the lifelong fate that keeps him deprived (he says) of Women, of Companionship, of the barest rudiments of a sense-making context. Woe unto the world therefore; woe likewise unto me.

This means for instance, since Deprivation of Women is a great theme, that he makes a whole chapter out of the few paragraphs in the earlier book about the girl who wouldn't let him get anywhere, and suppresses completely the affair with "Angelica," who "helped cure my Sundays in a hotel room in Oakland." The Angelica part is no longer usable. For it's a rooted premise in 1971 that nothing, absolutely nothing, comes through, and was ever man so ill-used?

Granted that both works are heavily fictionalized, it's *Because I Was Flesh* (1964) that's the more interesting. "I had matriculated at the University of California in the middle of my twenty-first year, enrolling as a special student. Most of my courses were in philosophy and anthropology. I soon found that the work and the talk in the classes at Berkeley were tiring and bootless. . . ." So 1964.

But in 1971 the same episode begins, "Now Rabble University loomed before me. And as I stood at Wether Gate viewing the disorderly horde of students anathema was on my lips. 'What is the easiest digestion and excretion?' I asked, and replied, 'The crowd.' Then I recalled Le Sage's description of Academe: 'A common sewer of erudition.'"

More mental energy, less content; because the mental energy is being spent on phrases to array around a pose. Yes, a pose; which begins with calling it "Rabble University," and then asking us to believe that anathema was on his lips his first freshman day, and that self-interviews—even then, on that occasion—were yielding epigrams and citations from the likes of Alain René Le Sage (1668–1747).

That's too composed, too stagy a 20-year-old to credit. And for suspending so much disbelief, all the reward we get is the monotonous reward of sharing contempt for the easily contemptible, and the equally monotonous reward of a prose that consists of endless baroque figures carved in brown mahogany.

Dahlberg's prose has been much admired, often rightly. Montaigne remade, we are generally told; Sir Thomas Browne redivivus, Nashe new-minted. This time it resembles a Victorian interior, dark, massive, busy, relentlessly artistic, about as closely related to the 17th century models we're meant to think of as the Albert Memorial is related to Chartres.

Thank heaven, after page 185 the brown fog suddenly clears, though only to reveal Mr. Dahlberg with a narrative of grievances. Let him summarize it: "The flock of Laodicia who were neither hot nor cold and who had feigned to be my admirers—Edmund Wilson, Waldo Frank, Lionel Trilling, Horace Gregory, James T. Farrell, whom when obscure and hungry I had fed and helped, Kenneth Fearing, neglected and mourned by none, whom I aided to get published, Harvey Breit, to whom I furnished the hearth of friendship and nursed in his cruel illness, Charles Olson, who had looked upon me as father and mentor—all eschewed me. They forsook me to huddle together in the sheepfold of dungy comfort."

So that's what the sudden plain prose and naming of names is for—to particularize injuries. Unfortunately it's never quite clear what they were. We read 1,500 words on how Olson hurled Dahlberg "into the gullet of Cocytus" without finding out wherein his offense consisted, unless in not sitting at Dahlberg's feet with the old assiduity. And we may turn back with increased bewilderment to the 20-year-old Dedication to part VII of *Do These Bones Live*, in which Dahlberg seems to be coyly acknowledging that he lifted parts of that book from Olson's conversation. For now it appears that Olson never had a real idea of his own.

So "I shall always love Charles Olson and condemn him. Is that senseless? Then 'smite me on the other cheek' is the demand of a great tragic Madman. Ordinary people will attribute this to self-killing. It is far deeper than that. It is the human way."

Here, unless my nose for this labyrinth is faulty, we are passing a point of reference. Peel off the look of wisdom—a phrase like "It is the human way" sounds like wisdom—and we discern a greatly gifted man sunk into self-reproach because his governing impulse is now to attack his old friends who are his friends no longer, and because, try as he will, he can't quite make it evident that they were the offenders. So, entoiled in his own fatally mixed feelings, he troubles Heaven and us.

The *Confessions* is a book to have on one's shelf as a curiosity. Genuis self-entangled is chiefly only that—a curiosity. The genius in *Because I Was Flesh* remains: that's the Dahlberg book to read. As for his current phase, it deserves his own sort of missile, the recondite, allusive quotation lobbed like a grenade. Not having his gift for discovering such quotations, I offer the best I can think of: W. B. Yeats in a letter to T. Sturge Moore, writing of Wyndham Lewis: "What an entangled Absalom!" For makeweight I'll add what he never does, a footnote: II Samuel, xviii, 9.

1971

Gerard Manley Hopkins

GERARD MANLEY HOPKINS,
by Bernard Bergonzi. Macmillan, 1977.

We still aren't sure quite what to do with Hopkins. Locate him in his age? He was born in 1844, the same year as Verlaine, the year of *The Luck of Barry Lyndon*. Henry James and the Liddell-Scott *Greek Lexicon* were one year old, Robert Browning's meeting with Miss Barrett still one year off. None of these contexts encloses him, except (slightly) the Liddell-Scott.

Milieu? The family was prosperous (marine insurance) and abundant (nine children, the eldest GMH). Two brothers became artists, a sister composed. Another brother, sometime H.M. Consul in China, detested poetry (and lived till 1952). Hopkins *père* wrote widely: poems, *A Manual of Marine Insurance*, a treatise on *The Prime Numbers*. There was even a dog named Rover, who on 25 August 1868 bit Robert Bridges, future poet laureate.

Max should have drawn that incident, as he should also have drawn the middle-aged GMH grading Greek exams with a wet towel round his head, and assigning for fractions of sentences fractional marks he had difficulty adding up correctly.

But anecdotage doesn't locate Hopkins either. It accretes, what there is of it, because his life gives a narrator so little to work with. In devoting most of his short book to straightforward biography, Mr. Bergonzi inadvertently documents Elisabeth Schneider's remark that no other considerable English poet wrote out of so little experience of secular life. GMH passed from Oxford into the Jesuit novitiate as though through an air-lock, and lived the rest of his short life in places of semi-visibility, Dublin finally, his superiors in a quandary what to do with him.

For pastoral work he was nigh hopeless. Even his great verbal skills went awry in transmission. One practice sermon, still admirably cogent on the page, for some reason set hearers rolling on their chairs with laughter, so flustering Hopkins he muddled the final paragraphs, which unluckily contained several repetitions of John vi. 10, "Make the men sit down." So his lot was an eternity of exam papers, "331 accounts of the First Punic War, with trimmings," and all those fractions. He died in Dublin of typhoid in 1889, a few weeks short of 45, and is buried in Glasnevin, since known round the world as the resting-place of Paddy Dignam and of Leopold Bloom's mother. Joyce was seven in that year.

Like his preaching, his first jottings toward poems are risible; commencing one, he'd seemingly screw up his mind the way a first-grader in Penmanship screws up his face. "No more: off with—down he dings / His bleached both and woolwoven wear"—this of a Victorian male shedding his pants for a bathe, and his boots "last he off-wrings / Till walk the world he can with bare his feet."

Well we read this may with blinking our eyes, so remote is it either from spoken idiom or from any expressive efficacy. He seems to have jotted it while proctoring an exam, and never have subjected it to those sessions of toil during which his slag put on poetic glory. With the achieved results there's no arguing:

> Thou mastering me
> God! giver of breath and bread;
> World's strand, sway of the sea;
> Lord of living and dead;
> Thou hast bound bones and veins in me, fastened me flesh,
> And after it almost unmade, what with dread,

Thy doing: and dost thou touch me afresh?
Over again I feel thy finger and find thee.

Its base is indubitably odd. GMH seems to have felt "mastering me" not as anything English but as a compound "Homeric" epithet. The rest is a grammar of contrived indeterminacies. "Strand" is both rope and shore, "sway" both movement and rule. The "me" in "fastened me flesh" is direct and indirect object simultaneously, and "what with" is also "with what." But the propulsion, the sureness of pause and stress! (Now slow down, and reread all that.)

Rhythmic authority helps weld the whole, and behind the rhythm stands the engulfing example of Swinburne. Ahead, predicted by the stanza's eccentricities, looms Dylan Thomas, tormenting idiom in the faith that he can overcome us by what GMH abjured, personality. Hopkins is the man in the middle. Between Thomas's diction, merely self-regarding, and Swinburne's rhythms, merely self-perpetuating, he occupies an imperilled equilibrium, sustained in only a few irreplaceable poems.

He occupies other middles. A plaque by the onetime door of University College, Dublin, facing Stephen's Green, claims for this since-transmogrified institution the fame of three shades: "John Henry Cardinal Newman, First Rector; Gerard Manley Hopkins, Professor of Greek; James Augustine Joyce, Student": an enticing sorites.

All three situated minute phenomena by transcendental coordinates, along which sudden changes of scale and scope might occur momentarily. They bond by pairs several ways. Newman hadn't Hopkins's and Joyce's fierce interest in particularity. Joyce had abandoned Newman's and Hopkins's sacramental orthodoxy, the world subsisting in the Creator's purposes. Newman shared with Joyce a patient regard for the social realities of which Hopkins was innocent. (And Joyce admired Newman's "cloistral, silverveined prose," and Newman received Hopkins into the Church. An intricate Trinity altogether, its symmetry damaged only by the fact that Joyce so far as we can tell never chanced to hear of Hopkins.)

These ways of locating him aren't opted by Mr. Bergonzi, who mentions Swinburne fleetingly, Thomas not at all, Newman anecdotally, Joyce peripherally. In general he doesn't know what to do with the poetry except prowl round it respectfully, and Hopkins's life, lacking the poetry, is slight and bathetic. There's work to be done on it still, notably on its interaction with Latin, Greek, Welsh, but a die-extruded volume in the "Makers of World Literature" series isn't the place for that, nor is Mr. Bergonzi, for whom "magnus opus" is Latin, the designated man. Meanwhile Elisabeth Schneider's *The Dragon at the Gate* (California, 1968) remains the book about Hopkins to read.

1977

All the Angels
Have Big Feet

THE PURPLE DECADES: A READER,
by Tom Wolfe. Farrar, 1982. 396 pp.

Wheeeeeeeeeeeeee! went the Sixties, and Tom Wolfe was *there*, on the scene, in the scene, in Sulka four-in-hand and four-piece suit—make that *five*-piece?—yellow piping running round the grey like lemon neon, the lime weskit deep-lapeled and double-breasted; the Sixties, back when there was still a Walter Winchell, and Truman Capote was oooh, *big;*

and Thuddathud-*kerbump*! went the Seventies like Paul Volcker falling downstairs, and *Life* itself folded, and Drew Pearson had departed earth's scenes unwhoreshipped, watch it, unhorsewhipped, and there was Tom Wolfe still, still as tall and just a tad greyer, still the nonchalant master of the neon-piped sentence,

and Gassssp, wheeeeze, go the Eighties, and, ta da! Heeeeere's . . . Tom!!!, the smile still tight, the amused candid eyes unblinking, with a *Reader*, no less (pages that won't stay open bound in hideous purple cloth that wrinkles up the spine because that is what book manufacture has come to in the Eighties, even at $17.50 and Farrar, Straus & Giroux should be ashamed), to show us in his mocking mirrors what we've all been through.

How intact we've survived it all is disputable, but Tom Wolfe has been there to help, not least by devising a style the range of which can get so much of it together. He is famous for his paratactic syntax hand in hand with typographic hi-jinx—

> . . . and boy, they run out like ants and pull those barrels and boards and sawhorses out of the way, and then—Ggghhzzzzzzzzhhhhhhggg gggzzzzzzzeeeeeong!—gawdam! there he goes again, it was him, Junior Johnson! with a gawdam agent's si-reen and a red light in his grille!

That's Junior Johnson running a revenooers' roadblock in a car he's disguised as a revenooer's by nothing more than a siren and a red light. That's also Tom Wolfe, in temporary disguise as a good ol' boy, letting you hear Junior's story the way the boys tell it in No'th Ca'lina where by damn they're *talking* not for gawd's sakes writing.

Such is his trick: disguise: sink into the woodwork: become the very *voice* of the woodwork. It's been misunderstood; when "The Pump-House Gang" (1966) voiced the very throb of adrenalin that drove mindless voyeurs through the Watts riots ("Watts was a blast"), *Partisan Review* did not fail to call the brilliant paragraph "a virtual endorsement of the attitudes it mimics." But literati always tend to think that mimicry betokens admiration (else why the trouble? They take trouble only over measured Presbyterian judiciousness). Literati also worry when horrid alienations aren't allowed to evanesce but get fixed in print: some reader might *acquire* them!

Literati, there's the problem. We're all literati, else we'd not be fixed on this page. We look to print for information and opinion, and most of America has more sense (though, alas, it looks to TV). Tom Wolfe writes (for literati—for page-turners) about people who seldom turn pages: stock-car drivers, a self-made "art collector" whose fiscal base was a taxi fleet, hangers-out with surfboards, cunning intimidators of bureaucrats, "The Girl of the Year" (whose name, if you've forgotten from '64, was Baby Jane Holzer), astronauts, Vietnam pilots. . . . Literati find such types strange, unless the *New York Times* reporter makes them talk like a *Times* editorial, as he normally does.

Wolfe's only recourse is to make them seem stranger than strange: either so purple their purpleness turns neutral and we get a fix on their world—that's what distressed the *Partisan Review* man—or so one-foot-after-the-other reasonable that we follow hypnotized the decisions of, say Chuck Yeager, who led mankind through the sound barrier after a night so wild he'd broken two ribs, and in sober daylight had to hide his condition from the higher-ups, then whang the X-1's door shut with his only operative hand, his left, abetted by a nine-inch piece of broomstick.

Wolfe's prose tends to swerve toward list-dominated or else verb-dominated passages. These reflect, respectively, people defined by what they *have* and by what they *do*. The list is the oldest of all written forms. (Writing had to be invented to preserve lists; stories you can remember.) And lists gratify imaginations fixated by *things*. When Linear-B was an undeciphered script, scholars hoped for hexameter uplift. But once cracked, its inscriptions proved to be storehouse inventories.

Linear-B was the tool of Minoan bureaucrats. Bureaucrats always need to know your inventory of wine jars or dark oxen or flush toilets. They flourish among thing-centered people, who likewise live amid lists, as Flaubert and Joyce knew, and Wolfe knows. Leopold Bloom's thousand-word beatific vision of 1904 was confected by his creator from hardware-store catalogues:

> . . . watercloset on mezzanine provided with opaque singlepane oblong window, tipup seat, bracket lamp, brass tiered brace, armrests, footstool, and artistic oleograph on inner face of door . . .

Here is a Tom Wolfe equivalent, 1981:

> . . . The couch would be a mattress on top of a flush door supported by bricks and covered with a piece of monk's cloth. There would be more monk's cloth used as curtains and on the floor would be a sisal rug that left corduroy ribs on the bottoms of your feet in the morning. The place would be lit by clamp-on heat lamps with half-globe aluminum reflec-

tors and ordinary bulbs replacing the heat bulbs. At one end of the rug, there it would be . . . *the Barcelona chair.* . . . When you saw that holy [i.e., $550] object on the sisal rug, you knew you were in a household where the fledgling architect and his young wife had sacrificed everything to bring the symbol of the godly mission into their home.

Another, 1965:

Out front there are two gasoline pumps under an overhanging roof. Inside there are a lot of things like a soda-pop cooler filled with ice, Coca-Colas, Nehi drinks, Dr. Pepper, Double Cola, and a gumball machine, a lot of racks of Red Man chewing tobacco, Price's potato chips, Okay peanuts, cloth hats for working outdoors in, dried sausages, cigarettes, canned goods, a little bit of meat and flour, fly swatters, and I don't know what all.

Another, 1966:

. . . apartments where the lobby and the doorman look so great you feel you have to dress up to step on the sidewalk or you're letting down the building, esoteric New York day schools for the younger children and boarding schools for the older ones, lunches at La Grenouille where expensive matrons in Chanel suits have two bloody Marys and smile—teeth!—at tailored young men with names like Freddy, Ferdi, and Tug . . .

Things have no social existence save as they are valued. These are lists of *choices*, of acts of precious attention. Their contours yield the fever-charts of subcultures. (And your UHF circuitry picks up Wolfe's preference for the store with the gumball machines, the choices it offers being less pressured by mere chic.)

At the bottom of a *thing* subculture is appetite, which is static: when you have the Chanel suit or the gumball, you have it. (Though appetite soon gets bored, and wishes it had something else.) Against his cultures of lists, which encompass parts of America no other literatus has visited, Wolfe plays the cultures of *deeds*, which are normally relegated to the Huntin' Shootin' Stock Car magazines and to Action Comics. For twenty years he has been fascinated by this polarization. His book on art as a collectible (*The Painted Word*, 1975) derives from the earliest piece in the present *Reader*, "Bob & Spike," 1966. His fascination with the test pilots and astronauts of *The Right Stuff* (1979) is continuous with his interest in stock-car racer Junior Johnson, "The Last American Hero" (1965).

Certain moral discriminations do not waver. Bob & Spike Scull's drive to collect "art" is untouched by timeless contemplation: they are magnetized by the money and the status it brings. Of Junior Johnson and Chuck Yeager on the contrary we cannot define something that they want to accomplish. Hemingway talked of a Code, and Wolfe gets little further. They exemplify the Right Stuff.

As a satirist, therefore, Wolfe can complete his arc; as a laudator, he remains a stiff-lipped romantic. We're not yet past Hemingway in that domain. "The Truest Sport," a day with two naval pilots and as fulfilling a piece of writing as came out of the Vietnam mess, finally tells us only that such pilots lock themselves into a stoical myth of their own survival.

And Tom Wolfe? No, unlike Hemingway he's not locked into a myth. His mobile viewpoint still saves him, and his self-mockery. Despite appearances, he has no self-dramatization. The double-breasted weskits, the ivory-handled rolled umbrellas, these are not him, nor even his values, but appurtenances to speak for him.

They say, "Absurd. I am no part of identifiable society; in New York a transplanted Southern Gentleman perhaps, though in the South an anachronism. No, I am a *writer*, as absurd as that. I cannot help it if chic readers condescend to my subjects. On the side, I amuse myself with the resources of the printing-press, the ultimate resources a writer has. They permit me to write down strings like 'Gggghhzz zzzzzhhhhhhgggggggzzzzzzzzzeeeeeong!,' and if you think that absurd, or me absurd, or (heaven help you) Junior Johnson absurd, then your mirror is clouded indeed."

1983

Writing by Numbers

At the age of half past five, noted Ernest Hemingway's mother, he could count to 100 and "spell by ear very well." At forty-nine he still spelled by ear ("haveing," "makeing," "loveing") and would sum up a fortnight's toil with English prose in a string of numbers appreciably larger than 100.

> In April have written 556, 822, 1266, fished, 631, 0, 966, 725, 0 (4500 words of letters and business) 679, 0 (Sunday—laid off) 466, 905, 763 in what has run of this month. Hope it isn't all shit.

There were his day's word counts; and *The Old Man and the Sea*, he told Charles Scribner, Jr., in 1951, was *"exactly* 26,531 words. My previous count was on an incomplete copy. . . .

"This is the prose that I have been working for all my life that should read easily and simply and seem short and yet have all the dimensions of the visible world and the world of a man's spirit. It is as good prose as I can write as of now."

As it was; and yet that compulsion to count the words, each day's words, the achieved total of words: what was he proving? How many there were, or how few? Many showed a world that thought he did nothing save drink and fish that he was *working*. Few, though, showed how well he was working. A page of this magazine holds about 1,000 words. Hemingway seldom managed a *Harper's* page in a day, and that fact bespoke virtue. The fewer words the better was a principle Ezra Pound had convinced him of in Paris, in those miraculous years when Hem and Hadley lived up over the sawmill in the rue Notre Dame des Champs. By 1929 he could summarize: "I always try to do the thing by three cushion shots rather than by words or direct statement."

> Troops went by the house and down the road and the dust they raised powdered the leaves of the trees. The trunks of the trees too were dusty and the leaves fell early that year and we saw the troops marching along the road and the dust rising and leaves, stirred by the breeze, falling and the soldiers marching and afterward the road bare and white except for the leaves.

The elegiac cadences, the dust, the leaves, suffice to tell us that those troops have marched off to disaster. A few years ago Michael S. Reynolds allowed us to see how Hemingway conjured this wonder into existence from a less distinguished draft.* "It is time to question constructively all of the explications we have inherited," Mr. Reynolds wrote. "The vein of psychoanalytic exegesis has been overworked. The misleading thesis that Hemingway is always his own protagonist has littered the critical landscape with so much debris that it will take another generation of critics to restore the ecology." The time had come to watch the craftsman.

He added, citing appropriately Romantic instances, "Hemingway's reading is as important to his art as that of Coleridge; his textual revisions are as significant as those of Keats."

This year, Reynolds is back with *Hemingway's Reading, 1910–1940: An Inventory* (Princeton University Press, 1981), complete with a revised claim: "Hemingway's reading was more important to his art *and to his life* than Coleridge's was to his." Almost simultaneously, Hemingway's biographer Carlos Baker has sponsored 900-plus pages of *Selected Letters*, apt to confirm the darkest prejudices of the skeptical. Has a distinguished reputation ever been hitched to so many square yards of trash? That soon comes to seem a fair question.

*Michael S. Reynolds, *Hemingway's First War: The Making of "A Farewell to Arms,"* Princeton University Press, 1976.

Corp Shaw and I were on an enormous party at the Toledo Club. We both lay on the grass out side of the club for some time. Your old pal Hem established the club record. 15 martinis, 3 champagne highballs and I don't know how much champagne then I passed out.

Or:

Lots of things happen here. Gertrude Stein and me are just like brothers and we see a lot of her. Read the preface you [Sherwood Anderson] wrote for her new book and like it very much. It made a big hit with Gertrude.

Yup, bet it did. For 150 pages or more this dreary leering and muscle-punching taxes patience, relieved by an occasional break such as (1921, to a sister): "It was a glorious night. We'd come out of some place where we'd been waltzing and into the outer air and it would be warm and almost tropical with a big moon over the tops of the houses. Kind of a warm softness in the air, same way it used to be when we were kids and we'd roller skate or play run sheep run with the Luckocks and Charlotte Bruce." Suddenly, a flash of the Hemingway Style, linked with his surest topic, nostalgia. He might have written it in the first draft of a story, after which he would have reworked it with sureness.

But the Letters aren't reworked, ever. He liked writing them, he told Scott Fitzgerald, "because it's such a swell way to keep from working and yet feel you've done something"; or, as he told Bernard Berenson, "I write them instead of stories and they are a luxury that gives me pleasure and I hope they give you some too." More than once he hoped no one would print them. "I write letters because it is fun to get letters back. But not for posterity." They were byproducts. "Should you save the hulls a .50 cal shucks out for posterity?" (This says, "I am a gun." He said many unguarded things.)

What happens when they're printed is that they make a Book, such a book as the fastidious craftsman would have disowned. For the style was not the man; the style was what the man could achieve after he had before him something to revise. Nothing is more striking than the painful distance between his deft three-cushion shots and what he would spill onto paper when he just felt like gabbing. There are writers—Henry James and Virginia Woolf come to mind—who exist in their letters as we expect them to from their books: poised, guarded, grammatical, careful of nuance.* It is not accidental that Hemingway cared for neither of them.

Here, for instance, is Virginia Woolf, sampled at random: "About Rupert's letters. I'm all in favour of printing them and giving some sort of correction to that impossible sentimental fashion plate of Eddies. If Gwen, Dudley, and you (—what about Noel though?—) all contributed, that should be wiped out. I hadn't heard of the Bryant scheme; but Morgan talked to Leonard about your suggestion that he should write something."

That's about a 1936 proposal to publish still other letters, those of the poet Rupert Brooke, by way of correcting Edward Marsh's 1918 memoir. It is written from within a circle where first names suffice, and even Marsh, who requires correction, is no remote malign bungler but simply "Eddie." The literary game had tacit but specifiable rules. People knew other people well, and hints sufficed. When you picked up a pen, as when you picked up a teacup, your obligations included deftness.

An equally random dip turns up this from Hemingway:

> The word count is Wed. 577 and yest morning, my birthday, 573 before breakfast. Weight 200 even. To celebrate my fiftieth birthday (in what other goddamn country where you've spent your life writing as well as you can wouldn't you receive one wire from an American when you'd made fifty against considerable odds) I fucked three times, shot ten straight at pigeons (very fast ones) at the club, drank with five friends a case of Piper Heidsieck Brut and looked the ocean for big fish all afternoon. There was nothing although the current was strong and the water very dark.

Far from reaffirming his identity with a tight-knit circle, Hemingway is concerned to define himself *against* his correspondent's every

*By coincidence, the Belknap Press at Harvard has just issued the third volume of James's *Letters* (ed. Leon Edel, 1883–1895, 579 pp.) and Harcourt Brace Jovanovich the sixth volume of Woolf's (ed. Nigel Nicolson and Joanne Trautmann, 1936–1941, 556 pp.). In the present state of publishing, the letters of safe authors are a safe enterprise. Yale recently emitted, with relief, the forty-second and last volume of the correspondence of Horace Walpole, with a mere six volumes of indexes yet to come.

sense of how a normal life is conducted. He begins with the affirmation that he spends his life writing as well as he can (who else, he constantly implies, does that?), goes on to a list of things he does in Cuba that no one can do in New York, such as shooting pigeons and going after big fish, casually brandishes a brutal taboo word, and affects indifference to the utter neglect he doesn't forget to complain about. Writing is a lonely occupation; so is the nightlong reading on which Hemingway's writing fed, and Hemingway was an intensely lonely man, in exile more than half his life.

Hemingway's exile did not commence when he left his native country for Paris; it commenced when he returned. After 1928 he was always where people he valued weren't: in Key West, in Cuba, in Ketchum. Letter after letter begs for their company. Four of the fourteen sentences of one letter to John Dos Passos say, in slightly varied words, "For God's sake come down." To collect the typescript of *A Farewell to Arms* for Scribner's, Max Perkins will have to "come down" (he did). At work on *Death in the Afternoon* in Wyoming, he pleads for a visit from Mike Strater: "Wire me as soon as you get this if you can come. . . . Why the hell don't you come out here. . . . Hope I'll hear you're coming . . ." (Strater didn't).

Many letters are cries from an exhausted man. What exhausted him was inventing, a thing he did with the aid of books and maps and topographical memories and remembered incidents. "Every writer is in much of his work. But it is not as simple as all that," and Philip Young's book "which proves that I am all my heroes" would have profited from more exact information. A scrotal infection had set Ernest wondering what a man's life would be like if his penis had been lost and his testicles and spermatic cord remained intact. "I had known a boy that had happened to. So I took him and made him into a foreign correspondent in Paris and, inventing, tried to find out what his problems would be."

And the trouble with *Tender Is the Night*, he told Scott Fitzgerald, was that the real people Scott had put in it clashed with the lives he had invented for them. "If you take real people and write about them you cannot give them other parents than they have (they are made by their parents and what happens to them) you cannot make them do anything they would not do. . . . Invention is the finest thing but you cannot invent anything that would not actually happen.

"That is what we are supposed to do when we are at our best—make it all up—but make it up so truly that late, it will happen that way." In his best work Hemingway made it up so truly that there have always been readers to believe it had already happened that way, and to Hemingway himself. Carlos Baker's fine biography, published in 1969, allows us to suppose that *A Farewell to Arms* tells the story of an affair he had in 1918 with a nurse in Milan, Agnes von Kurowsky; "the story ached to be told." At seventy-nine, Agnes talked to Michael S. Reynolds:

> Q: I think he wrote a lot of things he never experienced.
> A: Well, that one in Spain—I know that doesn't sound like anything he would do. Some of the books are fine. *The Old Man and the Sea*—that one stands out in my mind more than anything he wrote. It's so to the point. Nothing comes in to interfere.
> Q: Of course the experience never happened to Hemingway.
> A: Of course not! He would have put the skeleton of the fish up on the wall if it had.

She emphatically denied any but a platonic romance with young Ernest, and Mr. Reynolds concludes that she had contributed little to the novel's Catherine Barkley save presence and physical beauty. So much for the story that ached to be told.

Yet there had been a story that ached to be told: the story of a fantasy. One of Carlos Baker's notes is astute in citing a fellow patient who thought that Ernie "must have dreamed a good part of the story during his tedious stay in the hospital." "It is not *un-natural*," wrote Hemingway, "that the best writers are liars. A major part of their trade is to lie or invent and they will lie when they are drunk, or to themselves, or to strangers. They often lie unconsciously and then remember their lies with deep remorse. If they knew all other writers were liars too it would cheer them up."

Maybe it would. Here's a story Hemingway wrote in a 1936 letter, recounting, of all things, a "Wallace Stevens evening." Stevens having come to Key West "sort of pleasant like the cholera."

It starts with "my nice sister [Ursula] . . . crying" over Mr. Stevens "telling her forcefully what a sap I was, no man, etc." (A touchy theme in those years; in 1937 the suspicion that Max Eastman had implied something similar earned Eastman a slam in the face and some moments of terror.)

Next, out in the rainy street, our hero "met Mr. Stevens who was just issuing from the door haveing just said, I learned later, 'By God I wish I had that Hemingway here now I'd knock him out with a single punch.'" This is hardly the Stevens we know, but Hemingway was not following his own counsel against putting real people into stories. The Mr. Stevens of the story next "swung that same fabled punch but fertunatly [sic] missed and I knocked all of him down several times and gave him a good beating." The location of Stevens's fall was "a large puddle of water."

Someone then requested that Hem take off his glasses, desiring "a good clean fight without glasses in it." Next "Mr. Stevens hit me flush on the jaw with his Sunday punch bam like that. And this is very funny. Broke his hand in two places. Didn't harm my jaw at all and so put him down again and then fixed him good so he was in his room for five days with a nurse and Dr. working on him."

Finally, "I have promised not to tell anybody and the official story is that Mr. Stevens fell down a stairs."

That's the story. It omits the shabby detail that Stevens was 56, Hemingway 36. Is it a true story? Who's to say? Six years later Wallace Stevens called Hemingway "a poet and I should say, offhand, the most significant of living poets, so far as the subject of EXTRAORDINARY ACTUALITY is concerned." Just the man, Stevens goes on to say, to lecture on poetics at Princeton.

Hem at the lectern, making an academic point? Stevens was fantasizing a story too, and just on this theme his story may have been the truer one.

1981

The Poet in the Grey Flannel Suit

PARTS OF A WORLD: WALLACE STEVENS
REMEMBERED, *an oral biography by Peter Brazeau.*
Random House, 1983. 330 pp.

Biography is a minor branch of fiction; of fairly old-fashioned fiction too. It's hard to think of a biographer's stratagem that hasn't its antecedents in Walter Scott or Dickens. No matter whether you've invented your central character or gleaned his dossier from "sources" you can footnote, what you do next is nothing but tell his story in the way of the Victorian masters. So Joseph Blotner's Faulkner, Mark Schorer's Sinclair Lewis, Richard Ellmann's Joyce, are all for better or worse fictional creations. Each biographer had no choice save to flesh out his man from his idea of his man: from what he was capable of imagining. "Creation of character," it used to be called.

When we lack a biography of a major writer, we may guess that his executors haven't authorized one. But nonauthorization has not so far prevented two "lives" of T. S. Eliot, with an authorized one said to be a-simmer on a British back burner. For a plausible Eliot hasn't been too hard to imagine: the celluloid-collar protagonist in a tale of thwarted love. That Prufrockian construct may not be Tom's very self, but it will serve to propel a narrative.

By contrast, nobody has yet imagined a plausible Wallace Stevens. That, not the legalities of "authorization," is what has deprived Stevens-watchers, so far, of a *Life* (though we've 890 pages of *Letters*). What to make of the Hartford insurance executive who gave so little away? Eliot too gave little away, and Eliot too (like Stevens, a Harvard man) was in non-bohemian "business": a banker, then a publisher. But you can pretend he was also Prufrock, as you can't pretend that Wallace Stevens was Canon Aspirin, or Crispin. The people in the Stevens poems are cartoons by Peter Arno. (Prufrock too is a cartoon, but by Daumier.)

Peter Brazeau has not attempted an impertinent biography. He has interviewed some 150 people who knew Stevens in the second half of a long life, and edited the transcribed testimony. If his book leaves us with no single imagined Stevens, it affords copious witness.

So hear this: "At one time he used to get big shipments of Gramo-phone records; they came from Europe. He would have me go down to the post office and pick up this big box, and he'd go down with me and pay out quite a bit of money. . . . We went up to Pomfret. At one time there was an opera house there. Mr. Stevens knew about every-thing, I guess. Mr. Stevens said, 'An Italian opera house used to stand right here, but it burned.' And in the back of the opera was a big florist, a garden. He'd spend half of the evening walking around this green-house, looking for oddball flowers, something that no one didn't have in the gardens some other place. . . . He'd mostly be silent, and he was a very good observer. He was just looking around all the time—the scenery and stuff like that."

—so Naaman Corn, factotum/chauffeur at the Hartford Accident and Indemnity Corporation, as taped by Peter Brazeau in 1977. And you'll find "Slice the mango, Naaman" in the poem called "Certain Phenomena of Sound," the poem that also says—of someone else—

> You were created of your name, the word
> Is that of which you were the personage.
> There is no life except in the word of it.

Naaman, a Biblical name, means "beautiful, agreeable."

And here's Samuel French Morse, recalling how, a graduate student, he got taken for lunch at the Canoe Club: "very civilized and pleasant. It was well-sustained, but it wasn't anything for Boswell to take down. . . . These were business acquaintances and he was one of the boys. Back of the bartender were pictures of nude girls; he wanted to make sure that people understood that he appreciated this, nudging me and saying, 'See!'"

And Betty (Mrs. Richard) Eberhart: "Wallace was always the prosperous businessman with the big house, but his wife was always upstairs in some mysterious way."

In some mysterious way, friends of Wallace Stevens found they seldom got into the house. William Carlos Williams, visiting, got put up at a hotel. And Stevens told a business associate, Charles O'Dowd, "Mrs. Stevens and I went for a walk yesterday afternoon. We walked to the end of Westerly Terrace, and she turned left and I turned right." And in 1949 he wrote to a Cuban friend, "The moon which moves around over Havana these nights like a waitress serving drinks moves around over Connecticut the same nights like someone poisoning her husband": an odd image.

"I never heard him speak of Mrs. Stevens," an associate's wife remembers. Yet in August '42 two other associates ate her cooking ("consummate"; "asparagus tips, creamed, with this pie covering"), and earlier, because a sculptor named Weinman had admired Elsie Stevens, it is her profile we see on the 1916 dime and half-dollar. Choosing to marry her, it seems, he chose between her and his own family—he never saw his father again—and the choice later proved to have been not all ice cream. "He treated his wife as if she were ash," wrote a '52 visitor. "I saw her at the door, and she disappeared."

All of his poetry evades what it's talking about, and much of it isn't talking about anything: finger exercises, to keep limber his formidable knack with diction. "Slice the mango, Naaman, and dress it"—that appropriates nothing of Naaman Corn save his name. Naaman Corn was bewildered, as we may be.

He's the cliché Babbitt, anxious to be one of the boys and in the right club. He tipped orchestra leaders to play "Have You Ever Seen a

Dream Walking." He generally had "a few martinis." He read his poems the way Babbitt would read poetry. He riffled the bills in his wallet in such a way that one witness thought it evident "he was tight with money."

. . . "As he riffled those bills, one could see dominance there." And he wrote "The Idea of Order at Key West"—

> . . . And when she sang, the sea,
> Whatever self it had, became the self
> That was her song, for she was the maker. Then we
> As we beheld her striding there alone,
> Knew that there never was a world for her
> Except the one she sang and, singing, made.

Imperishable. And he wrote "The Auroras of Autumn." He died a converted Catholic. For years he and Elsie had lived in different parts of the house.

And we still can't imagine him. For a start, we'll have to sort his poetry out: what's alive, what's evasive, what's as empty as were whole domains of the life he barely let associates see.

1983

Seraphic Glitter:
Stevens and Nonsense

From "Notes Toward a Supreme Fiction" (*Collected Poems of Wallace Stevens*, p. 383):

> We say: at night an Arabian in my room
> With his damned hoobla-hoobla-hoobla-how,
> Inscribes a primitive astronomy
>
> Across the unscrawled fores the future casts
> And throws his stars around the floor. By day
> The wood-dove used to chant his hoobla-hoo
>
> And still the grossest iridescence of ocean
> Howls hoo and rises and howls hoo and falls.
> Life's nonsense pierces us with strange relation.

Question from Hi Simons: who or what is/was the Arabian?

Stevens to Hi Simons, Jan. 12, 1943 (*Letters of Wallace Stevens*, p. 433): "The Arabian is the moon; the undecipherable vagueness of the moonlight is the unscrawled fores: the unformed handwriting."

A reader is apt to be more intrigued by this information than grateful for it. To know that the Arabian is the moon is to know something about the content of Stevens' mind but little about the poem in front of us, since the identity won't fit into the poem. It doesn't help us with the hoobla-hoobla-hoobla-how, which comes better from an Arabian than from the moon (synaesthesia for the moonlight's persistence?), nor with the way stars are thrown around the floor, and to have to think that the moon is inscribing something across its own handwriting, which is what the rest of the note requires us to think, is to wrestle with difficulties we hadn't known we had. No, the lines read much better if we forget the moon and go back to imagining a noisy intrusive Arabian who does ungovernable things: a harbinger of "life's nonsense." Stevens reads gratifyingly as what he was, on the evidence of the *Letters*, strangely reluctant to be: the most insouciant of all Nonsense poets, apotheosis of an honored métier, he for whom even a Carroll or a Lear came but to prepare the way.

In *The Field of Nonsense* Elizabeth Sewell argued acutely that what France ritualized as *symbolisme* was the very impulse England banished to the nursery: the impulse to use words as counters in an arbitrary game whose criteria are pattern, symmetry, and elusive quasi-sense. So Stevens' look of getting at something profound isn't threatened by a little remedial stress on his nonsensicality.

Much of *Harmonium* co-opts effects from sophisticated nursery verse:

> Chieftain Iffucan of Azcan in caftan
> Of tan with henna hackles, halt!

or,

> And, "Why are you red
> In this milky blue?"
> I said.
> "Why sun-colored,
> As if awake
> In the midst of sleep?"

And "The Plot Against the Giant," with its three girls offering their three entrapments, reads like a fairy-tale archly rethought to go with Beardsley designs.

In calling this Nonsense we don't belittle it but establish its genre, the same genre an avowed admirer of Edward Lear ornamented when he wrote

> I grow old . . . I grow old . . .
> I shall wear the bottoms of my trousers rolled

and,

> o o o o that Shakespeherian Rag—
> It's so elegant
> So intelligent.

And "all styles can come down to noise," William Empson has reflected; and any utterance is potentially nonsensical, so little do we say of what we intend. Talk of the rosyfingered Dawn is nonsense until we agree in deferring to Homeric sense. Poetry walks closer to nonsense than prose, simply in making us more conscious of its separate words and their distance from one another. It depends on an agreement to understand, as Elizabethans agreed to understand sonnets (Dr. Williams wanted an agreement to stop understanding them).

Eliot's Nonsense and Stevens' Nonsense is moreover American Nonsense, like Poe's, not English Nonsense, like Lear's. Both exploit a grandiose poetic tradition, the English High Romantic, but differ in the way they regard it. American Nonsense works from outside the tradition, convinced that traditional and nonsensical effects are alike synthetic. It admires the tradition's skill at synthesis (". . . strange synthetic perfumes, / Unguent, powdered or liquid") but rejoices in its own skills too and is unabashed. But for an English Nonsense-expert—say for Lear—the tradition inhered in seamless natural process, a passion-flower rooted in one's back yard, a norm from which the syntheses of Nonsense subtly deviated. Lear was a contemporary and friend of Tennyson's, and like Tennyson a legitimate poetic inheritor of Coleridge. The discovery he made was unsettling: that the effects of Coleridgean verse depend not at all on sense or the show of sense, that a ritual of syntax and auditory recurrence co-opting not moons and maidens but Pelicans and Dongs will erect paper pleasure-domes as stately as any in Xanadu. This discovery fascinated Tennyson, who did not pursue its implications, and also fascinated Eliot, who did. What inhibited Tennyson was doubtless the reflection that Lear's nonsense called into question the credentials of the only tradition Tennyson knew: rendered doubtful its grip upon the world of public experience, to which the Laureate had affirmed allegiance. What was catalytic for Eliot on the other hand was precisely the future that could be deduced from Lear's deracination of romantic rhetoric. No longer rooted in one island's literary history, that rhetoric could grow in a sort of international void, could reach toward the zone of arcane *symboliste* frisson, could hint at Laforgue and Mallarmé and Dante in an English seemingly timeless and unlocalized, neither Missouri nor London, neither 1880 nor now.

Nonsense freed both Eliot and Stevens from a poet they longed to be freed from, Whitman. It permitted an American to manipulate the rituals of certified Poetry (the resonant turn of phrase, the mighty line) without sounding the way Whitman had made Tennyson sound, provincial. Whitman's was no longer the only way around an Anglophile provincialism.

The way of Nonsense is analytic: to detach the rituals of high poetry from their normal structures of meaning, and to draw more or less explicit attention to their self-sufficiency as rituals. "A Primitive Like an Orb" offers one of Stevens' many comments on the working of his own verse:

> . . . And in bright excellence adorned, crested
> With every prodigal, familiar fire,
> And unfamiliar escapades, whirroos
> And scintillant sizzlings such as children like,
> Vested in the serious folds of majesty,
> Moving around and behind, a following,
> A source of trumpeting seraphs in the eye,
> A source of pleasant outbursts on the ear.

Not-quite-Milton, a sort of Origami Milton, the paper phoenix fluttering in the wizard's hand, this scales infernal pomp down to "whirroos," alliterations down to bedtime fireworks ("scintillant sizzlings such as children like"); yet "Vested in the serious folds of majesty," it permits us glimpses of seraphic glitter, hearkenings to seraphic trumpets whose "outbursts" it coolly designates "pleasant." Would Milton have admitted his effects were "pleasant"? Yet they give pleasure.

A French connection remains to be explicated. Much as Stevens' rhetoric is comfortably post-Miltonic, not least in its comfort with the unrhymed five-stress line into which it insouciantly chucks little un-stressed jigs and skippings—

> . . . words about the nightingale
> In measureless measures, not a bird for me
> But the name of a bird and the name of a nameless air
> I have never—shall never hear. . . .

—so was *symbolisme* post-heroic, exploiting the French Alexandrine: bedecking itself in the glitter of a dead dragon, but for the sake of rit-ual, not of eloquence. Eloquence was a mere goose-neck to be wrung (*"Prends l'éloquence et tords-lui son cou!"*). Victor Hugo, eloquent on every state occasion, epitomized a vulgar adversary, Laocoon en-toiled in yards of *pompier* hose. To *say*, to offer to say, was risible. ("A poem should not mean but be.") To move with authority through what had been the motions of saying, that was the poet's new voca-tion.

The movement was staffed by lapsed Catholics, raised on august traditions of the efficacious ritual word: *Hoc est enim corpus meum.* Much power might inhere in ceremonious not-saying; poets did not give up the possibility that their words in not saying might yet be words of power; also Rimbaud and Verlaine had demonstrated that the poet lived a dangerous game.

Wallace Stevens was not a romantic of that sort. There was no in-compatibility between his poetics and a business livelihood, an or-dered routine. Seen over his shoulder, do the Frenchmen not seem a little absurd? Yet Stevens, we must conclude, believed as deeply as they in words of power; if we are going to explain the most extraordi-nary datum of his career, the long sequence of letters in which he calmly *explains* poem after poem, what it intends to handle and con-vey, we can only postulate his faith in his verbal forms, since the man who had no equal in his profession at drawing up a surety bond was far too intelligent to suppose that the words he had put on his pages could *mean* what he said he meant them to mean in any normal lexical way. "The Arabian is the moon." It is only the moon while Stevens is saying it is the moon; it would never have been the moon had he not written that note, and it ceases to be the moon as soon as we turn from the note to the verse. So how was it ever the moon?

A little later in the same letter to Simons Stevens concedes that "several things" in the "Notes Toward a Supreme Fiction" "would stand a little annotating." "For instance, the fact that the Arabian is the moon is something that the reader could not possibly know. However I did not think that it was necessary for him to know. Even without knowing———" One may wish he had finished that sentence; it is unusual for him not to finish sentences in his letters. The three dashes he substituted for an effort to finish it must stand for the deepest mystery in his poetic, the relationship between his words and the part of experience that is not verbal. Pure faith invested that mystery. Though he had to explain them to enquirers whose seriousness he respected, still the poems had power to *mean*: had perhaps potential power over men, "supple and turbulent," not yet born.

You cannot, F. R. Leavis long ago pointed out, paraphrase the doctrinal parts of Wordsworth whose insidious way is to seem supremely paraphrasable. Stevens resists paraphrase more airily, turning the latter end of a sentence aside into sheer non sequitur, with an aplomb that bespeaks his comfortable situation in the heart of the tradition of Nonsense. And yet, like Wordsworth, he had "something to say," and like Mallarmé he proposed efficacious rituals.

> He is the transparence of the place in which
> He is and in his poems we find peace.
> He sets this peddler's pie and cries in summer,
> The glass man, cold and numbered, dewily cries,
> "Thou art not August unless I make thee so."
> Clandestine steps upon imagined stairs
> Climb through the night because his cuckoos call.

1976

1680 Words on
Duncan's Words

"Give a poet a machine," Duncan said in delight, "and he'll *use* it." Pound, his point was, had found a poetic use for every character on the typewriter keyboard, not excluding / and @, two symbols which also remind us of what typewriters were "meant" for: business letters. Men of letters of course use them too, but by habit never stray from the keys that spell words (one reason to say "men of *letters*"). So used, the typewriter is a mechanized quill, introducing no new possibility save perhaps the carbon copy. But Pound—it's as if he'd recognized a keyboard instrument left lying around by inattention, and thought to find out what tunes it might be made to play.

That's a model for thinking about some of Duncan's playfulness, as when he noticed the word "locomotive" lying around and started taking it to pieces:

> loco-co co moto mo mo
> locomomo cotivecomo
>
> mocolotive
> motocolive

> moco lomo motive lomo
> co co co co co como co momo
> lo mo como lo mo tomo

> At Lake Como we saw mountains.

Though published among the "Imitations of Gertrude Stein," that poem derives from her only the jaunty non sequitur it uses to end with, Lake Como. For the rest, it's intent on four queer syllables: not, in Stein's way, undergoing their hypnosis, but in a tinkerer's way, undoing screws, refastening. And out of bits and pieces of the word "locomotive'" it contrives an acceptable imitation of how trains can sound, which is no more what the word was meant for than the Remington was meant for writing Cantos.

We may even want to reconsider "non sequitur." The mountains, at any rate, follow from "co co co co co como co momo," where the train is surely laboring up-hill. No, what Robert Duncan and G. S. have in common is chiefly a place of origin, Oakland. ("There is no there there," she said. I'm not sure he'd agree.)

It's curious how readily Duncan can detach his language from language:

> Calling up words—or calld in by words—
> the familiar comforting beasts in the dark
> come home toward our lanterns, and we,
> herdsmen of our language, call them by name.

The words are both the beasts and the sounds we use to summon them, and name them; there's a shift of signification that's like suddenly being asked for the name of the word "cow." More shifts lie just ahead:

> And the years return to us. Our own
> departed return. What do we know of them
> as they come thru towards us? but we are
> sure of them. We leave a light in the window.
> In the mind. We read in the evening as if
> they were about to enter. We sit
> about the round table.

That's so simple in itself it even recalls the cozy cliches of American stage melodrama: the parlor, the round table, the lamp in the window for the long-lost child. But on the page it doesn't exist in itself; it exists in a seamless typographic continuum with the lines about the animals and the language. So, does "Our own departed" hint at another way to think about language? "What do we know of them as they come thru toward us?"—especially if "they" are the words we invented in an earlier phase of history.

And—not to talk this to death—"we" in that case are the historic human "we," reaching back to the first speakers. So, on the next page,

> Even the subhuman Mousterian man left
> ashes of fires. . . .
> Outside
> the epoch of the greatest cold
> has driven
> the mammoth and the reindeer southward
> to wander
> in enormous herds. Storm
> has made an almost continual night. Inside:
> ears alert for the cave-lion or bear,
> the Cro-Magnon man workt
> the inaccessible rock-face
> and returned from the deepest recesses of the mind
> to the hearth,
> to the place where we too are gathered.

What he's working at is a *visual* language, drawing animals in a place so remote there's no way to draw them from the life. As he draws them out of "the deepest recesses of the mind," his ears are alert not for words but for the menace of lion or bear. And he's one of us.

. . . Which in paraphrase is perhaps a bit banal, but then what happens when a poem gets paraphrased can't be blamed on the poet. I'll risk the banality for the sake of the neat instance: Duncan writing, as so often, poetry about poetry, and teasing a few simple images apart the way you'd tease a dense knot apart, to examine its pattern of crossings, putting trust in its continuities. (What I was quoting from, by the way, is on the first two pages of "An Essay At War.")

The way he took the word "locomotive" apart: that's the way he's treating three or four scenes we all have in our minds: herdsmen and animals; the melodramatist's parlor set; the Cro-Magnon artist. His materials have the status of found objects, easily retrieved from imagination's bric-à-brac. Elsewhere he's commented on the process:

> An empty room lit by a single electric light
> reveals a little universe of its deserted things:
> menacings of enameld saucepan meanness,
> cruelties of bolts and door knobs,
> secretive stoveness in stove black.

(That's a detail of "Electric Iron," from "Domestic Scenes.") And, as Adam in "Adam's Way" says of dream-country,

>   A man can see there
> what is only a word in this
> here world and hear
> what men awake but see.

I'm insisting, you see, on the ordinariness of his materials—things no more exotic, taken one by one, than a typewriter—because Duncan's procedures have, to my mind, less in common with those of the continental surrealists he gets compared to than with those of, say, the American "primitive" painter who made the huge cat's head Dr. Williams admired. Part of the technique is to get *up close*, using any sort of lens that comes to hand, for instance a dictionary with copious etymologies:

> Let there be the clack of the shuttle flying
>   forward and back,   forward and
>   back,
>
> warp, *wearp, varp:*   *"cast of a net, a laying of eggs"*
>   from **warp-* *"to throw"*
>   the threads twisted for strength
>   that can be a warp of the will. . . .
>
> And the shuttle carrying the woof I find
>   was *skutill* *"harpoon"* —a dart, an arrow,
>   or a little ship,
>
>   *navicula* *weberschiff,*
>
> crossing and recrossing from shore to shore—

—So "Passages 2" takes us from Circe's loom (in *Canto 39*) back and out to vast contentions with wave and whale. And, yes, it sounds surreal; and, no, it needed no trances nor anointings with honey-dew but simply a willingness to enter free fall with the O.E.D. "Give a poet a machine"—here a reference-machine—"and he'll *use* it." Anyone might have done that? But no one else did.

Or give a poet a hint and he'll run with it. With hints from the newspapers his running may be no more distinguished than anyone else's; Duncan's anti-war rhetoric of the 60's simply dates.* But a hint from "testimony at the trial of the Forfar Witches—"*that Andrew Watson . . . altho he be a blind man yet he danced alse nimblie as any of the companye, . . . and that Isobel Shyrrie did sing her song called* Tinkletum Tankletum"— sufficed to propel three lively pages you'll find in *Roots and Branches*:

> . . . Sing your song, Shyrrie, and raise it high
> till a glare of the old Wildness comes into my eye
> and the dead begin hopping like toads from the stones,
>
> croaking and moaning "To die! to die!"
> Such kisses and fumblings there be in old bones!
>
> :and that Isobel Shyrrie did sing her song
> :and that the divill kist all and one.
>
> Give us Tinkletum Tankletum before we go,
> and let's us and the dead make merry once more.
> I can hear at time's door the first cock's crow. . . .

That bespeaks a gift for rhythmic deviltry "The Ballad of Mrs Noah" draws on too.

I know, I know, I'm not mentioning the "visionary" Duncan. I'm assuming that "visionary" roots reach down into the accessible: Blake's into the domain of engraver's copper and burin, Duncan's into the play-world whence he fetched "Tinkletum Tankletum" and "co co co co co como co momo" and the world of jostling information-atoms whence he fished up shuttle = shipling, lytel schippe. That second

---

*Though "Passages 26" has cunning wordplay about the B-52s obliterating peasantry they were too high to see:
    "The Industrial wiping out the Neolithic! Improver of Life
        flying his high standards!"
—flying planes the way you'd fly banners.

world is the classroom-world, closer to Tinkletum Tankletum than we often think. It's commonplace to read in a modern American poet's *vita* something like this from Duncan's: "University of California, Berkeley, 1936–38, 1948–50." Penn gave us Pound and Williams; Columbia, Zukofsky; Harvard, Eliot and Olson and Creeley. Let them inveigh against academe (though Eliot and Zukofsky didn't), still they're marked by its juxtapositions, its surreal detachments. Even the habit of conning such documents as can make you the gift of Tinkletum Tankletum is a habit classrooms encourage.

They encourage you also to stay loose with parts of speech: "Light song" can be a song not heavy, *and* a song about Light; a "moving picture" can be a picture that moves you. Scribes can also divide "aloud" "a loud." So can poets; and in Duncan's "Light Song" we even encounter the juxtaposition "Chaplin Lawrence" (how would either man have responded?) in the thick of a hymn to hymns:

> Chaplin Lawrence said was beauty in a man
> in 'City Lights'
> the silent moving picture speech or
> indistinguishable metropolis murmuring a loud
> we do not hear
> suggests
> the language we long for,
> Hidden.
>
> As in the measures the song is hidden.
> Heard as we sing her
> word upon word.   The design
>
> as we observe it.

1983

The Fiction of Free-Fall

E. M. Forster's *A Room with a View* starts with people arriving in Italy on vacation. Nothing new there; fiction was always about people on vacation—people in free-fall. Don Quixote was not punching a time clock. The great genre that extends from the *Odyssey* to *The Adventures of Augie March*—the picaresque, the tale of the unattached wanderer—is a saga of what we have learned to call vacation (interruption of routine). But Homer alike with Saul Bellow (before Chicago's Committee on Social Thought flypapered him) could see it as the normal shape of human life, a taking of things as they come. Here "Vacation" means, "back to normal."

It was the glory of Henry James that his people didn't "work." That meant: being free from predictable and fairly uninteresting pressures, they could expand, stretch and dart fire. Some were dull, true, but if they were you could seek the cause—and expect a most interesting pathology—in *them*, and not in their subjection to "9 to 5."

And the Hemingway hero—Robert Jordan in *For Whom the Bell Tolls*—has been cut loose to think about blowing up a Spanish bridge the way he might be thinking about damming a stream some footloose July, up in Michigan.

Fiction, 19th century English fiction especially, has its gridded and ineluctable particulars—the clock, the calendar, the railway time-table, the city plan, in fact just about everything pedantry assigns to "structure"—because as football needs its grid to persuade you mayhem is rulebound, so the untrammelled bouncing about of human volition needs a look of containment before we'll acknowledge a writer's tidy job. For of writers we expect "Plot," and plot is chaos. "Plot," come to think of it, is foreshadowed in the *Odyssey*, when the winds of Aeolus come out of their bag, and the scheme of any novel is:

> BEGIN
> Let the winds loose.
> (Chapters of blowing about.)
> A show of rebagging them.
> END.

I once heard the novelist Richard Stern confide that he began *Golk*, the saga of Herbert Hondorp, by "cutting Hondorp loose."

David Lodge wrote a story some years back about an English family's unsuccessful vacation. Their idyll had begun, it belatedly turns out, with the dog getting mortally run over, and the rest was of the same texture (sunburn, seasickness). The story's subtext seemed to be that vacations are without exception unsuccessful, something it needed the dog's demise to bring home. That is a bourgeois perspective (Lodge's point). Following the Trojan War, Odysseus had a ten-year vacation of spectacular unsuccess, losing his ships and crewmen, being humiliated by Cyclopes worse than mosquitoes, tied to the mast while listening to song (which you'd not put up with in the Acapulco Hilton) and having his dog drop dead the minute he's back in Ithaca. Paraphrased, the *Odyssey* might be the stand-up monologue of a *nebbish* comedian, and such a thing may have crossed James Joyce's mind.

Fiction tells us that to be on vacation is mankind's natural state. That it's normal to be accountable for every moment is a potent counter-fiction, endorsed by the IRS as by all listers of figures. Thus real fiction rejects figures. They pertain to the anti-world. The moment Bellow starts mentioning numbers he's clawing us down into unreality, and the deadpan listing of Bloom's budget for the day is one of the high comic moments of *Ulysses*.

Fiction, the hammock: those are symbiotic, as the *New York Times Book Review* knows. Eyes always on figures (#1? #2? #7 last week?) the *Review* stands in for an industry. No member of a holiday crowd is more alert than the pickpocket.

1987

From Lower Bellowvia

A genre has long since defined itself, Nobel-certified: the Saul Bellow Novel. This is the Novel as First-Draft Dissertation: a rumination on the sorry state of the world, insufficiently formal for the Committee on Social Thought at the University of Chicago, however well it may translate into Swedish, but not unworthy of that Committee's encouraging noises. About the sorry state of the world there is nothing to be done save accept it, as every Bellow protagonist must learn for himself the way Job did. And since the Bellow Novel is obdurately protagonist-centered, what the reader gets to do is share his learning process.

In *The Dean's December* (Harper & Row, 1982), the Dean—not a Jewish Dean from the Bellow Repertory Company, not at bottom an *echt* dean at all but a mere dean of students, moreover a moonfaced French-Irish ex-newspaperman named Albert Corde who has drifted into academe, and don't confuse him with his fox-faced creator—the Dean, if I could just finish this sentence, is stranded in communist Rumania waiting for his mother-in-law, Valeria, to die.

His wife, Minna, née Raresh, is an astrophysicist of the Palomar caliber; he cannot understand a thing she does, save that she brings together "a needle from one end of the universe with a thread from the opposite end." Here, Minna being preoccupied with her mother, he gets little solace from her. And it's cold and he speaks no Rumanian: plenty of time to ruminate. Herzog, left in solitude, wrote letters. Corde can simply run on, third-person imperfect.

What he has to ruminate about includes how the college administration reacted to his two-part *Harper's* article about Chicago. "Corde had let himself go, indignant, cutting, reckless." Here he is being reckless:

> The cabdriver who picks up and returns all these dialysis patients is an enormous black woman in red jersey trousers. Her feet seem quite small. Her shoes have high heels. Her straightened hair hangs to her shoulders. She wears a cabby's cap and a quilted jacket. . . . These passenger-patients are her charges, her friends. She wheels forward the television set. The sick woman asks for Channel Two, and sighs and settles back and passes out.

You have to suspend belief to imagine *Esquire*, let alone *Harper's*, publishing to the extent of two long installments these meanderings of an epigone of Saul Bellow's, and suspend it further to imagine a late twentieth-century urban American university being flustered by their indignant high-mindedness.

Has the creator of Augie March mislaid his street smarts? Augie wouldn't have asked us to credit "a flood of mail," no less, inundating *Harper's*, or the notion that at a worldly Chicago college the sight of "one of its deans taking everybody on" makes them "jittery," "upset." Who, by the way, is he taking on in that dialysis vignette? The taxi driver? The patients? Channel Two, maybe? No, just death. "These are dead men and women. The metabolic wastes obviously affect their brains." It's the *irremediable* that gets to a Bellow character.

Note that phrase, though, "a *flood* of mail." Saul Bellow's mind has been grooved by recurring images, and thirteen years ago—the very year Neil Armstrong set foot on the moon—Bellow imagined a more sardonic flood.

In *Mr. Sammler's Planet* his Corde of those days, Mr. Sammler, was arguing to the extent of twenty pages with a Hindu biophysicist named Lal about whether man ought to be fooling with other worlds at all, seeing his mess on this one. The discussion was not trenchant even in 1969, and time has not sharpened it, though inside that novel it did some useful chores. It helped keep active the slightly defoliated eloquence from which the book drew most of its continuity, and it resumed the larger debate that reverberates from one end of the Bellow shelf to the other: what reasons, if any, can be stated for going on with the human enterprise, given all the ways God and man appear to collaborate in thwarting it?

That grand debate is as old as the Book of Job. What the author of the Book of Job couldn't have foreseen was Saul Bellow's reverse perspective, the farcical. The debate between Sammler and Lal was ended like this:

> "So I suppose we must jump off, because it is our human fate to do so. If it were a rational matter, then it would be rational to have justice on this planet first. Then, when we had an earth of saints, and our hearts were set upon the moon, we could get in our machines and rise up. . . ."
>
> "But what is this on the floor?" said Shula. All four rose about the table to take a look. Water from the back stairs flowed over the white plastic Pompeian mosaic surface. . . .
>
> "Is it a bath overflowing?" said Lal.
>
> "Shula, did you turn off the bath?"
>
> "I'm positive I did."
>
> "I believe it is too rapid for bath water," said Lal. "A pipe presumably is burst."

So much for technology? No, so much for the human right to goof off on visions of grandeur. The pipe burst thanks to the greed of an elegant bum named Wallace, who was upstairs banging it open on the theory that it was a dummy pipe with money inside. He suspected his father of stashing about the house large wads of money tendered by the Mafia for medical favors.

Sheer farce. Yet since Wallace's father was the unequivocally decent character in *Mr. Sammler's Planet*, and was also at that moment scant hours from death by cerebral aneurysm, these researches into the plumbing were tasteless and nearly impious as well as inept, and the flood that came cascading down the staircase to drown out talk about spacecraft admonished like the waters with which God overwhelmed all earth long ago, out of exasperation with human folly.

That was the once and possibly future Saul Bellow: a sardonic connoisseur of Old Testament motifs, a moralist, a fabulist. His fictions, in reflecting a tribal penchant for arguing, revert to the topics over which God and Job once squared off. To invent a new impersonator of Job is more or less his formula for getting a new book started: someone whose "Why me?" can extend to "Why anyone?"

Six years ago last May, Mr. Bellow could be watched for an hour as he and astronaut Neil Armstrong accepted academic honors from the oldest university in Ireland. There was much to amuse a prickly ironist, not least the complex fate that had brought a puppeteer whose character called the astronauts "superchimpanzees" to the same platform with the very man whose foot first tested extraplanetary soil. He also heard himself eulogized in some 250 words of Latin, composed by a poker-faced wag. In the cribs they'd been issued at the door spectators could match *"Insanumne genus humanum? Testes plerique"* against Bellow's "Is the race crazy? Plenty of evidence."

There exists no Latin—or French or Swedish for that matter—for the crisp nihilism of "Plenty of evidence": the word "evidence" plucked from law and the sciences and steamrollered flat to do for street argot. It's quintessential Bellow, accurately chosen, utterly resistant to export. It also recalls, as did the whole Irish occasion, a Bellow who'd have judged *The Dean's December* dreary: a book (for one thing) so remote from reliance on idiom that there's nothing save the regime to impede a Rumanian version.

For along the way Bellow has acquired an alter ego named Herzog, who first surfaced in the 1964 novel of that name and promptly addled his creator's head by lecturing into generous stupor the bestowers of the James L. Dow Award, the International Literature Prize, *and* the National Book Award. Herzog—a Leopold Bloom with a Ph.D.— prides himself on the cogency of his moral reflections, as, you can tell, does Corde, does Sammler, does . . . oh, come on, as does their author, who promptly signed up the ruminative Herzog as collaborator.

That was unwise, seeing that one meaning of "ruminative" is "characterized by a mind like a cow's stomach." But soon Herzog was being entrusted with the pen for pages on end. Those swatches of *Mr. Sammler's Planet* you may remember skipping were the work of Herzog: the fictional intelligence enjoying time out while something got written that might go into *Partisan Review* (he's changed magazines since).

"Sammler thought that this was what revolutions were really about. In a revolution you took away the privileges of aristocracy and redistributed them. What did equality mean? Did it mean all men were friends and brothers? No, it meant that all belonged to the elite. Killing was an ancient privilege. This was why revolutions plunged into blood."

Solemn as Sherwood Anderson's in *Dark Laughter*, that voice is the voice of Herzog: never mind that the name on the title page is the name of Saul. "Sammler thought." O Lord, "thought." The mind cowers. "A Thought," an acquaintance of G. K. Chesterton's used to announce, uplifting a large hand; to whom someone once said in exasperation, "Good God, man, you don't call that a *thought*, do you?" Herzog would have called it a Thought, whatever it was. Corde, alas, thinks too. Here he is thinking aloud on an interracial encounter:

> "Race has no bearing on it. I see Spofford Mitchell and Sally Sathers, two separatenesses, two separate and ignorant intelligences. One is staring at the other with terror, and the man is filled with a staggering passion to *break through*, in the only way he can conceive of breaking through—a sexual crash into release."

We're to imagine him *saying* that to someone. Moreover, since what Spofford Mitchell did to Sally Sathers was lock her in the trunk of his car, rape her repeatedly, and finally shoot her in the head, there may be those among us who will reject platitudes from Communications 1A; will even opt for Jeremiah's summation (17:9), that the heart of man "is deceitful, and desperately wicked." Such readers may be thought of as unqualified for later Bellow, where much of the time the thread of the protagonists' lucubrations is the same thing as the plot itself.

Not that *The Dean's December* lacks all touch of as skilled a fabulist as you might want. Its opening is rich with possibility.

"Corde, who led the life of an executive in America—wasn't a college dean a kind of executive?—found himself six or seven thousand miles from his base, in Bucharest, in winter, shut up in an old-fashioned apartment."

In the bundle of worries he spends long hours unpacking, Chicago dominates, a place of terminal craziness: its rich without point, its poor without hope, its ongoings rife with jagged violence and sexual hysteria, its very jails full of rats and sodomizings and stabbings. There fate assigns each denizen his place in one or the other of two anarchies: the legitimate, the illegitimate. No melioration of Chicago seems thinkable.

Is there life after Chicago? If so, Bucharest seems to emblematize it. Bellow's Bucharest is neither a Lower Slobovia of ludicrous privations nor a Len Deighton playground for adventurous free-world spirits. It's a suitable limbo for Corde's introspections: a bleak, half-lighted city where informers and bureaucrats are endured like the weather, and the genteel who can remember other times are furtive in guarding their diminished ceremonies.

No writer has more authority with the feel of a place:

> December brown set in at about three in the afternoon. By four it had climbed down the stucco of old walls, the gray of Communist residential blocks: brown darkness took over the pavements . . . more thickly and isolated the street lamps. These were feebly yellow in the impure melancholy winter effluence. Air-sadness, Corde called this. In the final stage of dusk, a brown sediment seemed to encircle the lamps. Then there was a livid death moment. Night began.

Corde empathizes readily with the "air-sadness": with starker phenomena as well. At one baleful session with a Party administrator, he feels himself "the image of the inappropriate American . . . incapable of learning the lessons of the twentieth century; spared, or scorned, by the forces of history or fate or whatever a European might want to call them."

This means: he senses that a Rumanian colonel will despise his incomprehension of brute power, which scorns to bend regulations merely so that a defected astrophysicist with her American bogus-academic husband may visit a paralytic in intensive care. If you'll notice, Corde is empathizing with what he feels the colonel feels about what he feels about the colonel's nonfeeling. With the book only a few hundred words old and its exposition still crisp, already we're in that deep.

We swim at such treacly depths because in this way station for his stunned soul Corde has nothing to do but wait: for one more hospital visit, arranged by bribery; for Valeria to die; for a grim day at the crematorium; for the flight home. Not that when he does have, or will have, things to do (in Chicago) does *doing* any longer seem to signify. In his morass of seeing-all-sides, acts are irrelevant.

So his plight—killing time in limbo—is rather close to the plight of his author, who must fill a book with sheer inaction and has consequently piped in what's been all too fluent for him of late years, the Herzogian vitality to be gotten from *opinions*.

Hence, multipage excerpts from Corde's *Harper's* article (reruminated, even, with trial revisions), chapter-long replays of Chicago conversations, an audience with the American ambassador (on whom "he wanted to try out . . . some of his notions about the mood of the West"), expostulations with a boyhood friend, now a big-shot syndicated journalist; more, more.

And his drear December has left his creator bereft of occasion for the sort of comic epiphany that can salvage all: scenes like the miniature Noah's Flood in *Mr. Sammler*, or the page near the end of *Henderson the Rain King* (1959) where the hero (you have to believe this) climbs into a roller coaster with a mangy old trained bear, too old to ride a bike anymore.

> And while we climbed and swooped and dipped and swerved and rose again higher than the Ferris wheels and fell, we held on to each other. By a common bond of despair we embraced, cheek to cheek. . . . I was pressed into his long-suffering age-worn, tragic and discolored coat as he grunted and cried to me.

That's a high Saul Bellow moment, one of the highest. Devoid of reflections, it prompts them. It would have been understandable to the author of the Book of Job, who envisioned Leviathan drawn out of the sea with a kind of Hebrew safety pin, and tethered on a leash for laughing maidens. Impossible to imagine it in Latin.

1982

Beckett Translating Beckett

Eight pages "From an Unabandoned Work" was Samuel Beckett's autumnal sign of life in the September–October *Evergreen Review* of 1960 (4.14, 58–65): unpunctuated murmurs spaced down the page.

next another image yet another they'll soon cease it seems it's me from head to foot with my mother's face I see it from below my mother's face it is like nothing

we are on a latticed veranda tangled with verbena the perfumed sun spangles the red tiles good God

the huge head hatted with birds and flowers lowers on my pale curls the eyes burn with severe love while mine my head thrown back at the ideal angle offers her its pale upcast eyes my eyes

kneeling bolt upright on a cushion shapeless in a white nightshirt clasping my hands with all my strength I pray according to her instructions

it isn't over she drones a belief of the Apostles' Creed I look at her lips while she can't see me

she stops the eyes burn again I cast up mine in haste and repeat all wrong the air vibrates with the hum of insects

it's over it goes out like a lamp blown ouť

[65]

This was "Translated from the French by the author." The French appeared the following spring: 180 pages in three symmetrical parts, called *Comment C'est* (Éditions de Minuit, 1961). Minute differences suggest that the English corresponds to a penultimate version. But not revision of the French but rethinking of the English accounts for the fact that in *How It Is*, "Translated from the French by the author" (Grove Press, 1964), barely twenty consecutive words at a stretch can be found to tally with that 1960 specimen. For instance:

> we are on a veranda smothered in verbena the scented sun dapples the red tiles yes I assure you
>
> the huge head hatted with birds and flowers is bowed down over my curls the eyes burn with severe love I offer her mine pale upcast to the sky whence cometh our help and which I know perhaps even then with time shall pass away
>
> in a word bolt upright on a cushion on my knees whelmed in a nightshirt I pray according to her instructions

[15]

—where the mot juste is "whelmed," with "flottant dans une chemise de nuit' for the French and "shapeless in a white nightshirt" as the transitional draft. Then:

> she stops her eyes burn down on me again I cast up mine in haste and repeat awry
>
> the air thrills with the hum of insects
>
> that's all it goes out like a lamp blown out

[16]

Again the exact single word, "awry"; yet again, "thrills." And inconspicuous stabs of vividness, in this medium so spare that no phrase can go really unexposed: "the eyes burn again" becoming "her eyes burn down on me again." The French is "elle achève ses yeux se rallument je relève vite les miens et repète de travers"—to which the 1960 version was "closer," "the eyes" for "ses yeux" corresponding to the fact that French pronouns have more taxonomic than personal import. The English, however, Beckett elected to intensify: *her* eyes, and burning *down*, and *on me*. From beginning to end, *How It Is* is *Comment C'est* less translated into English than re-experienced in English drop by drop, with the unique authority of a great stylist equally master of both tongues and making each tongue do what it has never done before. Perhaps so much thought has never gone, twice over, into the disposition of such common words, the little nuts and bolts you and I screw in with our eyes shut, "her" and "the" and "c'est fini" and "that's all." In the age of Wittgenstein and Louis Zukofsky, whose "*A*" documents some forty years' concern with, among other rabbinical matters, the implications of the indefinite article, one can envisage whole languages reclaimed, little idioms cherished like Homeric formulae as being the commonest currency of speech, hence intrinsic to a million minds, hence marvelous. Comment c'est, for example: how it is: all of philosophy footnotes such a phrase.

I commenced adumbrating such matters twelve years ago on first opening the English *Molloy*, where we find at the bottom of the second page of text,

> This time, then once more I think, then perhaps a last time, then I think it'll be over, with that world too. Premonition of the last but one but one. All grows dim. A little more and you'll grow blind. It's in the head. It doesn't work any more, it says, I don't work any more. You go dumb as well and sounds fade. The threshold scarcely crossed that's how it is. It's the head. It must have had enough. So that you say, I'll manage this time, then perhaps once more, then perhaps a last time, nothing more.

What caught my ear, and holds my attention still, was the eight-word sequence "You go dumb as well and sounds fade," a cadence as achieved as any of Vergil's. Its magic plagued me. Three years later I was sufficiently immersed in the way of such phrases to be writing a book called *Samuel Beckett*. Fortified by the assurance that his prose canon was virtually achieved—he had said in 1958 that he did not see how he could write another novel—I was polishing in January 1961 a penultimate draft celebrating the master of the declarative sentence when the mail from Paris brought a copy of *Comment C'est*, a novel evidently, 177 pages, and with no sentence from beginning to end except where a Beckett phrase maps point for point what would elsewhere be called a sentence.

But of course he had merely (merely!) gone still deeper, discarding not simply capitals and periods but all those little beginnings and endings, using white space to breathe with while he articulates the very nervous system of language, the phrases, the single words. So I pried open joints in my typescript to receive new material, including an eighteen-page sequence on the new work with quotations in English for the reader's comfort. I translated most of them myself, stringing English phrases together in the sequence of the French ones, with that *Evergreen Review* specimen for exiguous model. This excerpt was printed in the Spring 1961 *Spectrum* (5.1, 3–20), and I sent Beckett a copy.

He seemed to like it but found the translations "groggy," and offered to try to improve them some time. I didn't press him—Sam Beckett had better things to do than retouch my paraphrases—but before long he was pressing Grove Press for thermofaxes of all the pages of the *Samuel Beckett* MS that had *Comment C'est* quotations. These came back to Grove with painstakingly calligraphed revisions. I saw them once. I wish I had them. Luckily between the *Spectrum* version and my printed book they can mostly be reconstructed. They are rather exercises than essays toward the ultimate version, which they seldom resemble, any more than does the *Evergreen Review* excerpt. But watch.

> sorti de là la route qui descend bordée d'arbres des milliers tous pareils même essence jamais su laquelle des kilomètres de rampe tout droit jamais vu ça grimper là-haut l'hiver le verglas les branches noires grises de givre elle là-haut au bout mourant pardonnant toute blanche
>
> [95]

From the last third of this I had extracted

> winter skim ice black branches grey with ice she up there at the end
> dying forgiving all white

of which Beckett made

> winter icy road black branches grey with rime she up there at the top
> dying forgiving all white

This (1) registers the fact that *verglas* and *givre* are different words, an important detail in a work where so much vocabulary is recycled; (2) by specifying the road supplies a glimpse of what my excerpting had excluded; and (3) takes care of the irrelevant affinity between *at the end* and *dying*. It does these three things without being one word longer than the attempt it corrects.

Or watch him distinguish undistinction:

> cette vie donc qu'il aurait eue inventée remémorée un peu de chaque
> comment savoir cette chose là-haut il me la donnait je la faisais mienne
> ce qui me chantait les ciels surtout les chemins surtout [. . .]
>
> [89]

My version:

> that life then he would have had invented remembered a little of each
> how to tell that business up there he gave it me I made it mine what he
> sang to me skies especially roads especially

Groggy indeed. I had misread "ce qui me chantait" as "ce qu'il me chantait"; blurred the syntax of "had"; made "business" mistakable for the direct object of "tell"; dissipated the dubieties that commence with the first subjunctive; and managed no rhythmic structure whatsoever. His rewriting:

> that alleged life then he had had invented remembered a little of each
> no knowing that thing up above he gave it to me I made it mine what I
> fancied skies especially roads especially

His key change, apart from correcting the downright error, was to alter "how to tell" to "no knowing": a terse idiom instead of a confected phrase. Being an idiom, and being pulled on by "alleged," it draws away from "that thing" so that we don't tend to read "no knowing that thing up above" as a constituent phrase. The ear finds the proper grouping:

> that alleged life then he had
> had
> invented
> remembered
> a little of each
>   no knowing//
> that thing up above
>   he gave it to me
>   I made it mine
>   what I fancied
>   skies especially
>   roads especially

Such minutiae, comparable to the spin of an electron, are imperceptible amid the spot welds of normal prose; but *Comment C'est* gets useful work from the microforces of language. One more cure for grogginess:

> un jour nous reprendrons la route ensemble [. . .] nous aidions mutuellement à avancer tombions de concert et attendions dans nos bras le moment de repartir
>
> [70–71]

My version:

> one day we should set forth together . . . help one another walk fall down in unison and await embracing the moment to resume

His revision:

> one day we should set forth again together . . . help one another forward fall down in unison and lie there in each other's arms till it be time to go on

—a "forward" for a "walk" (which I should have remembered isn't a *Comment C'est* mode of progression), and thirteen eloquent little words to replace a polysyllabic archness.

The reader who wants to see Beckett's final versions of these details may find them in the Grove text of *How It Is* at pages 77, 72, 57. In the three longer examples that follow I give all four—French, Kenner, Beckett improving Kenner, final Beckett—since much of the interest in these comparisons depends on inspecting his final decisions. My version of the first isn't in the *Spectrum* article; I've just located it amid carbons of old typescripts. It was a citation for page 86 of my book, to illustrate an Occasionalist courtship: the doll-like synchronization of two people's movements, reseen from a time and place of remote agony.

I

soudain hop gauche droit nous voilà partis nez au vent bras se balançant le chien suit tête basse queue sur les couilles rien à voir avec
nous il a eu la même idée au même instant du Malebranche en moins
rose [. . .]

[. . .] demi-tour vers l'intérieur fugitif face à face transferts rattache-
ment des mains balancement des bras dégustation en silence de la
mer et des îles têtes qui pivotent comme une seule vers les fumées de
la cité repérage en silence des monuments têtes qui reviennent
comme reliées par un essieu

soudain nous mangeons des sandwiches à bouchées alternées cha-
cun le sien en échangeant des mots doux ma chérie je mords elle avale
mon chéri elle mord j'avale nous ne roucoulons pas encore la bouche
pleine

mon amour je mords elle avale mon trésor elle mord j'avale bref noir
et nous revoilà nous éloignant de nouveau à travers champs la main
dans la main les bras se balançant [. . .]

COMMENT C'EST, 37

sudden hop left right we are moving nose up arms swinging the dog
follows head down tail on his balls nothing to see he had the same idea
at the same instant Malebranche but paler [. . .]

[. . .] half-turn inward fleeting face-to-face transit rejoining of hands
swinging of arms silent savoring of the sea and islands heads pivoting
as one toward the smokes of the city silent identification of landmarks
heads swinging back as though joined by connecting rods

suddenly we are eating sandwiches in alternate bites each his own
while exchanging soft words my dear I bite she swallows my darling
she bites I swallow we say no more mouths full

my love I bite she swallows my treasure she bites I swallow brief interval and there we are again crossing the field hand in hand arms
swinging [. . .]

KENNER DRAFT

Surprisingly easy, in this tissue of small hints, to miss the point that later
seems obvious. "Hop!" means "Get moving," but with no exclamation point
I didn't guess it emanated from the dog and took it for an Anglicism. And
"rien à voir avec nous" I split apart, attaching the first half to the dog's lowered
head and the second to "la même idée." And having supposed that "roucoulons" was an elegant variation of "échangeant des mots doux," I got from
"pas encore" "not again" instead of "not yet." Beckett requires of the reader a
delicate trust in normalities of idiom and rhythm.

suddenly yip left right off we go chins up arms swinging the dog follows head down tail on his balls nothing to do with us he had the same idea at the same instant Malebranche less the rosy hue [. . .]

[. . .] right about inward turn fleeting meeting face to face transfers and hand in hand again arms swinging silent relishing of sea and isles heads pivoting as one towards the city fumes silent distinguishing of monuments heads back front as though on an axle

suddenly we are eating sandwiches in alternate mouthfuls I mine she hers and exchanging endearments my sweet girl I bite she swallows my sweet boy she bites I swallow we don't yet coo with our bills full

darling girl I bite she swallows darling boy she bites I swallow brief blackout and there we are again off through the fields hand in hand arms swinging [. . .]

SAMUEL BECKETT, 86–87

The little packets of movement into which the comic vision dissects this scene are analyzed into little packets of idiom: hence such details as "hand in hand again" rather than "rejoining of hands." And though the content of their dialogue is negligible there is expressive and inexpressive negligibility: "my sweet girl" and "my sweet boy" preserves the mechanical alternation of genders (*chérie, chéri*). As for "dégustation" (as when Paris restaurants in spring placard *Dégustation des huîtres*), he apparently found "relishing" a more explicitly gastronomic equivalent than "savoring."

suddenly yip left right off we go chins up arms swinging the dog follows head sunk tail on balls no reference to us it had the same notion
at the same instant Malebranche less the rosy hue [. . .]

[. . .] about turn introrse fleeting face to face transfer of things swinging of arms silent relishing of sea and isles heads pivoting as one to the
city fumes silent location of steeples and towers heads back front as
though on an axle

suddenly we are eating sandwiches alternate bites I mine she hers
and exchanging endearments my sweet girl I bite she swallows my
sweet boy she bites I swallow we don't yet coo with our bills full

my darling girl I bite she swallows my darling boy she bites I swallow
brief black and there we are again dwindling again across the pastures
hand in hand arms swinging [. . .]

HOW IT IS, 30–31

Some darker pigmentation in this final version: "sunk" for "down" and "it"
for "he," extending the principle which in the previous version replaced
"smokes" by "fumes." "Repérage en silence des monuments" has now become "silent location of steeples and towers," an expansion of the French, my
version having obscured the fact that the landmarks were urban, and his first
version (still under the pull of French words?) having obscurities of its own.
"Mouthfuls" becomes the more abrupt "bites," and "blackout," "black": the
trend is toward monosyllables each with maximized semantic content. This
atom-age prose emits its meanings in quanta. The "dwindling" in the final
gobbet is a liberty only the author could have taken. And note the frigid "introrse" just as tender glances meet.

II

un tel amoncellement de sacs à l'entrée de la piste que toute progression impossible et qu'à peine donnée à la caravane l'impensable première impulsion elle se serait bloquée à jamais et figée dans l'injustice

alors de gauche à droite ou d'ouest en est l'atroce spectacle jusque dans la nuit noire des temps à venir du bourreau abandonné qui ne sera jamais victime puis un petit espace puis achevé son bref voyage aplatie au pied d'une montagne de vivres la victime qui ne sera jamais bourreau puis un grand espace puis un autre abandonné ainsi de suite infiniment

COMMENT C'EST, 165

Within the costive conventions of *Comment C'est* these paragraphs correspond, say, to an especially lurid page of Gibbon. A rhetorical current carried by unusual syntactic energy runs down each paragraph like lightning down a wall in hell. Ratiocinative energies have been gathering for pages; at long last the narrator grasps in its entirety a reality which may be wholly mental but at least unites his faculties in horror. Not only does the spectacle he has excogitated immobilize injustice, it impossibilizes all the preceding narrative.

such a heaping of sacks at the very start of the route that all progression impossible and the caravan having barely received its unthinkable first impulse would be blocked for ever and congealed in injustice

then from left to right or west to east the atrocious spectacle on into the
black night of future time of a tyrant abandoned who will never be a
victim then a short space then his brief journey halted flat at the foot
of a mountain of provisions the victim who will never be a tyrant then
a long space then another abandoned and so on infinitely

KENNER DRAFT

Nothing *wrong* with this, but still not quite right. It makes no effort to solve
two central problems: how to get equivalents for the French word couple
"bourreau" and "victime," words between which, as between such persons,
there exists a relationship of sinister intimacy, and how to keep the monosyllabic adjectives ("short," "brief," "flat," "long") from degenerating into rem-
plissage.

such a mountain of sacks at the very setting forth that all progress impossible and no sooner imparted to the caravan its unthinkable first impulsion than it at a standstill for ever and frozen in injustice

then from left to right or west to east the atrocious spectacle on into the black night of future time of a tormentor abandoned who will never be tormented then a little space then his brief journey over prone at the foot of a mountain of victuals the tormented who will never be tormentor then a great space then another abandoned and so on infinitely

SAMUEL BECKETT, 197

Beckett's characteristic small precisions: "heaping" has become "mountain" and "impulse" the more pedantic "impulsion." More characteristic still, a syntactic structure of conspicuous frigidity now governs the entire first paragraph. And "à l'entrée de la piste" has become "at the very setting forth," and "bloquée," "at a standstill," improvements on my version easier to apprehend than to particularize. "Tormentor/tormented" solves the "bourreau/victime" problem. The spaces are "little" and "great," not "short" and "long," because seen, not traversed, not even mentally traversed: this is a diagram. Against this diagram, "prone" is oddly human, like "victuals."

such an acervation of sacks at the very outset that all progress impossible and no sooner imparted to the caravan the unthinkable first impulsion than arrested for ever and frozen in injustice

then from left to right or west to east the atrocious spectacle on into the
black night of boundless futurity of the abandoned tormentor never
to be victim then a little space then his brief journey done prostrate at
the foot of a mountain of provisions the victim never to be tormentor
then a great space then another abandoned so on infinitely

HOW IT IS, 137

The new trouvaille, of course, is "acervation," which suffices to snap the
whole passage into a diagrammatic mode against which the grotesqueries
stand in contorted relief. This permits relaxing the syntax which in the previous version performed a similar function, so "that it at a standstill for ever"
can become the more natural "than arrested for ever." A little more oratory
has been suffered to seep into "the black night of boundless futurity," and a
little less Euclidean congruence is discernible in "tormentor/victim" than in
"tormentor/tormented." And did rhythm govern the change from "prone at
the foot of a mountain of victuals" to "prostrate at the foot of a mountain of
provisions?" Or did he want the overtones of prostration in "prostrate"? And
"provisions," not "victuals," would certainly, like "acervation," be Gibbon's
word.

III

le petit besoin d'une vie d'une voix de qui n'a ni l'une ni l'autre

la voix extorquée quelques mots la vie parce que ça crie c'est la preuve il n'y a qu'à enfoncer bien profond un petit cri tout n'est pas mort on boit on donne à boir bonsoir

c'était je cite de bons moments quelque part de bons moments quand on y songe

Pim et moi deuxième partie et Bom et moi quatrième partie ce que ça sera

dire après ça qu'on se connait personnellement même à ce moment-là

collés l'un à l'autre à ne faire qu'un seul corps dans le noir la boue

immobiles à part le bras droit qui s'agite brièvement de loin en loin tout le nécessaire

dire après ça que j'ai connu Pim que Pim m'a connu et Bom et moi que nous nous connaîtrons même fugitivement

COMMENT C'EST, 148

Wracked summation, between my time with Pim, whom I tormented, and my time with Bom, who is to torment me. I pan the agony for little flecks of gold, though it's not the gold but the act of panning that satisfies. The effort yields one fleck of gratification per paragraph.

the small need of a life of a voice by one who has neither

the voice extorted a few words life because that cry is proof one has only to break through profound good a little cry all is not lost we drink we offer a drink good night

they were I quote good moments in part good moments when you think of them

Pim and I part two and Bom and I part four to come

say after that that it was personal knowledge we had then of one another

glued together making a single body in the dark the mud

motionless but for the right arm which moved briefly at great whiles all that was necessary

say after that that I knew Pim that Pim knew me that Bom and I will know one another even fleetingly

KENNER DRAFT

One error in the second paragraph, where my eye scrambled "bien profond" and never rechecked it, and one frank inadequacy in the fourth, where *ce que ça sera*—"What *that* will be like . . . !"—defeated all attempts to find an equivalent that depended neither on italics nor on punctuation.

the small need of a life of a voice on the part of one who has neither

the voice extorted a few words of life because of cry that proves it in deep with the blade that's all is needed a little cry all is not dead we drink we give to drink goodbye

they were I quote good moments yes somehow good moments when you think

Pim and I part two and Bom and I part four what that will be when you think

to say after that we knew each other even then

cleaved together two bodies one in the dark the mud

motionless but for the right arm brief flurry now and then all the needful

to say after that that I knew Pim that Pim knew me and Bom and I that we'll know each other even for a moment

SAMUEL BECKETT, 196

"On the part of" completes "need" less ambiguously than did "by." The principle Beckett appears to follow throughout is that in the absence of sentences the unit of composition is the phrase, so far as possible shaped by spoken idiom. Hence "in deep with the blade," "all the needful," and (his solution for "ce que ça sera") "What that will be when you think"; hence also his deletion of "personal knowledge" as unidiomatic. Something about "making a single body" displeased him; hence "two bodies one" with in its vicinity "cleave" in a sense now rare.

the paltry need of a life a voice of one who has neither

the voice extorted a few words life because of cry that's the proof good
and deep no more is needed a little cry all is not dead one drinks one
gives to drink goodbye

they were I quote good moments somehow or other good moments
when you think

Pim and me part two and Bom and me part four what that will be

to say after that we knew each other personally even then

glued together like a single body in the dark the mud

motionless but for one right arm brief flurry on and off all the needful

to say after that I knew Pim that Pim knew me and Bom and I that we
shall know each other even fleetingly

HOW IT IS, 122–23

Phlebotomy; the previous version had a little more vigor than was needful.
Hence this diction is at many points closer to that of my version (that is, to
what one first thinks of on looking at the French); "glued" has replaced
"cleaved," and "ce que ça sera" is just "what that will be," which I'd rejected
as inexpressive, and "knew each other personally," the tiredest epistolary
cliché, has been admitted, and "like a single body" has ousted the stark "two
bodies one." A studied bleakness permeates every line. Which is to say that
the mot juste is at times overjuicy, a fact we tend to forget in our relish for
strong phrases. It is no rebuke to Ernest Fenollosa, the enthusiast of mascu-
line verbs, to reflect that flatness and abstraction have their purposes. Fenollosa understood, alongside his propaganda for the *chargé*, that the Oriental
art he so greatly admired had its aesthetic of calculated intervals, gauged
nonevents.

1970

Some Post-Symbolist Structures

Part of the discovery of Language that was going on in the early nineteenth century was the discovery of Anglo-Saxon, which fascinated the young Lewis Carroll by being not-quite-English. People were exclaiming over the "epic" qualities of *The Battle of Brunanburh* as though it were a fragment of the *Iliad*, and citing, in that Romantic-vernacular heyday, bits from which you could extract a kind of sense without knowing except in the most general way what any of the words might denote. Lewis Carroll's imitation of this effect is better known than any of the Anglo-Saxon models he had in mind—

> And, as in uffish thought he stood,
>   The Jabberwock, with eyes of flame,
> Came whiffling through the tulgey wood,
>   And burbled as it came!

"Somehow it seems to fill my head with ideas," said Alice, "—only I don't exactly know what they are!" This gets cited in books on linguistics nowadays, with careful demonstrations of how much we can actually know without knowing the words.

The Romantic enthusiasts had discovered how thoroughly reader and writer can rely on the structural pattern of English. "Structure," so understood, corresponds to a higher level of generalization than "grammar" and "syntax." It is thanks to our understanding of structural patterns that we can enjoy a feeling of inwardness with such an utterance as "All mimsy were the borogoves," connecting the verb-form "were" with the -*s* termination on "borogoves," divining (how?) an inverted construction, assigning adverbial rather than adjectival force to "all," and concluding, faster than thought, that the borogoves, whatever they may be, are in a state of total mimsiness of which we can form no idea.

To state in detail and in order of application the exceedingly intricate rules by which we make structural sense of any utterance that may confront us has been the work of a generation of linguists, the most recent of whom are suggesting that the job is barely begun. Though this work has nearly all been done in the twentieth century its field of operation was discovered in the nineteenth, and largely by poets confronting the baffling fact, much later formulated by Eliot, that poetry can communicate before it is understood. Elizabeth Sewell in her pioneering work *The Field of Nonsense* has pointed to the analogy between the work of Mallarmé in France and the work of the English nonsense-writers Lear and Carroll. Nonsense-verse builds intelligible structures without intelligible words; thus Lear discovered you could create Coleridgean or Tennysonian effects with a minimum of reliance on words that are in the dictionary—

> . . . over the stark Grumboolian plain.

And Tennyson, as though returning the compliment, dedicated to Edward Lear a poem whose first five lines feature three adjectives and two nouns of which hardly anyone is likely to know the exact significance:

> Illyrian woodlands, echoing falls
>   Of water, sheets of summer glass,
>   The long divine Peneïan pass,
> The vast Akrokeraunian walls,
>
> Tomohrit, Athos, all things fair . . .

This is very likely the only appearance anywhere of the word *Akroke-raunian*; one understands that these are very splendid and ancient walls without examining that word's credentials. Tennyson seems to have remembered *infames scopulos Acroceraunia* from Horace (1.iii.20) and inserted his pseudo-kappas to point up the derivation from Greek words meaning high-thundering. We are no doubt to imagine the sheer sides of mountains from which thunderbolts are hurled, and Acroceraunia, for that matter, is the Latin name of a rocky prom-ontory in Epirus. Yet, prompted as we are to think of walls, not of mountains, we feel curiously little need of such information. Akroke-raunian walls rise, it may be, from a Grumboolian plain, in a land-scape made wholly of linguistic structures, and once this possibility was under control poetry could never be the same. By 1853, the date of Tennyson's poem, acute eyes might have sighted on the furthest horizon, slouching toward Dublin to be born, the rough beast *Finne-gans Wake*.

If we look at Tennyson's line more carefully we discover that the structural and the rhetorical principles can be separated. Our sense of linguistic structures can establish with perfect exactness the relation-ship between words; thus anyone reasonably familiar with English knows at once that *Akrokeraunian* is an adjective: that it denotes some quality of those walls. We are drawing on a different order of knowl-edge when we divine from its formidable length and sound that the quality it denotes has to do with exotic impressiveness, and we are really doing more than the poem asks us to do when we poke into its etymology, assign it a meaning, and find that its meaning turns the meaning of *walls* into a metaphor for cliffs. From the structural point of view, *Akrokeraunian* is a six-syllable phenomenon that comes be-tween *vast* and *walls* and has the same kind of syntactic function that *vast* has. It is clear that Tennyson could have drafted the line with a blank in it, to be filled up later by six appropriate syllables, and seeing the line in his work-sheet with that blank in it we should know at once that the missing six syllables would constitute one or more adjectives. In fact a prose draft of the whole poem is quite conceivable, a floor-plan of its syntax, with blanks where all the interesting words were to be installed. The plan would be of no interest whatever; it would run,

> [A lot of things] you describe so well I felt I was there; and as I read I felt I was in the golden age; and for me [a lot of exotic images] seemed realities.

This is the substance of Tennyson's compliment to Lear; we can probably agree that it is as banal as that of a thank-you note, and that the handsomeness of the compliment will depend on his success with the parts in square brackets. Such a draft, in fact, is so trivial we may feel fairly sure Tennyson never wrote one, but rather devised his clots of gorgeous words and then cobbled together the connective matter in the middle. This is no more than most of us would expect. We have been taught to ask scornfully what poetry may have to do with prose drafts, and are unsurprised when paraphrase, which is like an attempt to recover a prose original, yields little of interest.

But not always. At Westminster School, late in the sixteenth century, the young Ben Jonson acquired from his famous master William Camden a precept he never forgot, that before writing verse he should work out his sense in prose, and knowing this we may often be astonished at how little alteration the prose draft seems to have undergone in the course of being transmuted. When he makes the stone speak to passersby over the grave of the lady named Elizabeth, what it has to say defies paraphrase because it is already identical in structure and diction with any paraphrase we might venture to make:

> Would'st thou heare, what man can say
> In a little? Reader, stay.
> Under-neath this stone doth lye
> As much beautie, as could dye:
> Which in life did harbour give
> To more vertue, than doth live.
> If, at all, shee had a fault,
> Leave it buryed in this vault.
> One name was Elizabeth,
> Th'other let it sleepe with death:
> Fitter, where it dyed, to tell,
> Than that it liv'd at all. Farewell.

The stone has three statements to make about Elizabeth, three ceremonious sentences, the middle one short. Before entering on these statements it asks if we want to hear them, and bids us pause if so. At the end it bids us, in one word, Farewell. That is all; and in working out the structure of those three central sentences Jonson worked out his poem also. This defeats the Romantic distinctions between prose and verse; it becomes verse only in becoming decorously neat, and in being neat and quiet it imitates the qualities of the neat quiet lady whose virtue is reticence now as it was when she lived.

> Would'st thou heare, what man can say
> In a little?

means both, observe the virtues of this poem, small as this stone, and still more, be instructed in the qualities of this lady, whose life was a statement here completed by death, a statement the poem rephrases.

We can scarcely think about this poem except syntactically, nor is it easy to imagine Jonson thinking his way into it, while it was unwritten, by any but a syntactic route. Neither are the words bright jewels to justify the structures, nor are the structures, as they were for Tennyson, an unobtrusive mounting for the words. We may find it profitable to adduce another pre-Romantic poem for which no one would claim decorous neatness, yet for which, as much as for Jonson, the structures that hold the words in relation are exactly as indispensable as the words they hold. That great baroque structure the opening sentence of *Paradise Lost* is grown from a kernel sentence Milton seems to have imitated from the beginning of the *Iliad*. *Mēnin aeide thea*, Homer commences, "Wrath sing, goddess . . . ," and Homer goes on to explain what he means by the wrath of Achilles and the mischief it did. "Disobedience sing, Muse," commences Milton, placing the key words in the same order as Homer's but appending his explanations directly to the words they amplify. Having specified "Man's first disobedience" he elaborates on it at once, summarizing the whole drama of loss and redemption in a circular structure which begins with "the fruit of that forbidden tree" and ends ("one greater man" having negated the disobedient man) with "regain that blissful seat," thirty-eight words occupying in the sentence the place of one word in Homer. Then comes, just where it comes in Homer, the imperative "sing"; then, as in Homer, the vocative, "Heavenly Muse," which he

proceeds to elaborate just as he had elaborated the word "disobedience," by way of establishing to what Muse a Christian poet may
address himself. The verb stands unadorned in the middle, "sing";
the words before it and after it, "disobedience" and "Muse," receive
parallel amplification.

Whether from the custom of diagramming sentences in classrooms or from the writings of Noam Chomsky, we are all familiar with
the notion of a long sentence elaborated from a kernel sentence, and
with the principle that there is no other way to arrive at syntactic English. We may be less familiar with the fact that the kernel sentence,
after it has generated the elaborate sentence, may or may not prove to
be of any rhetorical salience. For Milton the kernel sentence is clearly
salient. As he elaborates, he releases the latent energies of his predi-
cate and his subject, showing us all that may be implicit, since Adam,
in *disobedience*, all that may be implicit, since the Holy Spirit revealed
himself, in *Muse*: two words which, he allows us to feel, are expand-
ing across his page their own inherent orderly energies. The kernel
sentence does not simply permit all this, it contains all this, and if, as
we read on in *Paradise Lost*, we chance to forget those majestic elabo-
rations, it will remain true that the Muse singing of disobedience
comprises the poem's business.

But this is not an invariable practice; in particular, it is not Symbolist practice. In the minor Tennyson poem we have looked at, the kernel sentence, far from mapping the poem's business, reduces to nothing but "I felt . . . and I felt . . . ," the merest excuse for the rest of the
poem to assemble its sonorities and exoticisms. And we may say that
Tennyson was working toward a new poetic which he never succeeded in formulating, and that it got formulated instead in France.
About ten years after Tennyson's homage to Lear, we find the very
young Stéphane Mallarmé composing in ten Alexandrine couplets a
poem called "Soupir," a single long sinuous sentence whose subject
and verb are not huddled inconspicuously away, but so disposed as to
command a maximum of evocative detail. Its kernel sentence appears
to be "Mon âme monte vers l'Azur," my soul mounts toward the
azure, the azure of the infinite pale sky being already for Mallarmé, it
would seem, an ultimate and a word of great power. Arthur Symons's
translation is faithful to the features we are interested in:

SIGH

My soul, calm sister, towards thy brow, whereon scarce grieves
An autumn strewn already with its russet leaves,
And towards the wandering sky of thine angelic eyes,
Mounts, as in melancholy gardens may arise
Some faithful fountain sighing whitely towards the blue!
—Towards the pale blue and pure that sad October knew,
When, in those depths, it mirrored languors infinite,
And agonizing leaves upon the waters white,
Windily drifting, traced a furrow cold and dun,
Where, in one long last ray, lingered the yellow sun.

This is a subtle piece of syntactic engineering. Symons remarks that "a delicate emotion, a figure vaguely defined, a landscape magically evoked, blend in a single effect." So they do; they are present like over-layered transparencies, not sorted out as the first sentence of *Paradise Lost* sorts things out. But Mallarmé does not huddle these elements together and allow us to associate them; he makes use of the remarkable sentence he is constructing, a sentence the progress of which uncoils like a plot. "My soul," he commences, both beginning the poem and giving the sentence its subject; then "towards," so that we know we are to expect a verb of motion, and for three lines the poem relies on that expectation to assimilate details we would not have expected:

My soul, calm sister, towards thy brow, whereon scarce grieves
An autumn strewn already with its russet leaves,
And towards the wandering sky of thine angelic eyes,
Mounts . . .

Already we have the woman and the landscape, and the qualities felt in the woman have given rise to the landscape. We also have, it would seem, a sentence completed. And yet two-thirds of the poem is still to be produced, and produced not by tacking more things on but by generating a new syntactic necessity. He does this economically, in plain sight, with such assurance we hardly see it done, and are apt to wonder where the rest of the poem came from. Yet if we watch closely it is easy to see what he does: he effects a mutation in the kernel sentence.

We have said that the kernel sentence seems to be, "My soul mounts towards the azure." This is not strictly true. The kernel sentence is complete in the opening lines, before the azure has been mentioned. It is, "My soul mounts toward your brow and toward the sky of your eyes." That mention of "sky" prepares for the mutation; the mutation itself occurs immediately after the verb. For the line that begins with the poem's main verb goes on,

> Mounts, as in melancholy gardens may arise
> Some faithful fountain sighing whitely towards the blue!

—all very orderly, an adverbial clause telling how the soul mounts and comparing its aspiration to a fountain's. The fountain mounts toward the sky but never gets there: its energy goes into striving. But instead of leaving us with this trim analogy, Mallarmé commences a new line by reduplicating the phrase with which the last line ended: "—Towards the blue pale and pure that sad October knew . . . ," and since we cannot help connecting the energy of *towards* with *mounts*, we connect, without noticing, the subject of *mounts* and that aspiration toward blueness. And there is the soul, mounting toward the azure sky, the kernel sentence mutated by a fountain's intervention. This works because each of its key elements, *My soul*, *mounts*, *towards the blue*, occupies a rhetorical strong point where a line commences, while the previous constructions in "towards" have expended themselves in less prominent niches. And with the soul mounting toward the azure and the fountain playing, he can allow the rest of the poem to concern itself with the still water in the fountain's basin:

> —Towards the blue pale and pure that sad October knew,
> When, in those depths, it mirrored languors infinite,
> And agonizing leaves upon the waters white,
> Windily drifting, traced a furrow cold and dun,
> Where, in one long last ray, lingered the yellow sun.

Since *it* may refer to the blue or to October, there is some blurring of the relative pronoun, less evident in Symons's translation than in the French, where it governs not one verb but two. It appears to be a calculated blurring; Mallarmé shows every sign of interest in the sentence he is putting together, and of awareness that such linguistic chemistries as he aspires to need shaped vessels to contain them. His syntactic arrangements, unlike Tennyson's, are like the interconnected glass vessels on a laboratory bench, of virtually sculptural interest in themselves, yet functional and everywhere transparent, to let us watch the colors change within them. Yet they are unlike Milton's too, not to mention Jonson's, in being strangely devoid of independent interest. Confronted by "My soul mounts toward your brow and toward the sky of your eyes," we may legitimately ask what it may mean. Unlike Tennyson's kernel sentence, it contains words vital to the poem's chemistry as well as to its syntactic legitimacy. Yet it is already sufficiently a piece of opportunism to be saying, in itself, nothing very forceful: nothing of the order of "Disobedience sing, Muse."

We have seen that Mallarmé's formal kernel sentence is supplanted by a mutant version composed of words that open lines. Many of his poems exploit that order of nearly geometrical coherence. He will make of the first and the last words of a poem a thematic phrase which the intervening words fill in like a chord. His most famous sonnet begins "Le vierge . . ." and ends ". . . Cygne": "the virgin swan." His *Toast Funèbre* to the memory of Gautier is enclosed within the words "O . . . nuit": "O night." His memorial sonnet to Edgar Allan Poe not only announces in its first line that eternity will change Poe's mere self into what he was meant to be, but has for its first word "tel" and its last "futur." The Poe sonnet moreover is made of Poe-words, dark Gothicisms, sortilege and hydra and a black flood and a tomb and blasphemy; it does not fail to capitalize *Poète* in its second line to anticipate the *Poe* of its twelfth; it manages to resonate with basement metaphysics like *Eureka* itself; and amid its controlled semi-penetrabilities three isolated strong lines like bars of steel assert the aphoristic weight of the French Alexandrine. These may be the most important facts about the sonnet, and all of them except the presence of the three strong lines may be gathered by a scanning eye that does not actually *read* it. So far are we on the way toward *la poésie concrète*, and Mallarmé as we know from his last work was to carry that possibility still further, and dispose clusters of words in pure spatial contingency on a page otherwise white.

Such instances may help us describe Mallarmé's syntactic structures: they are ways, among other ways, of governing the exact relationship of the poem's elements, and all his ways, including his syntactic ones, have something of the geometer's economy about them. This is in part because the French language contains more syntactic orthodoxies than does the English. When the French writer does something so simple as place the adjective before the noun instead of after, he can anticipate a seismic dislocation in the sensibility of the French reader.

English usage being less rigid, the poet who attempts comparable effects in English must go to greater extremes. In 1896, after some years of hearing from Symons and others about what was going on in France, W. B. Yeats attempted some syntactic legerdemain of his own: a twenty-four-line poem that consists of one sentence, and like so many poems of Mallarmé's proceeds by systematic digression from its formal structure. Indeed the importance of the kernel sentence is vanishingly small. It is simply "I press my heart . . . and I hear. . . ." And so little are we likely to ask what it means, that we are even unlikely to notice it, amid Yeats's exploitation of the pliancy of English subordinate structures.

HE REMEMBERS FORGOTTEN BEAUTY

When my arms wrap you round I press
My heart upon the loveliness
That has long faded from the world;
The jewelled crowns that kings have hurled
In shadowy pools, when armies fled;
The love-tales wrought with silken thread
By dreaming ladies upon cloth
That has made fat the murderous moth;
The roses that of old time were
Woven by ladies in their hair,
The dew-cold lilies ladies bore
Through many a sacred corridor
Where such grey clouds of incense rose
That only God's eyes did not close:
For that pale breast and lingering hand
Come from a more dream-heavy land,
A more dream-heavy hour than this;
And when you sigh from kiss to kiss

> I hear white Beauty sighing, too,
> For hours when all must fade like dew,
> But flame on flame, and deep on deep,
> Throne over throne, where in half sleep,
> Their swords upon their iron knees,
> Brood her high lonely mysteries.

Are we prepared to say without hesitation where those flames come from, and those swords and those thrones? Their ring is Miltonic (pre-Raphaelite Miltonic), but we are far from Milton, whose effort in his long sentences is to keep clear whereabouts we are from moment to moment as the sentence works itself out. Yeats's effort is nearly the opposite, as we can tell from the way he revised this ending. The version he published in 1896 heard white Beauty sighing, too

> For hours when all must fade like dew
> Till there be naught but throne on throne
> Of seraphs, brooding each alone,
> A sword upon his iron knees,
> On her most lonely mysteries.

This is clear enough, at least in structure: Beauty sighs for those hours when everything will fade except the seraphs who brood on Beauty's mysteries. "Till there be naught but . . . ," runs the governing structure: we cannot mistake it. But he seems to have disliked a structure we could not mistake, and three years later the ending was revised to run as it now does in the definitive edition:

> I hear white Beauty sighing, too,
> For hours when all must fade like dew
> But flame on flame, and deep on deep,
> Throne over throne where in half sleep,
> Their swords upon their iron knees,
> Brood her high lonely mysteries.

This not only substitutes "high lonely mysteries" for "seraphs," it makes everything turn on an "all but" construction which we are almost certain not to notice. The phrase "when all must fade like dew" has such a ring of completeness that only by nearly scholastic effort, and with a printed text to pore over, can we force the "But" that opens the next line to give up its air of magisterial disjunction and link itself with "all."

Yeats is willing to dissolve one strong effect into another, leaving us with no clear idea how they are supposed to be related, though structural relations are specified in the text if we choose to undertake the work of recovering them. Thus we can determine that eleven successive lines develop from four nouns (*crowns, tales, roses, lilies*) that are all in apposition to the noun *loveliness*; that three lines about the pale breast and the lingering hand return us to a person we had quite forgotten, the *you* of the poem's opening; and that a new kernel sentence in parallel with the first one, *when you sigh I hear* . . . , paralleling *when my arms wrap you round I press* . . . , presides over the second lobe of the poem. Yet the way these kernel sentences preside is curiously oblique. Each serves to introduce an abstract noun, the first one *loveliness* and the second one *Beauty*, which nouns are the real seeds from which the enchanted thickets grow. And these nouns are not the objects of the main verbs in the kernel sentences, but abstractions produced within subordinate clauses which those verbs have produced. The effect is to move our attention as far as may be from the thrust of subject–verb–object. The structure is formal, elaborate, symmetrical, and syntactically faultless; and yet only by a very great effort of attention is the reader likely to discover what it is.

Tennyson's structures, which are equally unassertive, turn out when we disengage them to be informal, asymmetrical, and unimportant. They enable him, while he deploys his sumptuousness of diction, to fulfill the schoolmarm's requirement that the sentence shall parse, and they tend to comprise its least effectual words. The Yeatsian structure, though elaboration encumbers and conceals it, has been an object of the poet's careful attention, and though it may never chance to attract our notice its presence does matter, and not merely to the schoolmarm in us. Its presence underwrites the feel of ceremony and formality Yeats's poems of the 1890s characteristically yield. Those were the years when Yeats was being a Symbolist, meeting people familiar with what was going on in Paris, listening during the year he roomed with Symons while Symons talked out the still-unwritten *Symbolist Movement in Literature*, or expounded the translations he was then making, which Yeats called "the most accomplished metrical translations of our time," adding that the ones from Mallarmé "may have given elaborate form to my verses of those years, to the latter poems of *The Wind Among the Reeds*, to *The Shadowy Waters*." In 1937, looking again at Mallarmé in a translation, Roger Fry's this time, he called that way of working "the road I and others of my time went for certain furlongs. It is not the way I go now, but one of the legitimate roads."

Yeats did not abandon the intricate long sentence; each stanza of *Byzantium* is one sentence, each stanza of *Coole Park, 1929*, each stanza of *Ancestral Houses*, each but three of the twelve stanzas *In Memory of Major Robert Gregory*. What he abandoned was the Mallarméan way of proceeding by digressions from the sentence's main business. By transposing this particular method into English, and discovering its possibilities and limitations, he may have saved other poets time. Other poets, certainly, whose later work is quite unlike Yeats's later work because they did not adopt Yeats's final attitude to syntax, display in their early as well as their later work a debt to Symbolist syntax which is less than obvious if only because Yeats had already explored the obvious.

Thus instead of progress by digressions we encounter progress by ellipses. In Mallarmé's "Soupir," we may remember, Arthur Symons discovered a delicate emotion, a figure vaguely divined, a landscape magically evoked, three things that would seem not to be related but are blended into a single effect. The trick of the blending was to make the elements digress from a kernel sentence which holds them firmly in relation to one another and allows the reader's mind to overlay them. But if they can be held firmly by some other means, the kernel sentence may simply be omitted.

One way of holding them, giving each element in the poem its identity and still persuading the mind that they relate, is by metrical definition, as in Ezra Pound's 1912 poem "The Return," in which a strong metrical figure—

Góds ŏf thĕ wíngèd shóe!
With thĕm thĕ sílvĕr hóunds,
                    sníffĭng thĕ tráce ŏf aír

—dominates the part characterized by verbs in the past tense, enforc-
ing the contrast between the emphatic way the gods once *were*, and

                    the tentative
          Movements, and the slow feet,
          The trouble in the pace and the uncertain
          Wavering

that expresses their unstable way of returning *now*. The poem encom-
passes a long historical span, from Sappho's time, say, to H.D.'s, but
no kernel sentence makes a statement to that effect. The sentences of
which the poem is made are very simple: "See, they return"; "These
were the souls of blood"; while no syntax specifies the coherence of
the poem as a whole. We may feel that a statement of some length has
been made but that important syntactic members of this statement
have dropped out. And yet nothing has dropped out; we have,
thanks to the rhythmic definition, every necessary element, held in
place in the poem's continuum so exactly that alterations of tense will
specify everything.

Or we encounter progress by incantation, as in Eliot's "Marina."
Some parts of "Marina" can be treated as sentences and some parts
cannot; nor can "Marina" as a whole be treated as though it were a
long statement, even a statement of which parts are missing. Its or-
ganization is not syntactic at all. One probably wants to call it "musical," based on associations and recurrences, among them the Shakespearean associations aroused by the title. It is as far as Eliot ever went
in that particular direction, but the direction is implicit in most of his
work, and confirmed as well by work of Valéry's: the poem faced toward a domain of waking dream, so certain of its diction that we concede it a coherence it need not find means of specifying. It has no paraphrasable structure at all, and yet seems to affirm its elusive substance
as authoritatively as Mozart.

Eliot admired Tennyson when Tennyson was out of fashion, and now that Eliot too is out of fashion it is pertinent to recall his great indebtedness to Symons's *Symbolist Movement in Literature*. Everyone remembers how he discovered Laforgue in that book; we tend to forget how quickly he dropped Laforgue, and also tend not to notice how tenaciously he developed hints from Mallarmé, of whom he and Valéry are the principal heirs. I think Donald Davie has been alone in insisting that Eliot's sensibility is post-Symbolist. Yet surely he imitated the unseen eyebeam that falls in *Burnt Norton* on flowers that seem looked at, from "le regard diaphane" which in *Toast Funèbre* rests on unfading because verbal flowers; surely the intent insistence on a silence into which "words, after speech, reach" (for "that which is only living / Can only die") reflects Mallarmé's best-known preoccupation. *Burnt Norton*, by intention a counter-poem to *The Waste Land*, is also a sustained homage to Mallarmé, the austere codifier of its difficult art. The art is in touch with Tennyson's as well, and with Edward Lear's. The inventory of its structures remains to be made, so long, ironically, despite all Eliot's warnings, was criticism preoccupied with his "ideas." What Mallarmé wrote darkly of Poe, that the dipsomaniac who went by that name would be transformed by the operations of Eternity not into some myth but precisely into himself, we may see exemplified, more convincingly than in Poe's case, when Eliot is sufficiently forgotten to be rediscovered. His work may then seem a compendium of examples for such a survey of post-Symbolist structures as this paper has hinted at.

1972

Who Was Leslie Fiedler?

Who was Leslie A. Fiedler? Once upon a time, sighed the Mock Turtle to Alice, I was a real turtle; and once upon a time, says Leslie Fiedler (b. 1917; Ph.D., U. Wisc. 1941), I was a real professor, almost. But I never *quite* believed in it.

Ah, ah, those days, those days! In '41, straitjacketed in his new doctorate, the burly Fiedler was bundled by implacable Fate into the train that would haul him off kicking and fuming to the academic Gulag in Montana. Folklore has cherished and doubtless improved the scene at his departure: the sighs of commiseration on the platform, the indomitable leonine head at the coach window, its defiant shout through roars of escaping steam: "I'll publish my way out in five years!" (Tactical delinquencies stretched the years to twenty-three.)

What Fiedler was supposed to do in Montana was what any English Ph.D. is supposed to do anywhere: Uphold Standards. Since none of the students has ever heard of the standards, you have to lay them down before you can start to uphold them. The students don't come from homes where Shakespeare and Dickens and Mark Twain are read, since by Fiedler's reckoning there are no such homes. These authors, long ago mass entertainers, are now read only in classrooms, where they are part of High, i.e., compulsory, Literature.

What is read in the absence of compulsion is (make your own list).

We learn in *What Was Literature?* (Simon & Schuster, 1982) what the list was for Fiedler's generation: "Zane Grey, Edgar Rice Burroughs or Margaret Mitchell." By classroom norms, to take pleasure in such is "shameful or regressive." One is *required* to take pleasure in Shakespeare et al., and kids soon learn to fake it. Thus are Standards transmitted, with the distinction they imply between high literature and low.

The academic's other obligation is to publish his way out of wherever he commenced by getting stuck, until he arrives at a desirable place. There he publishes his way *up*, or else takes the golden years easy by swearing off ink altogether. Publishing means assembling leaden sentences under titles like "Archetype and Signature" or "In the Beginning Was the Word: *Logos* or *Mythos*" (actual Fiedler titles) for journals unread save by promotion committees (affinity for the wrong journals was one thing that slowed Fiedler).

The time he is not spending in this joyless pursuit he is supposed to spend exhorting captive classes to take joy in *Silas Marner*. Does he go to the movies? Watch sitcoms? Late at night, does he reach for a handful of easy joy like *Cujo*? If he does, he lets no one hear of it. A preacher's wife's recreations in Sodden, Tennessee, are not more circumscribed.

His abnegation has negligible effect on the taste of the public, which goes on preferring pictures to words and vulgar words to subtle. Yet he and his colleagues are financed by that same public: "by a society which considers them part of the 'professional' cadre that turns raw English majors into the next generation of fully-credentialed critic-pedagogues, capable of training a third generation, etc., etc."

This picture, though, is already a little old-fashioned; in particular, it omits the salient development of the Forties and Fifties, the "broadening" of the curriculum. "Formerly despised modernists" were let in, "along with certain American writers hitherto neglected in the academy." The sole result, says Fiedler, was to turn these writers, too, into difficult and uplifting classics, "like the *Aeneid*," and "once started, the process never stops. What we have done for the novels of the nineteenth century we can do for those of the twentieth, whether

Herzog, V., The End of the Road, Portnoy's Complaint or *Slaughterhouse-Five.*

"Finally (*mea culpa!*) such books come to seem as hermetic, esoteric and inert as *The Faerie Queene* itself. . . ." "In the end, the institutionalized taste of the late twentieth century regards as substandard almost everything which naïve and uninstructed readers are likely to recognize as a 'story' or a 'poem.' But this means in effect the exclusion of anything which the children of such readers can comprehend, even after they have entered college, without the aid of a qualified teacher."

This account makes hilarious reading, much as does the fourth book of *Gulliver's Travels*, from which Fiedler has learned some things about the persuasiveness of zestful narrative. With his account of what professors really do, compare Gulliver on lawyers:

> For example. If my neighbour hath a mind to my cow, he hires a lawyer to prove that he ought to have my cow from me. I must then hire another to defend my right, [and] . . . my lawyer, being practiced almost from his cradle in defending falsehood; is quite out of his element when he would be an advocate for justice, which as an office unnatural he always attempts with great awkwardness, if not with ill will. . . . And therefore I have but two methods to preserve my cow. The first is, to gain over my adversary's lawyer with a double fee; who will then betray his client, by insinuating that he hath justice on his side. The second way is for my lawyer to make my cause appear as unjust as he can; by allowing the cow to belong to my adversary; and this if it be skilfully done, will certainly bespeak the favour of the bench.

All this is being explained to a highly intelligent horse, whose qualifications for doubting it are nil. Swift's reader is apt to be disoriented because he forgets how much he knows that the horse does not, notably the long history of Western jurisprudence, with the aid of which we can justify its institutions against an adducer of particular abuses.

Swift's trick is not to let you think of history. Where Fiedler goes him one better is in preempting the historical account as well. No sooner has he uncurtained a new tableau in his chamber of horrors than he is launched on a brisk account of how its protagonists came to be frozen in those particular positions.

Early in this process he slips past us an article of faith, that "the culture of the United States [was] from the beginning 'popular' beneath a thin overlay of imported European elitism."

He goes on: "Our national *mythos* is a pop myth and our Revolution consequently a pop revolution." It was "cued by a boy's dream"— "grown men dressing up as Indians and dumping into Boston Harbor that supreme symbol of effete European civilization, British tea"— and the boy's dream had to be subsequently equipped with philosophical apologies and "the high-falutin phrases of the Declaration of Independence."

This sounds very like his account of how *Slaughterhouse-Five* has fared in the classroom: a boy's dream onto which professors glue chic semiotic jargon. In either case it is in the dream that he locates authenticity. If only our mentors would linger amid such dreams! Pausing to register for future use the query whether by Fiedler's own showing the impulse to abstract from the dream isn't an equally authentic American custom, we come to his statement of what is centrally American: "a 'revolutionary' model of politics and culture, challenging to all civilizations with graveyards or museums to defend—to whom, therefore, the past is reassuring and the future a threat."

That puts in lively words a familiar whim: that Americans are uniquely disencumbered of the past, the better to welcome nobody knows what. Such people exist, to be sure; I have even met them in disciplined, history-crazed Germany. But no *society* of such people, it is safe to say, exists or has ever existed: least of all in America, where traditions of protest against alteration—*any* alteration—run from *Walden* clear to *The New Yorker*, where rural Southerners and New Englanders live in social architectural museums, and where an autochthonous art form, the western, celebrates in clear-lighted timelessness the rituals of a mythical but optically documented Past.

Let's call on a new witness, Robert Nisbet, who writes in *Prejudices**:

"Man is a time-binding creature. Living with the past is vital to individual and society alike." Lest we dismiss him as a sentimentalist, Nisbet is quick to reprove *nostalgia*, "at best a rust of memory, often a

* Harvard University Press, 1982.

disease," which "makes of the past a cornucopia of anodynes and fancies" and betrays itself by isolating a particular slice of the past where all its golden oldies congregate: the 1890s perhaps, the 1920s.

Confined to the same room under Queensberry rules, Robert Nisbet and Leslie Fiedler would talk past each other for hours. Nisbet believes in the authority of the past: in tradition. He does not attribute to genius any wish to break with the past; rather, to rediscover "the spirit of the best of the past despite efforts of the establishment . . . merely to freeze or ritualize the past." The enthusiasms on which he casts his skeptical eye are generally crystallized into *ideas*, with names like Alienation, Technology, Originality. His *Prejudices* gives a few pages each to seventy such topics, arranged in alphabetical order because any order will do.

Fiedler's interest in ideas is comparatively slight (in his youth, he tells us, he entertained some radical ones but got tired of them). Myth and dream, the surging of archetypes in the semiconscious: such forces of fantasy and folklore preoccupy him (and are never mentioned by Nisbet). And where Nisbet likes being tethered to a topic round which he can ruminate all the golden afternoon, periodically dropping an aphorism ("Woe to the misguided who set out to be original, for verily they will produce a two-headed calf"), Fiedler prefers the bull elephant's headlong progress, slam-bang through straw villages and their shrieking natives toward that ultimate waterhole in the sky, a place whose deeps give back the lurid reflections he calls America's Inadvertent Epic, and of which the second half of his book presents, if not a deep drink, a plausible mirage.

Having complementary limitations, these are good men to read in conjunction. Against Fiedler's epiphany of the Boston Tea Party, grown men in Indian costumes, "a boy's dream" ideologized later, we can weigh Nisbet's belief that all revolutions are *incited* by ideologues, roused to frenzy by the sight of a government grown weak.

The granting of "reforms" is one mark of a weak government. "The position of the American colonists of all classes was much better in 1770 than it had been several decades earlier," Nisbet says. "But such improvement only quickened the desires of the pamphleteers which for a combination of religious and secular reasons had reached apocalyptic intensity by the 1760s, with millennium-by-revolution [their] increasingly ecstatic dream . . ."

Long afterward, one of the ideologues, John Adams, wrote that the revolution "was in the hearts and minds of the people," and "substantially effected before hostilities commenced." That's closer to Fiedler's view of it, though not close enough, since no more than Nisbet does Adams allude to the bizarre detail Fiedler seizes on, the Indian costumes in Boston harbor. Though Fiedler doesn't *dwell* on that detail, it's a clue to his phantasmagoria.

How to read the Revolution is crucial to his sense of American academe's plight and what's to be done about it. To demonstrate the irrelevance of imported and aristocratic "standards," he needs a pop America, different in essence from any other society. Nisbet demurs. All revolutions, he thinks, are alike, and at bottom unnecessary (he's persuasively sharp about the idea that "history" ever renders anything necessary). Ours, we gather, is a society like other societies, disintegrating as others have disintegrated, from confusion, from inflation, from loss of nerve. But No!, cries Fiedler in thunder, it's been a fructive and *necessary* disintegration. What's been disintegrating is an irrelevance, an imposed crust, represented in college curricula by what elderly professors call "English as we have known it."

That, he exults, is dead. "It began dying at the moment that people like me were permitted to join the profession. I am not proposing, as some have charged, to 'open the gates to the barbarians,' since I *am* a barbarian, already within the gates. It becomes me therefore to urge that, having nothing to lose, we venture to find out what might be gained by abandoning our last and dearest snobbism, the conviction that print is inherently superior to movies and TV, even though everyone must presumably be taught (by *us*) to read words on a page, whereas no one has to be instructed in reading images on the screen."

This does not mean courses in "cinema," with their "jargonizing about 'montage' and 'tracking shots.'" Such courses, like analogous literary courses, simply daze students' perception of whatever drew them to movies in the first place. Moving "from ethics and aesthetics into ecstatics," the teacher needs to avoid "even the semblance of celebrating already established works at the expense of those still despised, much less those preferred by an elite at the expense of those loved by the great majority. Only in this way will he be able to make clear the continuity of all song and story, pre-print, print and post-print, high, medium and low."

Even if Nisbet ever raised his voice (which he doesn't), Fiedler would be by this time far out of his shouting range, charging through a mythic jungle still scarcely mapped. This entangling dream place has at least two chief domains, on one of which he reported in his famous 1948 essay, "Come Back to the Raft Ag'in, Huck Honey." That was the myth of Huck and Jim, Ishmael and Queequeg, Natty Bumppo and Chingachgook, in which "the new Adam lives in innocent anti-marriage" with a noble savage of another color. The new Adam in this myth is "an anti-Odysseus, who finds his identity *by running away from home.*" It is the Home-as-Hell myth, and a certain sexual innocence is secured when Twain turns the new Adam into Huck Finn, a boy who won't ever grow up. (Imagine an adult Huck! Twain couldn't. It's easy to imagine an adult Tom Sawyer. His name is Babbitt.)

The other American myth is called Home-as-Heaven, and the interplay of the two of them can be "read as a single work, composed over more than a century, in many media and by many hands." This is America's Inadvertent Epic, "unequaled in scope and resonance by any work of High Art." (Don't buy *that*; but read on.) The best sellers that compose it "have been loved by the majority audience, which considers them not epical at all (the very word turns them off) but 'good reads.'"

Such myths don't create ideas; like dreams, they release feelings, which the waking life may ideologize. Thus if, thanks to the myth of Home-as-Hell, "All Americans . . . including girls and women . . . at levels deeper than ideology perceive white women as the enemy"— Huck's Aunt Sally, she who must be escaped from because she'll "civilize" us—that not only explains why "even the most enlightened of us, male and female alike, end up cheering McMurphy's attempted rape of Big Nurse" in the movie version of *One Flew Over the Cuckoo's Nest*, it can also explain "why, after all, ERA may never become part of the Constitution." ERA ideologized women as the Oppressed; but between waking and sleeping we question that categorization; is it not they who are the mythical oppressors?

But that myth is a detail in this book, which spends its time on the myth of Home-as-Heaven. This myth, unlike the other, has been the province chiefly of women authors, extending from Louisa May Alcott and Harriet Beecher Stowe all the way to the scripters of the soaps (where, if no marriage lasts long, that is not because marriage is precarious but because it is "the sole conceivable Happy Ending, and the soap opera can never end").

TV has its Home-as-Hell plots too, the "men's" shows: the westerns, the cop shows, the sci-fi spectaculars, in which "we head out for the Territory once more" and Jew Starsky is paired with Gentile Hutch, black Tenspeed with white Brownshoe.

And so much do the two myths differ as day and night that daytime is TV's soaptime, nighttime, coptime. Let no commonsense bore protest that programs are shown when their intended viewers are most likely to be near the screen; no more than the mass dreams themselves is their analyst bound to take cognizance of trivial fact.

The "feminine pop tradition" begins with *Uncle Tom's Cabin, or Life Among the Lowly*, a book that puts on display "the most compendious gallery of homes in American literature": the Cabin itself, the St. Clares' villa, Miss Ophelia's New England farmhouse, Legree's decayed mansion, more, more. Mrs. Stowe, who had published "a kind of domestic guidebook called *House and Home Papers*," in effect sketched for her successors "the myth of the Utopian Household."

Reading her mythically is justified by the way she wrote mythically; her characters, Uncle Tom, Eliza, Topsy (who, as everybody knows, just "growed"), Little Eva, Simon Legree, "emerge mysteriously from the collective unconscious and pass, scarcely mediated by her almost transparent text, into the public domain, to which, like all authentic popular literature, they properly belong." That's a way of stating the fact that most of the people who can name them have never read the novel.

What continually interests Fiedler is this strange capacity of certain literary constructs to slip past the confines of the text, a thing the apostles of pure Text who are currently pipelined into every academy give no heed to at all.

If the word "myth" puts you off, as it generally does me, then give your attention to that strange phenomenon: the way, for instance, Sherlock Holmes is known to millions who've neither read a page of Conan Doyle nor even seen one of the perfunctory Holmes movies.

Mrs. Stowe never got closer to the real South than Kentucky, and it was in Brunswick, Maine, seated at a communion service in February 1851, that she was visited by the hallucination from which *Uncle Tom's Cabin* started: the vision of a white man beating an old black man to death. The book commenced serial publication before she was well launched writing it, "sustained, it would appear, by other hallucinations as vivid as the first." Where they came from, why they've proved so contagious, we needn't venture to say. Their source, at any rate, was not the nightmare of slavery. That was only her vehicle for a deeper nightmare: the nightmare of Home cosmically violated: Uncle Tom's home, all homes.

It was because the central myth did not pertain to slavery that its voltage could survive a transposition of Mrs. Stowe's story into anti-Negro forms. This was effected in *The Clansman* of Thomas Dixon, who survived until 1946, though his novel had been totally forgotten except in D. W. Griffith's film version, *The Birth of a Nation*. Dixon was faithful to one theme of Stowe's, the centrality of the Home. Rape epitomizes the ultimate threat to this, so when Dixon turned Reconstruction Negroes into rapists, in total reversal of Mrs. Stowe's benign darkies, the continuity of America's Inadvertent Epic was not breached at all. In *The Birth of a Nation* Klansmen ride to head off rape while audiences cheer.

"I myself once saw" (Fiedler writes) "the members of a left-wing ciné club in Athens, believers all in the equality of the races and the unmitigated evil of the Klan, rise to their feet at ten o'clock in the morning . . . to scream with blood lust and approval equal to that of the racist first-nighters of 1915 as white womanhood was once more delivered from the threat of black rape." God knows, he adds, in the nightmare they plunged into open-eyed, "what ultimate enemies of their own were threatening what prized and virginal darlings."

And Dixon recognized Margaret Mitchell as his literary heir. In *Gone With the Wind* (1936), where the threatened home is Tara, we encounter once more the supreme indifference of myth to medium. For the blockbuster movie, with two directors and eleven or twelve script-writers, "proved to be as aesthetically undistinguished as her prose," and yet became the most popular spectacle of the age. Rape and vengeance is the formula still, and the continuity with *Uncle Tom's Cabin* still perceptible. (The rape in *Uncle Tom* was flagellation, and the vengeance that of God working on an evildoer's conscience.)

And on, into *Roots*; but rather than try to show how that fits in (a task that gives even Fiedler trouble), I'll ask again his own question: what was Literature?

It was, he would have us think, popular entertainment, subsequently transformed by the academy into an elitist bore. By attending to myth, he says, he is showing the academy how to get the excitement back: a *popular* excitement. But at what cost!—jettisoning what from age to age has always been preserved by a minority, some exact perception of the satisfactions of art.

Shakespeare, yes, was one popular playwright among many others. But his plays rise above theirs, such of theirs as have chanced to survive, by the local quality of his writing: the vigor of the page, the felt jostle of word against word, the absoluteness of phrasing ("a mole cinque-spotted"; "the beggar's nurse, and Caesar's"). True, Mrs. Stowe's "most mythically resonant tableaus are . . . usually the 'worst' written," shrill and sickly sweet; but from the fact that "the words she finds or does not find simply do not matter," it does not follow at all that words don't matter.

To perceive words, to sense rhythms, to distinguish phrase from phrase, these are aspects of a rare skill, of which it is no use pretending all students are capable. The greatest literary works—the *Iliad*, *Hamlet*—owe their distinction to what only that order of perception can discern: the union of a powerful myth with expression just as powerfully adequate. Such perception needs defending against the pedantries Leslie Fiedler rightly lambasts. It needs defending, too, against his pretense of having discovered "the continuity of all song and story," accessible in its most widely circulated avatars.

Why Shakespeare's admirers (and no other hack dramatist's) thought his plays worth collecting for publication in an expensive folio within seven years of his death is a question worth pondering. Messrs. Heming and Condell were prompted by a rare order of detailed perception that deserves our gratitude: a perception of how one way of saying differs from another, a kind of perception that lapses for Leslie Fiedler when he offers "The boy stood on the burning deck . . ." as denoting Longfellow's "Wreck of the Hesperus."

That line, of which he quotes a parody to show the persistence of Longfellow among kids, is not by Longfellow or by any American but by Mrs. Felicia Dorothea Hemans (1793–1835), also known (to elitists) as the author of "The stately homes of England/How beautiful they stand!"

No American boy stayed to the death on a burning deck. The myth is all wrong, and a myth critic should have known better. From Poe through Melville to *Catch-22*, the myth for Americans is self-preservation. Fidelity to the death is an *English* myth, in America attributed only to dogs named Fido. Robert Nisbet would be the man to write a meditation on that.

1982

The Invention
of the "Other"

T. S. Eliot said of Ezra Pound's *Cathay* that Pound in that little book was the inventor of Chinese poetry for our time: in short, had persuaded his readers that in opening *Cathay* they visited an authentic China of the mind. After 69 years the accomplishment is undiminished. By now, though, it's permissible to scrutinize the credentials of English free verse and wavering elegiac rhythms when, as in *Cathay*, they offer to deputize for strict rhymed forms and percussive patterns of recurrence. And what about that Tennysonian title, *Cathay*? "Better sixty years of Europe than a cycle of Cathay"; when Victoria's Laureate wrote that, he stated an utter disjunction between Europe, aspin down ringing grooves of change, and a far-off no-place where nothing at all spins: nothing new seems to happen at all.

The modernist enterprise has repeated and repeated such acts of invention. Eliot himself invented an English Laforgue; Joyce invented a very odd kind of Homer, master of every expressive wile; Leishman and Spender re-invented Rilke; Kenneth Rexroth and Gary Snyder have synthesized alternate Japans (and take your pick); lately, Ethnopoetics has invented American Indian rituals which Walt Whitman would have thought were barbaric yawps. William Carlos Williams, aloof from such exotica, derived idioms, he said, from "the speech of Polish mothers": not Warsaw or Lubin Poles, but American Poles whose babies he'd delivered. After fifty years it gets easier to see Williams inventing too: a highly formalized American informality, as much a contrivance as Wordsworth's "real language of men."

Every time someone looks for a way to be newly authentic, what ensues, apparently, is not "the natural" but an invention. This is next equipped with credentials which include "being natural": returning poetry to the way people really behave when they open their mouths. Poetry, if we are to believe the poets, keeps straying into artifice and needing recall to the natural: which, a generation later, is disclosed as yet one more artifice.

My education in these matters took a quantum leap some 15 years ago, when an accident of scheduling stranded me at the Newark, N.J. airport in the company of the director of the Fogg Museum at Harvard. The papers were full of the latest museum scandal: an Etruscan horse which had just proved to be a 19th century forgery. Chemical tests of the bronze had been decisive. And it occurred to me to ask my captive museum director how it was that someone had thought to send the piece to the lab. What had aroused suspicion?

Her answer was simple and profound, and amounted to this: *the style of your own period is always invisible.* Into that horse, she explained, the sculptor had incorporated every Etruscan mannerism he knew about, and every 19th century mannerism he didn't know about. The result, in its time, was most satisfyingly Etruscan. But its time did not last; no time lasts. The horse occupied its case in the Metropolitan, and the decades slipped past, and styles imperceptibly altered. This continued at a glacial rate, until one fine morning someone said, "That horse looks 19th century." When someone else agreed the piece was rushed off to the lab. It was not the horse that had changed, but the modalities subject to which it was possible to view the horse.

This, I was given to understand, is perfectly general, perfectly reliable. No fabrication will deceive for more than a couple of generations. One has only to wait: the invisible style of the time will rise inexorably to visibility. It follows that whatever we are doing today, in our own time, that characterizes us as denizens of the 1980's, is something we literally cannot know. We mistake it for being natural. It is our successors who will know it as artifice.

We are now in a position to say some sensible things about the initial plausibility of the artifice. To exemplify that I'll return to Pound's *Cathay*, nearly 70 years old and by now demonstrably of its time, which was 1914–15.

The first thing to ponder is that "free verse" seemed plausible, though the Chinese poems are not "free" at all but rhymed and counted according to strict conventions. One's first thought may be that Pound got by with free verse because neither he nor his readers knew any better. But Pound did know better, since the Fenollosa notes are quite explicit about the Chinese formalities. And at least one of his readers, Arthur Waley, knew better, being a sinologue of certified accomplishment; and we should note that when Waley published his own versions from the Chinese, he sometimes followed Pound and employed free verse, though he didn't understand its principles at all well and wrote it as though he thought it a kind of prose you set down until you felt like ending the line. "Free verse" was exotic stuff for the likes of Waley; an incomprehensible thing they did in Paris.

And here, I think, we are close to a simple answer: "free verse" in those days was an exotic form, even called *vers libre*. Chinese poetry, that was exotic, too. And how better represent one exoticism than through another? This general principle is a subset of one still more general, Saussure's claim that communicative systems are systems of differences. To map an extreme difference, use another extreme difference. Thus something as remote as Cathay in time and space seemed adequately impersonated by something as remote from English practice as imitation French *vers libre*. ("Cathay," by the way, is not even on the map, where you find only "China." In a time of institutionalized cartography—the British Admiralty, the National Geographic Society—you can't get more geographically remote than to be off maps altogether.)

What other marks of China needed preserving, to render an invented China plausible? Many of them came to Anglo-American sensibilities in those days via blue china, the designs on plates made in

England, where blue bridges crossed blue rivers beneath blue wil-
lows, and on them sat blue fishermen, patient, patient. As a child in
Canada I took my breakfast toast off a plate like that. It lent access to a
time-warp, connecting my 1920's to 1914 of the Pound Era. "Blue,
blue," the second poem of *Cathay* begins:

> Blue, blue, is the grass about the river
> And the willows have overfilled the close garden . . .

When I first met that I understood it at once.

   I've since had students who wondered about grass being blue.
Rather than recall a Canadian breakfast, I can offer them learned
words. When the Chinese poem was written, about 140 B.C., the language had not yet distinguished blue from green; it is perfectly philological to write, as H. A. Giles did in a version Pound knew,

> Green grows the grass upon the bank,
> The willow-shoots are long and lank . . .

or, as Waley wrote in implied correction of Pound,

> Green, green,
> The grass by the river-bank,
> Thick, thick,
> The willow trees in the garden . . .

. . . philological, but not plausible. China, they knew in 1915, was
blue.

   China was also a place for simple permanent happenings: separa-
tions, lonelinesses, yearnings. Such things happen too in Montana,
but in Montana they are also filling out the same Internal Revenue
forms confronted by Angelenos, a consideration that somehow trivi-
alizes Montana's hold on the great permanent griefs. It is Cathay's absolute otherness, like the moon's, that guards and circumscribes
poems of parting, and prevents anyone's objecting to so restrained a
detail as

> Our horses neigh to each other
> As we are departing . . . ,

on the ground that much is being made of mighty little.

There is no denying that invention builds with cliche, with the regnant cliches of its own time. For it is always cliche that looks natural, and to look natural, we were saying, is what this order of invention aims at. A cliche is something later deemed uninteresting because overfamiliar; cliches mark the style of a period after the period has passed. But in our own time we cannot identify what will someday seem to be our time's cliches: to us, now, they are vital elements of our active awareness.

A final observation: to the inventor—for instance, to Ezra Pound in 1914—these cliches look fresh. We've been saying that two generations later they look routine. (Not *Cathay* itself: his technical intentness, syllable by syllable, keeps it wholly alive.) We should add that in their own time, to anyone but an inventor, the cliches are apt to look barbarous. Saussure's system of differences may prompt us to see how in being useful to an inventor of something alien they are, by definition, elements other than routine. Stravinski made savage noises in 1912 out of combinations of tones that shock no one in 1983 but could once provoke actual riots. What provoked the riots was their difference from the combinations allowed by the practice of Mozart, Beethoven, Berlioz, even Wagner. That is a difference we can still perceive. To hear *The Rites of Spring* after the Jupiter Symphony is like moving from Williamsburg, Va., to ruddy arid Mars.

Stravinski having made that point, Prokofieff next managed a further novelty by recreating a synthetic Williamsburg, called *Classical Symphony*. Mozart would not have recognized it as "classical," i.e. Mozartian. It is we who recognize it as pseudo-Mozart, synthesized in the lifetime of Stravinski. In short, once Stravinski had invented savagery, to be identified with the future, it was possible for Prokofieff to invent Mozart, and identify pseudo-Mozart with the future too.

In summary: (1) you cannot expect the natural, only the invented; (2) the elements of the invented are the cliches of the living; (3) we invent pasts as well as presents and futures.

The only failure, in these domains, is a failure to invent: a willingness to assume that what looked natural to some other people in some other place or time can be natural to us. But no: there was nothing less natural to the French of the 1880's than *Symbolisme*; nothing less natural to Renaissance men than the Renaissance; nothing less natural to American Indians than their chants. These, it seems feasible to suggest, have all been innovations, inventions: defiances of the obvious, which is to do nothing, or to do mindlessly what was done yesterday. The mindless perishes.

A perpetually renewed decision to cooperate with the earth spirits and the corn spirits lies at the heart of a culture dedicated to earth and corn. Decisions are actions; decisions to repeat are decisions to act. "Do it again" can be a formula for an avant-garde. "Let us go then, you and I" is the opening formula of a cliche, the best-known poem, among freshmen, since the Rubaiyat. It was also, in its time, a daring way to get a poem started. It is still the generative formula of all ritual and all reading, since reading is enacted ritual: "you and I." I write, you read; you write, I read; someone has written, we read together. And the present, when there is one, gets reinvented, perpetually.

1984

Breaking the Line

By the best count available, that of the 1980–81 *Directory of American Poets and Fiction Writers* (published by Poets & Writers, Inc.), 3,536 poets are more or less at large on this continent; the alphabetical sorting runs from Aal, Katharyn Machan to Zweig, Paul, not omitting David UU of Kingston, Ont., and Verandah Porche of Brattleboro, Vt. You qualify as a poet if you have published ten or more poems in three or more different U.S. literary magazines, at least one of them since 1960; and "Books do not substitute for the magazine publication requirement." Only half that many fiction writers could be turned up; writing prose tires the hand.

In the days before computerizable criteria, it was only intermittently a matter of public record that William Carlos Williams was a poet at all. It pleased him pathetically that he had been asked to read poems, amid the Christmas rush, in, as I remember, a Newark department store. Next to the escalators it would have been, with the Santa-bells jangling and the numbed throng ascending toward lawn-jeray and p'fume. One time an American crowd had been an element in which his mind flashed, dolphinlike:

> . . . It is summer, it is the solstice
> the crowd is

        cheering, the crowd is laughing
        in detail

        permanently, seriously
        without thought

Did he read "At the Ball Game" to the December crowd? It was four
decades since he'd written it. You envied his stamina. A heart attack
and his first two strokes had still not killed him.

And his voice could carry. Up from the cellar one evening came a
brandy he'd been paid for delivering a baby and not uncorked all
those decades. His right arm was near-paralyzed and it would be up
to me to measure out amber drops older than I was. I bent my wrist,
a-quiver in the web of his injunctions: "Careful, careful." The stuff
was precious: I was careful, careful. But then eyeing the stinted portion, "More! More!" A sharp rising inflection, the kind that brings
charge nurses scurrying. Folks must have heard that second "More!"
down the street.

The urgencies of his own crisp, propulsive voice were what rang in
his head as he worked, ejaculating the phrases, shaping the measure.
Was it 6 A.M., or was it 5, that the typewriter woke me? Not clickety-
clickety, but a dogged clack . . . clack . . . clack. He grasped the wrist
of his right hand with his left, steered the forefinger over a key, and let
it drop.

He was seated at a wonder of the 1950's, an electric typewriter, presented by the hospital staff when he retired. Now that slapping a car-
riage rightward the old way had gotten awkward, there was virtue in
the automated return. He had only to aim and drop the heavy finger,
and lo, a new line. No poet started new lines as deliberately as Williams, or on as elusive a principle. Through his head ran another
rhythm than the clack . . . clack . . .

        The measure intervenes,
            to measure is all we know,
        a choice among the
            measure . . .
                the measured dance
        "unless the scent of a rose
            startle us anew" . . .

—letter by letter, too intent to notice his sleepy spectator.

Nine Ridge Road, Rutherford, N.J., was a big wooden exercise in the Victorian idiom; what you'd expect of a small-town doctor's house except that walls were hung and attic trunks filled with mementoes of American Modernism. What sort of life had been able to manage that combination?

The *Autobiography* Williams dashed off in three months of 1951 weaves its underplayed vignettes out of details as often as not misremembered. The first stroke terminated his ability to revise it. The Reed Whittemore biography of 1975 conveys, through its arch readability, a Connecticut ironist's reluctance to quite believe in any "Poet from Jersey." Joyce Kilmer, it reminds us, was also from Jersey, and it's he, not Williams, whom they honored in naming a rest stop on the Jersey Turnpike.

> (I think that I shall never see
> A W. C. W. WC.)

And now Paul Mariani's *William Carlos Williams: A New World Naked* pours out more information than we'd dreamed of, in a rush that seems to have overwhelmed copy editing (McGraw-Hill, 1982). (Pound's Confucian *Unwobbling Pivot* even gets cited as "Wobbling.") It's a shaggy, prolonged bear-hug of a book; hardly a sentence couldn't be quickened by excisions. "At home there were the usual domestic satisfactions and difficulties of any young married couple." (Delete either "at home" or "domestic," either "usual" or "any.") "Next day—Saturday—Williams had a chance to hear George Antheil play his own modern atonal music. It was, he thought, startling but quite good in its own way." ("Modern" is redundant with "atonal"; also strike "own"; and is the last phrase an indirect quote—Williams at his slackest—or a paraphrase—Mariani at his usual?)

"His was a life devoid of the dramatic tragedy or intense pathos of some other poets. . . ." More adjectival saturation bombing—"dramatic," "intense"—no, the point is not that Strunk & White weren't digested, the point is that one's mind tires in discarding such words throughout a long book that seems twice as long as it is, and hence half as faithful to its subject's celerity as the imitative form it aspires to would require.

Imparting speed to his idiom was the poet's lifelong concern: not Hemingway laconism, which is a role, but energy like an inside pitch, to whip round the endings of those impossibly short lines: an energy that seems to inhere not in the speaker but in the language, and can quicken any banality. What it seems to handle, its red wheelbarrow, its leafless vines, its cod's head, is but necessary pretext. A Williams poem is no more "about" anything it names than a game of baseball is about a ball. But no ball, no game; and no wheelbarrow, no poem.

"No day has passed since 1970 that I have not thought about Williams," writes Mariani in a sentence to be believed, which also tells us that he can somehow write as he does with models like

> The pure products of America
> go crazy—

ringing in his ears.

Yet his sheer devotion has engendered a book that helps: the generous Williams-eye view of the life of Williams that (in contradistinction to Reed Whittemore's amused distance) preserves *no* distance, conveying the daily urgency of the house calls and letters and talk and anguish and elation and bedroom escapades and sea voyages and writing and frenzied rewriting through which Williams achieved what he triumphantly did: the definition of an American poetic idiom.

"Williams enters me but I cannot enter him," Robert Lowell wrote in 1961. "He sees and hears what we all see and hear and what is most obvious, but no one else has found this a help or an inspiration. . . . When I say that I cannot enter him, I am almost saying that I cannot enter America." Yes.

"No one else has found this a help or an inspiration," but Williams did, with his inarticulate persistence that could never quite formulate what needed doing yet could find the way to do it: at what cost! Thousands of hours of frantic naïve work, hundreds of thousands of crumpled sheets of paper, no one knows how many junked typewriters, ruptured friendships, immense drafts on his wife's patience . . .

His wife. Her name was Florence (Floss); she had been his second choice after her glamorous sister Charlotte got betrothed to his brother Ed, whom she later didn't marry (and that betrothal estranged Bill for good from Ed). "Hard and useful as the handle of a spade," Floss sustained every disorder, stemmed every crisis. After his eyes couldn't find the beginning of the next line it was she who read to him. Chapman's *Homer* I can testify to: the two of them on the sofa, Bill's hands clasped between his knees, his head inclined to catch through Flossie's low, loved monotone the cadence in which John Keats had caught "deep-brow'd Homer."

It was Floss who placed the phone call to Verner Clapp, of the Dogpatch name, to find out what he'd meant by his 1952 letter about a "full investigation" before Bill could take up the Library of Congress poetry consultantship they'd offered not once but twice. Well, answered Clapp of the Library's Loyalty Board, Dr. Williams had sure gotten around a lot. What did that mean? Well, hadn't her husband been in Germany and Austria? Yes, back in 1910 and 1924 (she might have added, to study pediatrics). Well, resumed Clapp, he sure had gotten around.

Whatever he was charged with—the indictment seems to have included publishing in *Partisan Review*—he was never cleared, never not cleared, and never served. The ordeal sent him for eight weeks into a madhouse.

Biographers are at the mercy of their material. The Clapp episode is reconstructed in detail from the letters by which Floss kept various friends posted. Something we'd much rather hear about, Bill Williams's earliest encounters with Wallace Stevens, is wholly absent from the narrative; on page 125 Stevens is suddenly "his plump, groomed, fastidious friend." How did that come about? Presumably in 1915, when contributors to Alfred Kreymborg's *Others* used to meet in some unheated shack on the lower Palisades to hear one another read. But no record survives.

By page 473 (it is now 1942) Stevens is "one of the few poets he deeply admired," though the Stevens *Letters* disclose a cooler view of Williams, whom he'd admonished to "settle on 'a single manner or mood' and let that position become 'thoroughly matured and exploited,' rather than keep going after his incessant new beginnings." They were antipodal. Stevens's was a mandarin poetic, metered speech keeping its distance from the vulgate, deriving its periphrases and its dislocations of sense from fin-de-siècle mannerisms he'd imitated in his 'prentice days. Yet the two kept in often-guarded touch; it's a pity to have so sketchy a reconstruction of the tensions.

It was Stevens who, in introducing the Williams *Collected Poems* of 1934, gave a generation of commentators their catchword, "anti-poetic," a term that missed the eager impartiality with which a Williams poem can traverse its materials. A thorough romantic he supposed Bill was, cherishing from his tower (tower!) his "exceptional view of the public dump and the advertising signs of Snider's Catsup, Ivory Soap and Chevrolet Cars": items with no tickets of admission to a Stevens poem, save (obliquely) "Man on the Dump," which we can even read as an effort to imagine being Williams.

> Is it peace,
> Is it a philosopher's honeymoon, one finds
> On the dump? Is it to sit among the mattresses of the dead,
> Bottles, pots, shoes and grass and murmur *aptest eve* . . . ?

No, that was not how it was, not a murmured yearning. We have still no terminology for his innovation, radical as the discovery of the transistor, which was to find the way of making into part of a poem such an arrangement as this:

> (To make the language
> record it, facet to facet
> not bored out—
>   with an augur.
> —to give also the unshaven,
>   the rumblings of a
> catastrophic past, a delicate
> defeat—vivid simulations of
> the mystery .)

Try it this way: most "free verse" implies regular verse. Behind it, as Eliot wrote sixty-four years ago, lurks the ghost of some regular metric. That ghost says, "I am in my singing robes. I am not disregarding norms, I am raising their ritual to a ritual still more arcane. If I use the twelve-tone row I remember Mozart. Hear my ancient voice behind this jagged page." Even Whitman's free verse says, "Remember the King James Bible, the Psalms; remember the catalogues in the Song of Songs."

This happens because line divisions, in reinforcing syntactic ones, make us conscious of pausing where we'd pause anyhow, thus moving the casualness of the sentence to the plane of "art." Eliot:

> The winter evening settles down
> With smell of steaks in passageways.
> Six o'clock.
> The burnt-out ends of smoky days. . . .

Williams in his early days did that kind of thing too:

> I will teach you my townspeople
> how to perform a funeral . . .

. . . a 1917 poem that was read at his graveside. But syncopate those divisions—

> the dirty
> snow—the humility of the snow that
> silvers everything and is
> trampled and lined with use—yet
> falls again, the silent birds
> on the still wires of the sky, the blur
> of wings as they take off
> together . . .

—and suddenly the speed of nonredundant words serves to separate the utterance from casual speech without ritualizing it, so off-balance do those odd breaks throw our rhythmic habits.

We read in something like a natural voice, while at the edge of attention something is *tugging*.

For decades no one knew what to say about this quality. As long ago as 1933 Williams himself wrote of the difficulty of saying something about "new" work; most often, he said, "we set in motion an antiquated machine whose enormous creaking and heavy and complicated motions frighten the birds, flatten the grass, and fill the whole countryside with smoke."

Despite creakings, Mariani's biography is no such machine. Saved by its love and by the details it preserves, it contains many pages to which readers will turn again: the one, for instance, that contains the tribute to Whitman Williams never published. Since he'd thought it might do to end *Paterson 4* I can surely use it to end this:

> and the waves
> called to him and
> he answered, drilling his voice to
> their advance
> driving the words above
> the returning clatter of stone
> with courage, labor and abandon
> the word, the word, the word. . . .

1981

Williams's Rhythm of Ideas

"The American idiom," William Carlos Williams used to say; and "the Variable Foot." These encompassed all that he had achieved or hoped to achieve. Visitors in his last decade heard him repeat those phrases with the urgency of a man recalling clues from a treasure map glimpsed in a dream. Explicate them he couldn't. The American Idiom has accordingly been written off as Jersey chauvinism and the Variable Foot ridiculed as a rubber inch.

His problem was inherited terminology. "Idiom" was not the word he wanted, nor was "Foot." These were simply nouns he could hear learned men uttering in the general vicinity of what he meant. The adjectives were his: "American," "Variable." Our most useful clue is the fact that he seldom used either phrase without the other. Something rhythmic, something American, those went together. So let me try to sketch what he may have had in mind.

You've surely at some time or other tried to reconstruct the words of a familiar song, only to discover for the first time that you had no idea what some of them were. You'll search your memory in vain. Whole phrases aren't there; you literally never heard them. They were masked by the piano or by slurred intonation. And yet you had the illusion of total lucidity. So how did you follow the song when you were hearing it?

As you listened, you relied on a pattern the music sustains: a pattern of intonations, pitches and pauses, with no inherent semantic content at all. This pattern locates key phrases; it holds them in relation amid ascents and descents of key, amid instances of urgency and linger; and it lets you imagine you've discerned what came between. The structure of meaning is a kind of rhythmic envelope within which we connect the dots between perceived words. We do this without knowing we do it. Poets know about it and know we do it. It's a skill of ours they can count on.

Day by day, we rely on this principle more than we know, not just when there's music, but whenever we're face-to-face, listening. The tunes of English sentences run in our heads, and if we can seldom repeat back a sentence exactly, that is because it's seldom we really discern every word. We've learned to rely on experience with key words and on the tune.

Robert Frost, for one, understood this. To illustrate the most fundamental kind of communication a poet has in his control, Frost adduced what you can hear of a conversation in the next room when you can't make out any of the words. What you are hearing then is a rhythmic pattern: an envelope of stresses and pitches that won't dissect into "feet," though we're right if we call it "rhythmic." It's the local shape of meaning: what T. S. Eliot was relying on when he said that poetry could communicate before it was understood. If it doesn't communicate that way, it's not poetry, just semantic addition, hitching meaning to meaning by syntactic hook and eye.

The local shape of meaning is a pattern we have no name for. That's one reason Williams floundered. He was right in sensing that its initial shapes are regional. We can tell when the conversation in the next room is being carried on by American rather than British voices, even when we can't discern "elevator" from "lift" or so much as isolate determining vowels. There's an American way, distinct from the English way, of distributing stresses and pitches the length of a sentence.

                    I have eaten
                    the plums
                    that were in
                    the ice-box.

That's American, with its odd stress on the preposition "in." A probable British phrasing would be:

                    I have eaten the plums
                    that were in the ice-box.

Americans tend to hit prepositions with a rising inflection, and Williams tends to break lines on prepositions. I'm suggesting that these two facts are connected. That different English-speaking people pace their stresses differently in the sentence, also that a rising inflection is one form of what we loosely call "stress": these are truisms we're apt to forget when we talk of poetry, where "meter" is supposed to be supranational. But meter codifies the small units of rhythm, and Williams was right about the individuating rhythms that run sentence-long, utterance-long, and aren't usefully described by the micro-units of meter, the iambs and anapests. They are the distinctive patterns of the voices you hear in Rutherford, in Toronto, in Dublin or in the Cotswolds.

If you try to fit metrical units to a rhythmic pattern that encompassing, the "feet" you'll be marking off will be far from regular in duration or in content. So we see why Williams talked of the Variable Foot, a manifestation of the American Idiom. And since what Williams wrote won't scan by "feet," it gets called "free verse," though free verse it isn't.

Free verse, in order not to be cut-up prose, has been insistently cadenced, almost liturgical. Beneath its American prototype, the verse of Whitman, we hear not the live voice but the ritual parallelisms of the King James Bible: living idioms but not living rhythms. To Whitman's sanctioned, "poetic" rhythms, once he'd got used to the strangeness, Mr. Emerson could respond. You don't hear those in mature Williams. You hear the rhythmic envelope of American utterance, Variable Feet and all.

By listening—he once mentioned listening to "the speech of Polish mothers"—Williams acquired a repertory of patterns that served him the way known meters or chanted cadences had served former poets. Listen to these lines from "The Poor":

> It's the anarchy of poverty
> delights me, the old
> yellow wooden house indented
> among the new brick tenements.

That has the run of speech, and it's printed in four lines whose phrasing exactly models it. "Delights me, the old" makes no sense as a "mighty line." The event is not the line, the event is the line break. What isolates "delights me, the old" is a pair of rhythmic events, one before it, one after it. The event before it is a break in pitch after "poverty"; the event after it is the recovery of pace after a lingering on "old."

Arranging such an utterance into a stanza was an act as decisive for Williams as arranging speech into iambs was for Shakespeare. We know from papers preserved at Yale University and the State University of New York's College at Buffalo how Williams would type the same sequence of words over and over, breaking it into lines in different places. That was how he made poems, as we can learn by unmaking them. Here are the very same words in the same sequence with the authenticity of the rhythmic envelope destroyed:

> It's the anarchy of poverty delights me,
> The old yellow wooden house
> Indented among the new brick tenements.

That groups the words "by sense," but listen to what it loses! If you heard the first version spoken under Frost's conditions—in the next room, the words themselves inaudible—you'd know the speaker was excited about something. The second would sound like three lines from the minutes of the Bergen County Mosquito Extermination Commission.

"Unless there is / a new mind," he wrote, "there cannot be a new / line. the old will go on / repeating itself with recurring / deadliness."

> without invention the line
> will never again take on its ancient
> divisions when the word, a supple word,
> lived in it, crumbled now to chalk.

It's important to introduce "invention" lest anyone suppose that composition according to the American Idiom and the Variable Foot is simply a mimetic notation of what can be heard in the street, the line fitted to the spoken phrasing. That's how it begins, but the final pattern, Williams reminded Mike Wallace in an interview, may have "as much originality as jazz." The words to which it's fitted need not even be speakable words, maybe, as in "Two Pendants: For the Ears," what Mike Wallace correctly called "a fashionable grocery list":

> 2 partridges
> 2 mallard ducks
> a Dungeness crab
> 24 hours out
> of the Pacific
> and 2 live-frozen
> trout
> from Denmark.

"If you treat that rhythmically," Williams said, "ignoring the practical sense, it forms a jagged pattern. It is, to my mind, poetry."

So patterns made, though built on patterns heard, can tug against the pattern we'd normally hear. That's analogous to the way Shakespearean verse rhythms will pull against the pattern of spoken idiom; it's when the two exactly coincide, when someone seems to be dutifully speaking in meter, that metered verse goes slack: "I must go down to Bedfordshire tomorrow," as we read in *The Stuffed Owl*.

Shakespeare wrote in an age of speech just discovering printing, Williams in an age of print when the short poem is, almost by definition, something to look at. Accordingly, his favorite tension is between the look of the poem and the sound of it. It's by eye that we discern the division into lines, by ear that we follow the enveloping cadence. These may nearly coincide—we've discussed an example— but they normally pull away from coincidence.

At one extreme, in the famous "Red Wheelbarrow," a symmetry of syllable count and lineation is imposed on a sequence of simple words impossible to read aloud at all—try to find the voice in which you can begin a sentence with the words "So much depends on"!

At the other extreme, in the prose letters spliced into *Paterson*, the "natural" idiom takes over completely because there's no meaningful division into lines at all.

And between those extremes, where Williams was tirelessly inventive, line break nearly coincides with some local event of speaking cadence but doesn't quite. That's contrapuntal. I'll end where he ended "Paterson V," by affirming just this fact:

> We know nothing and can know nothing.
>   but
> the dance, to dance to a measure,
> contrapuntally,
>   Satyrically, the tragic foot.

That's an international jubilation. "Counterpoint" is a word from the 16th-century Italian keyboard masters. "The tragic foot" is by etymology Greek and goat-footed. And we dance "satyrically" not as satirists but as satyrs, goat-footed too. Such creatures have danced through our language before:

> Meantime the rural ditties were not mute;
> Tempered to the oaten flute,
> Rough satyrs danced, and fauns with cloven heel
> From the glad sound would not be absent long.

Milton, of course, in "Lycidas": the last time in English that an explicit dance went satyrically. Between the Cambridge classicist and the New Jersey master of American Idiom and Variable Foot—of what Milton would have condescended to as "rural ditties"—there's a contrapuntal interplay if we can hear it.

1983

Maynard Mack's Pope

ALEXANDER POPE: A LIFE, *by Maynard Mack.*
Illustrated. W. W. Norton, 1986. 975 pp.

Not a classic of our poetry, wrote the great Victorian critic Matthew
Arnold; no, Alexander Pope was "a classic of our prose." There are
fashions in feeling as there are fashions in costume, and within fifty
years of Pope's death in 1744 people were expecting a poet to stir
thoughts too deep for tears. If he didn't do that, then the best he could
seem to be doing was apply his feather-duster to verbal surfaces. And
when he left them tidy, as did Pope, well, tidiness was a prosaic virtue
at best.

As late as 1933 an American critic, Horace Gregory, was dismissing
"the mere perfection of a regulated line of verse," and stating that
"Pope's recitation of the dogmas of his day is hollow": not "basic
moral values" but "a ritual of devotion." And so much for the Pope of
the Ethic Epistles, who is made to sound like a fastidious Jerry Fal-
well.

But then there was Pope the Satirist, a Pope whom Victorians
thought a nasty little man, sometimes "actually screaming with ma-
lignant fury." He was small and crippled, which was made to account
for much: "a fiendish monkey," Lytton Strachey wrote, at an upstairs

window dropping boiling oil "upon such of the passers-by whom the wretch had a grudge against." Strachey, being post-Victorian, smirked with delight.

It was just 50 years ago, in *Revaluation*, that F. R. Leavis assembled the above quotations and more, by way of indicating a disarray of judgment. No one, it was clear, had a fix on Pope at all: on the Pope whom Leavis, in 30 of his finest pages, went on to display as a master of far more variety than he'd ever received credit for.

And "it is . . . a pity," Leavis astutely remarked, "that we know so much about Pope's life. If nothing had been known but the works, would 'envy,' 'malice,' 'venom,' 'spite,' and the rest have played so large a part in the commentary?" True. The great danger of absorbing writers' biographies is that you can begin to think you understand writing you've not troubled to come to terms with. Like a crime fiction fan, you dwell zestily on motives.

Those pseudonyms in the Epistles—"Sporus," "Atticus"—who were the men really? Lord Hervey of Ickworth the courtier, Joseph Addison the pundit. Aha! And what had those two done to Pope, pray tell, that explains his venomous rage? Next thing we know, instead of reading Pope, we're sorting the unwashed linen of the 18th century, that consummate age of gossip.

But what they may have done to Pope is the wrong question. The right question is, what is Pope doing with them? And in his new biography of Pope, Professor Mack is persuasive about that. Pope is doing much more than relieve his personal feelings. His concern is with a cherishable order, which such men's psychic pathologies endanger. "Sporus," Mack writes, "is simply the climactic instance of a form of prostitution bedeviling the entire society that the poem depicts." "Prostitution" is the right word: an intercourse that turns on *quid pro quo*. I'll flatter you if you will flatter me, since we both understand how life's deepest itches are the ones relieved by flattery.

That's an understanding not unknown in Washington, and it bespeaks "a selfish individualism which was anathema to Pope's reverence for the moral tradition and the possibilities of private and civic order." Of the great English poets, Pope has the most to say to the American 1980's.

For half a century, readers whom Leavis has aided to a first-hand view of Pope have already known such things. But we've seen Leavis wishing we could disregard biography: in effect directing attention away from it. When even as great a critic as was Leavis in his prime must bid us look away, we've an unstable situation.

Professor Mack's *Life* takes the opposite tack. He will tell us the story of Pope's life as it needs to be told if we're to perceive the poetry, and its rich grasp of civic tradition, growing naturally out of what the man saw and experienced. That means a leisurely telling, with none of the compression that can lead to inadvertent caricature.

The Popes were papists, and we start with scenes of outrage, hysterical Englishfolk burning effigies of the Roman Pope. In 1677, eleven years before the poet's birth, the annual effigy had "a belly filled full of live catts who squawled most hideously as soon as they felt the fire; the common people saying all ye while it was ye language of ye Pope and ye Divel in a dialogue betwixt them." As Mack notes, "the intensity of the aggressions released may be plainly read in the screams of those burning cats." An English Catholic in the 1680's was a sort of 1920's Georgia negro, with the difference that the latter could never renounce his negritude, while the Catholic lived with the cruel knowledge that by going through a rite of "conversion" he could ease all pressures. He was made to feel that he *chose* his persecution.

The Popes left London for the village of Binfield in Berkshire (pop. 300). Before he was 20, young Alexander, irregularly educated, could turn some lines of Homer's Greek into this:

> Cou'd all our Care elude the greedy Grave,
> Which claims no less the Fearful than the Brave,
> For Lust of Fame I shou'd not vainly dare
> In fighting Fields, nor urge thy Soul to War.
> But since, alas, ignoble Age must come,
> Disease, and Death's inexorable Doom;
> The Life which others pay, let Us bestow,
> And give to Fame, what we to Nature owe. . . .

That says: what all men must do, let us do freely: we shall "bestow," not "pay." And typically, those two words get contrasted in one neat line on which all the sense turns, and all the passion. That was what would later get dismissed as "mere perfection."

Translation, yes, but you can't miss the feeling behind it. The greatest translator between Chaucer and Ezra Pound, Pope like them could invest what had long been there with what was personally his and publicly his time's. Mack offers a fine analogy:

"The aim is still to work within a known vocabulary of motifs and patterns . . . not forgetting (to borrow an image that would have fascinated Pope had he known of it) that like the genetic double helix they contain much encapsulated wisdom, and therefore not neglecting to appropriate their strength. In this sense, Pope's poetry is as strongly 'conservative' as that of the Romantics is revolutionary."

"Conservatism" as respect for the double helix: yes, that would have pleased Pope, who some years later would move the motifs of Homer into the salon-world of the *Rape of the Lock*. Go back and reread the Homer. Then read this:

> Oh! if to dance all Night, and dress all Day,
> Charm'd the Small-pox, or chas'd old Age away;
> Who would not scorn what Huswife's Cares produce,
> Or who would learn one earthly Thing of Use? . . .
> But since, alas! frail Beauty must decay,
> Curl'd or uncurl'd, since Locks will turn to grey,
> Since painted, or not painted, all shall fade,
> And she who scorns a Man, must die a Maid. . . .

And what can she substitute for the Homeric hero's vow that he will "bestow" the life which others "pay"?—

> What then remains, but well our Pow'r to use,
> And keep good Humour still, whate'er we lose?

Loss, yes, loss is inevitable: mankind's doom. But our power inheres in what we can control, our "good Humour." And Homeric DNA has transmitted that message: our power inheres in what we can control. Never mind if it's something so undervalued as "good Humour." A century whose greatest novel is an Irishman's total rewriting of the *Odyssey* ought to reach for such transpositions.

Pope was doing things like that when he was sounding pretty silly in letters. How does one assemble a world?

He was four feet six, and crippled with Pott's Disease: tuberculosis of the bone, doubtless contracted from the milk of his wet nurse Mary Beach. (It's typical of that documented age that we know her name.) The symptoms include "debilitating bouts of high fever, severe inflammation of the eyes, a harsh cough, abdominal pain, and a persistent chill or numbness in the legs that frequently brought on in later years a considerable or total loss of use." Later "the vertebrae collapse both sideways and backwards into what is clinically called a kyphoscoliosis." "That long disease my life," he once wrote. Yes.

When his father died, the Anglican Dean of Westminster wrote to suggest that he had now no reason left not to obtain the advantages of conversion. (He might, for instance, buy a house in London, unobstructed by the 10-mile rule for Roman Catholics.) And he replied,

"In my politicks, I think no further than how to preserve the peace of my life, in any government under which I live; nor in my religion, than to preserve the peace of my conscience in any Church with which I communicate. I am not a Papist . . . I am a Catholick, in the strictest sense of the word. . . ."

In short—it is a tactful civil letter—he was, though not a fanatic, not to be bought. In another 11 years he had written the first version of the *Dunciad*, which Mack groups with *Gulliver's Travels* and Gay's *Beggars' Opera*. They ask questions "about ourselves and the societies we have built or tolerated to which in the latter decades of the twentieth century we can only return embarrassed and sometimes shameful answers." All of them suggest ways people can be bought.

The *Dunciad* would absorb Pope for years. The 1728 version was but the first of four. Its final version (1743) is sprinkled with names that could ring little bells then—names of the "poets" and "criticks" who get heard of. Today we could make our own list. But the *Dunciad* trusts we'll see past names soon forgettable to a general busy buzz and buzzy biz. An elder critick:

> . . . am I now fourscore?
> Why, O ye Gods, should two and two make four?

That man has the air of preparing to stir things up importantly. He next climbs high, to dive far into Thames mud.

> The Senior's Judgment all the Crowd admire,
> Who but to sink the deeper, rose the higher.

American weeklies, too, have offered such spectacles.

If Mack is reminded of Breughel—all those little scurrying figures—it's only to remind us how "actual persons on entering a work of fiction forfeit . . . their historical reality and become subject to the needs and themes of the new world they have been placed in." The Dunces did not see it that way; Pope after publishing the poem never fared abroad "except in the company of Bounce his Great Dane, and with pistols in his pocket." "What he calls writing," ran a 1731 attack, "is his poisoning Paper and Reader; he lives on Scandal, like a Maggot on Putrefaction, or a Fly on Excrement."

These slanders managed to stick. Pope the Maggot, Pope the Fly, is essentially Lytton Strachey's Pope, except that from a safe two centuries' distance Lytton Strachey could relish the spectacle. So we're slam-bang in the world of "personalities" which has been the 18th century's most poisonous legacy. If Pope didn't flatter let him not be flattered. Flatter, flatter: what else can matter?

What else can matter is the solemn burden of the *Dunciad* and of the other satires, the part Strachey didn't notice: all that's conveyed by Pope's deep command of rhythm (misread as "finish"), by his accuracy of distinction ("pay" vs. "bestow"), by his hold on the deep roots of the European legacy (Homer). "What mortal can resist the yawn of Gods?" There is vacuity by which the gods know enough to be bored. We mortals need to be firm about it. In doing so we'll sound Tory, which according to the most audible authorities is no way to sound. That may, in the long run, unnerve us.

I'll not conceal how even Maynard Mack, vulnerable to the century of Doctorow and Kermode, does show a need to shuffle from foot to foot. Beginning with "that vanity which impels us all to impart to the world a more or less flattering image of ourselves," Mack moves to what "sociologists will see" as "aspects of resocialization." Sociologists—today they are totem-sages. Invoke them in a mumble and feel safe.

"Nature had set [Pope] apart with a crippling and disfiguring disease. Upbringing had set him apart through membership in a disfranchised and always suspect minority." Hence "the resulting urge to redefine, almost re-create himself, within the poems and elsewhere." Yes, yes, we've heard such things. A self-redefining Pope, a Pope of urges, is not the Pope to hold us long. Now and then, this most sympathetic of biographers seems uncertain whether or not his man wasn't, perhaps, on the whole, a neurologist's "case."

Better not to quote such clunkers; best to dwell on Mack's slow unfolding of Pope's career among the great and the pseudo-great and the entrepreneurs who'd buy, for resale, what he had to sell. He lived in the first age to discover literature as commodity, and the shock of that never left him.

Odd indeed by our lights, he put faith in words like "order," which we have learned we must rescue from redneck sheriffs. As much as biography can disclose the substance of such a faith, Professor Mack does disclose it. And he quotes enough Pope, and appositely, to lead fit readers to the only place they can profitably go, if they'd see why Pope's life was worth writing in the first place: to Pope's own lines, like the ones that gravely celebrate

> . . . The Pow'r who bids the Ocean ebb and flow,
> Bids Seed-time, Harvest, equal course maintain
> Thro' reconcil'd extremes of drought and rain,
> Builds Life on Death, on Change Duration founds,
> And gives th'eternal Wheels to know their rounds . . .

If you can decline to argue with the force of that, Maynard Mack's book can help you find your way into the world it came out of.

1987

The Traffic in Words

MULLIGAN STEW, *by Gilbert Sorrentino.*
Grove Press, 1987. 464 pp.

On page one, addressed to the author ("Dear Gil") and signed "Harry White, Editorial Director," a letter rejecting the manuscript from which the book we are holding was printed. Next, rejection letters from eleven more editors who try out other ways of sounding honest. The way of this first one is frank and hearty:

> . . . one of the most remarkably conceived and executed novels it has ever been my pleasure to read in manuscript. . . . However, the sheer cost of doing your book. . . . To be frank with you, I must show a profit to the parent company. . . .

And then:

> Don't misunderstand me: I will not publish schlock so as to make the money that might justify doing MULLIGAN STEW, or books like it. But I feel that the books on the Fall list are not only *good*, but have definite market appeal. . . . One . . . is, it seems to me, a necessary addition to "Beatle lore"—*The Compleat Beatle Wardrobe Book.* The other

two—*The Films of Roy Rogers* and a zany, wonderful novel about life in California, *Screwing in Sausalito*, are risky but have received great word-of-mouth publicity. . . .

That last clause helps define "good." In the other letters words are less definable. An editor named Frank Bouvard (where have we heard that name?[1]) is afraid that "the narrative doesn't rise above its own irony—although one of our readers, a Sorrentino 'fan,' felt that the irony hasn't the precision to cope with the strong narrative." Derrida couldn't put that better.

Chad Newsome, who had a taste for the high life back when Henry James employed him in *The Ambassadors*, liked "the orgy scene . . . and the descriptions of the girls' costumes in the nightclub scene," but sure couldn't figure the whole thing out. He and his firm were "out to lunch on this one."

Claude Estee ("maybe I'm just 'old fashioned' ") found it "neither engaging nor exhilarating, nor was it full of the simple zest of life, as novels really must be to be novels that compel the reader," and Sheldon Corthell's gang "admired the writing just as *writing*," but "could not respond to the book as a *book*." Ah so.

A fistful of such letters, not all of them troubling even to get his name right, may reinforce a novelist's suspicion that most publishers' first readers are chimpanzees, reporting to editorial directors who lie on the floor and hiccup. In less-paranoid moments, like those in which the high spirits of a Gilbert Sorrentino may conceive a *Mulligan Stew*, he may recognize the voices assumed by human beings trying to pretend they aren't serving a venture in mass production, a theme concerning which it behooves us to be less naive than they'd like.

Mankind's first mass-produced item was surely the brick, the second probably the book, the manufacture of which J. Gutenberg had mechanized by 1454. "Mass production" means that expensive make-ready, mystifying to an unschooled observer—What is the man in the apron doing with all those metal cubes?—enables you to turn out with little trouble a large number of identical artifacts, such as Jeeps or Bibles.

---

[1]François Denys Bartholomée Bouvard was Flaubert's Oliver Hardy. His ventures into literary criticism were unfortunate.

Indeed you can produce with intoxicating ease more copies than people can be found to want. Detroit had its Edsel, and in 1716 Oxford University Press overestimated the press run of David Wilkins's edition of the Gospels in Coptic, and were 191 years getting rid of the last copy. That should have taught the industry a lesson.

And though printing's ostensible role was to copy with ease what had formerly been copied by hand, it grew evident almost at once that mankind's existing stock of verbal treasures was too small to feed the new technology. Hence instant treasures: books composed solely because entrepreneurs with a press and some type needed something to print. William Caxton himself in the 1480s was translating French romances with his left hand, for printing with his right.

Such books were long suspect. One wanted not to be caught in their company, and keeping *out* of print was at one time a real writer's mark of distinction, like staying off the *Donahue* show. John Donne managed to keep his *Songs and Sonnets* from printers' hands right up to his death in 1631, and Swift's *Tale of a Tub*[2] in 1696 regards the interlocked industry of bookselling, printing, and scribbling with the sour suspicion professional literacy would direct toward TV in the 1950s. Who needed all those blurry little pictures, Aldous Huxley used to ask; and, Swift asks in effect, who needs all those millions of penny-a-line words.

But people with a need are finally the principal thing mass production produces: hence in these late days something called The Reading Public, a human subspecies imbued with the line-scanning, page-turning habit, that will go mad if long deprived of lines to scan (POWs would read and reread the labels on packages) and must at all costs not be traumatized by novelty. Much investment rides on The Reading Public's well-being; Argentinian sheep are tended no more carefully. It is ministered to by Sunday Book Pages and by designers of gadgetry to support a book above one's bathtub. Its whims are tabulated weekly by computer-processed sales figures from 1,400 stores. And knowingly pastured, it keeps a solicitous industry so healthy

---

[2]Which he never admitted writing. Nor, for that matter, though his printed works fill a yard-long shelf, did Swift proclaim his connection with a single one. "Lemuel Gulliver" took the blame for the most famous.

that the likes of RCA and Gulf + Western have come to esteem publishing firms as choice investments.

Publishing firms in turn think up things like *The Compleat Beatle
Wardrobe Book* and *The Films of Roy Rogers*. (Come, come, you didn't
mistake those for the brainstorms of minor Miltons?) Each publisher
works on the scale he can maintain and be maintained by. He knows
how many books his 1982 list will contain long before he knows what
most of them will be. He observes two seasons, spring and fall. Spring
culminates in vacations and novels; fall in Christmas and thirty-dollar
books you buy for somebody else. He is fertile in commissioning Beatle Wardrobe Books at need. And by a persistent misunderstanding,
every publisher is beset with correspondence from people who think
his main function is the maintenance of the life of the mind.

James Joyce, prone to such illusions, pestered publishers for years.
It was finally necessary for a couple of ladies in Paris to rig up an *ad hoc*
firm solely to issue his *Ulysses* (which may, after all these years, have
been the fiction best-seller of the century).

Pros like James Michener are under no such illusions. They tend to
their business, which is tending to The Reading Public. And between
the busy Micheners and the deluded Joyces stretches a sad half-world
peopled by such as "Anthony Lamont." So back to *Mulligan Stew*.

Leafing past the rejection letters we come upon a Reader's Report,
allegedly commissioned by Grove Press (which did in fact publish
Mulligan). It is signed "Horace Rosette" and postures accordingly ("A
humor so fragile and evanescent that one reads it while almost literally holding one's breath"—imagine raunchy Grove succumbing to
that), but it does let us know what we're in for, and should we get lost
we can turn back to it for guidance.

What we're in for includes slabs of a variously titled novel-in-
progress by "Anthony Lamont," who keeps rewriting the opening;
and also the scrapbooks, journals, and correspondence of the same
"Anthony Lamont"; and also the diary kept by one of his characters,
"Martin Halpin," who fears that working in a novel by Lamont ("this
scribbler, this unbearably pretentious *hack*") marks a coming-down in
the world.

For we are to understand that fictional characters, if like members of a repertory company they work long hours and take pride in doing what they are asked to do, nonetheless have their standards, and Halpin resents having been plucked out of the footnote "in which I have resided, faceless, for all these years in the work of that gentlemanly Irishman, Mr. Joyce."[3] "I can't understand how Mr. Joyce allowed him to take me away! Surely, it can't have been for money! Or does Mr. Joyce even *know* that I have gone? Maybe he's dead."

So, in the accents of 1930s fiction, might a man speak who'd lain silent forty years in a footnote. Mr. Joyce is indeed dead, since 1941, and some of his property unclaimed; rummaging about while their employer is engaged on something else, Halpin and his co-star even stumble upon what aficionados cannot but recognize as several books that belonged to Leopold Bloom.

Halpin's co-star, Ned Beaumont, has worked for Dashiell Hammett ("An actor—a *Hollywood* actor—even impersonated me in a movie they made from a book I worked in"). That was in *The Glass Key*, where Beaumont took one of the longer beatings in the history of the genre, and you'd think he'd welcome a job where, introduced as a corpse from the start he's at leisure save during flashbacks. But characters in the Seventies seem an ungrateful lot, and Lamont furthermore is a uniquely repulsive employer. He writes absurd dialogue and keeps changing his mind.

Both Beaumont and Halpin are gaga over madcap Daisy Buchanan, who never seems to remember a previous employer, Scott Fitzgerald. She's still married to Tom, who writes her lovers stiff letters.

The hack Lamont lives a hectic life of his own. He aspires toward cash. He also aspires toward respectable celebrity, defined as inclusion in a course on the experimental novel that a Professor Roche is designing. From the *curriculum vitae* he writes out for Professor Roche we learn that he acquired his perseverance from his illiterate father,

> and from my mother [*he continues*] my love of books and music. My
> mother read to me from the Bible, *Treasure Island, Pilgrim's Progress*,

[3]On page 266 of *Finnegans Wake* is a note that reads in its entirety, "I have heard this word used by Martin Halpin, an old gardener from the Glens of Antrim who used to do odd jobs for my grandfather, the Rev. B. B. Brophy of Swords." Joyce put Mr. Halpin to no further work.

Growing Up Straight and Sound, Scales and Feathers, Modern Business English,[4] and other books in our little library.

My schooling was haphazard. . . . To this day, long division and fractions are beyond my powers. . . . In 1942, when I was about fifteen[5] I won a prize for an essay I wrote in school competition, "What I Can Do To Help The War Effort."

This is the Barefoot school of author's reminiscence. Elsewhere we are offered the Mandarin variety, a clipping of an interview with Lamont's favorite author, Richard McCoy, who lives with his wife in the Hotel Splendide, where the concierge gives satisfaction:

"There are not many left who can read, let alone spell," [McCoy] continues. "This exquisite *bijou* gets every message perfectly correct—a pleasure to read. R-e-a-d." McCoy himself loves to spell and often amuses himself after writing by doing so for hours. It is suggested that he will spell anything. "Not quite *anything*," he grins slyly.

Phantasms swarm; one might even suspect "McCoy" of being Vladimir Nabokov, except that he detests Nabokov. It's at least fairly clear that these are interviews and reminiscences we seem somehow to have read before.

As a young man, he wrote with a red-lacquered penholder and fine nib. Later, as he mellowed, he switched to a green penholder, then to an Eversharp fountain pen. Now he uses a Parker Jotter and makes his corrections with the Bic and the Venus. He must use black ink. "There is purity in black," he explains.

The Portrait of the Author as a Successful Man is an unacknowledged subgenre of the Book Supplements, part of that great enterprise of pasturing The Reading Public. *Mulligan Stew* is most easily described as a contour map of those pastures, executed with *National Geographic* vividness.

But we're still forgetting Lamont, who stumbles down the hack's *via crucis* loaded with cross upon cross. His sister Sheila has up and married none other than Dermot Trellis, a truly despicable hack whom Sorrentino borrowed from a novel by "Flann O'Brien"—to

---

[4]Probably the shortest list in *Mulligan Stew*. The longest occupies six pages. Connoisseurs of the list, take heed. (*The Book of Lists* sold umpty whillion copies.)
[5]Subtraction also is beyond his powers, since he was born in 1925.

whose memory, under his *real* name, Brian O'Nolan, *Mulligan Stew* is dedicated. This fact may prompt a fit readership though few to refresh its memory of "O'Brien"'s *At Swim-Two-Birds*, a 1938 book that won't stay buried. (It was most recently reprinted as a Plume Books paperback three years ago. Yes, there *is* a Plume Books. Yes, there *is* an *At Swim-Two-Birds*. Read it.)

In *At Swim-Two-Birds*—and if you ask me to explain that title I'll drop all these balls: I can't possibly manage another—Dermot Trellis is a character in an undergraduate's novel, where he performs as a novelist whose characters are conspiring against him. Sorrentino's point in ostentatiously lifting the whole device—which "O'Brien" derived, maybe, from Unamuno's *Niebla*—is in part that Jeeves is more real than Wodehouse, Holmes than Doyle, Bloom, even, than Joyce (you invest yourself with reality, therefore, by inventing).

More than that, characters recur, under various names, in various books by various authors, tokens and touchstones of permanency. *New* characters, really new, would drive The Reading Public to television. Bloom, the most "realized" character in all fiction, is a huge cliché.

And the world of fiction? It is a shadowy half-world of trees without roots, houses without kitchens, bathrooms without toilets, where forgetful authors equip revolvers with fifty cartridges, change pen to pencil in mid-letter, and force hard-put characters to remove stockings but not shoes. In that world The Reading Public daydreams for hours.

A Joyce or a Flann O'Brien can render its landscapes in hologram by laser-accurate command of stylistic variousness. Sorrentino, like any American you can think of, is imperfectly equipped with such resources—his parodies of silly rhetoric depend more on silly ideas than on inappropriate tropes—so he tends to rely on sheer energy. When the band plays fortissimo for seventeen hours people do not notice haphazard key-shiftings.

We're still forgetting Lamont. His sister, we were saying, has married Dermot Trellis, and has been drawn by the despicable Trellis (so thinks Lamont) into courses of vulgarity, not to say treachery. Is it the hand of Trellis we are to discern behind the flagging interest of Professor Roche? That course in the Experimental Novel, alas, will contain no niche for Anthony Lamont, his *Baltimore Chop* supplanted by Trellis's *Red Swan*.

And was it the conjoined wiles of his sister and Trellis that procured Lamont's humiliating evening with the poetess Lorna Flambeaux, whose palpitant *Sweat of Love* (twelve X-rated poems, printed entire for our reference) was inconsistent with her vigorous riposte (umbrella, handbag) to his advances?

Was it . . . But enough of his paranoia. The book-pushing scene is no fit habitation for even so squalid a spirit as Lamont's, and we begin to grasp why, in his novel-in-progress, he has cast Halpin and Beaumont as a publishing partnership, and arranged for one to kill the other and not know if he has done it or not. Moral catatonia, not knowing what you're doing or have done, that's his gut verdict on the milieu where they pass time programming letters to authors from stock phrases, e.g.,

3. while we felt . . . we also thought
4. while we thought . . . we also felt
5. lack of narrative structure
6. undeveloped character of

Catatonia also solicits the avant-garde fictionist he fancies he harbors within him. "Halpin doesn't know whether he killed him or not," he writes in his notebook. "Must be clear that Halpin really doesn't know whether he is lying or not about the murder." Sustaining that empty nescience at novel length will be a *tour de force*, and Lamont's *Guinea Red*, later retitled *Crocodile Tears*, aspires, albeit fumblingly, to membership in the avant-garde, Robbe-Grillet division.

And surely *Mulligan Stew* . . . ? No, surely not *Mulligan Stew*. *Mulligan Stew* (for all that the meter of its title, and more of its minor debris than I thought to keep track of, bespeaks *Finnegans Wake*)—*Mulligan Stew* is a send-up of the avant-garde, which we'd better have a talk about.

The writers—a few of them per century—who make a permanent difference: we're not talking about them, the Joyces, Eliots, Becketts. And apart from them, avant-garde writing is almost exactly as perishable as is Reading Public writing, from which it differs chiefly in soliciting the approval of a smaller group, ranging in size from a group of one, the writer, up to a group of perhaps 1,100, say five per million of the U.S. population. (I derive this figure from the normal circulation of literary quarterlies, the typical press runs of small houses like Jargon and Black Sparrow, the confidences of itinerant publisher-editors, and observation of the moss on the north side of trees.)

How many such partially overlapping groups of up to 1,100 there may be is anybody's guess. Their members are mutant members of The Reading Public; discerners whose Book-of-the-Month Club days are behind them. Their cravings are diverse: novelty, a regional ethos, insidership with what's going on out there, simple honesty, just the shock of word on word, or, rarely (and as rarely encountered), genuine autonomous imaginative life. There are writers to provide all these, the best of them differentiated from the Schlock avant-garde by a quality of care about something, be it only typography or vowel sequences.

But the Schlock avant-garde: ah, that: Anthony Lamont's natural home: vain, self-deceiving, as driven as NBC by the winds of fashion: it discerns baleful magic in words like *plastic* and *lostness* and pins its faith on fatuous strategies. "Indianapolis and New York are interchangeable in this novel," writes Lamont of an early work. "The names of streets, parks, restaurants, etc., are identical: I thought to use this technique to get across my feeling that our world has become featureless." Writing-Seminar *Angst*.

Still, we can use any number of avant-gardes, if only to enforce the one point they all agree on, that despite its numbers the great Reading Public is as factitious as they are. More's the pity that sustaining them has become factioned, fragmented, each group left to grow fixed in the illusion that it contains the only 1,100 literates in the Republic.

Time was when much that's now left to small presses could stay beneath commercial tents: as when Alfred Knopf published Wallace Stevens steadily, from *Harmonium* to *Opus Posthumous*, or Horace Liveright used the proceeds of things like *Replenishing Jessica* to underwrite Ezra Pound's *Personae*.

But small sales won't do any longer, nor will slow sales, not with conglomerate accountants breathing heavily. They breathe especially hard at the mention of a Backlist, in practice a warehouseful of miscellaneous titles sold copy by copy on special order. The prestige of a firm used to derive from its Backlist. But to the accountant it's as though Ford in Detroit kept on hand, at huge cost, a small stock of Model T's and A's to gratify whimsical nostalgias. Get rid of it all! Concentrate on what moves quickly! And avant-garde publishing, the best like the worst, is almost wholly an affair of backlists. Where first novels can be sent now I've no idea.

Hence—to epitomize all this and more—Anthony Lamont struggling to make it both ways, on the big time and on the circuits of esteem, without the talent for either; and going mad from the strain (and writing better); and all those ghostly Characters complaining that times are not what they were; and Gil Sorrentino in irrepressible spirits confecting his intricate Stew (I've outlined perhaps a quarter of the plot) and filling its interstices with his beloved Lists (for another such virtuoso of the List you'd have to resurrect Joyce): and (in real life, if you follow me) twenty-five publishers—yes, there are still twenty-five publishers—rejecting it.

And (old-fashioned Happy Ending) one publisher—Hurrah!—was mad enough to take it.

Did the other twenty-five perhaps divine its subversive content? No, I think not. I meditate in this connection upon a rejection letter I heard about recently, which wasn't for a subversive book at all. It deserves preservation as the generic rejection letter from these latter days of big-time word-merchandising. "I cannot recall reading," it said without irony, "a novel as learned, as intelligent, as witty as this, and one with so exact a sense of its place and time. However it is not right for us." Think long on all that tells you about "us." Then go and engrave it on the tomb of Rabelais.

1979

Wyndham Lewis:
Satirist as Barbarian

Satire, unlike song or epos or simple narrative, is a radically *written* genre, impossible—inconceivable—without the textual storage and recall that has been possible for only twenty-eight centuries. It requires that the language by which we recount events be externalized for inspection, the way only writing externalizes; externalized moreover into literature's defined genres with their concomitant apparatus of expectations. By contrast, the talker, performing as he must amid shared acoustic fluidities, can mock, can cruelly mock, but he cannot satirize. Satire's technologies are not at his disposal.

The spoken, as any crowd knows, is experience we share; whereas the written, as English Augustans understood, is an artifact for men of sense to appraise. We share speech by participation; in joining the mocker we turn against his victim, who will be fortunate if he is not booted out of the tribe before nightfall. But writing is assessed by judgment, cool and external; in detecting the manipulations of the satirist, we come to perceive his victim (and likely ourselves) as entrapped in a kind of metaphysical warp. Something has proven to be wrong on a very large scale, and in a way resistant to our analytic habits. These habits may even be part of what is wrong. What were we doing, sagely nodding our heads as the Modest Proposer prattled about the sheer nuisance of being assailed by beggars? Is *that* a way to state the Irish Problem?

Accordingly, satire manipulates whole systems of perception, notably the literary genres and their potential for overlayering. It addresses itself to book-people like ourselves, persuading us that we have picked up a pamphlet about economic distress in Ireland, or a narrative of voyages into several remote nations of the world, or a brief epic to celebrate a lady who kept her virtue at the cost of some hairs.[1] We had expected the apposite satisfaction: social zealotry's lubricious narcissism, the voyage-reader's vicarious escape, connoisseurship's judicious self-congratulation that can appraise a genre-bound performance. But sooner or later, and perhaps abruptly or perhaps by gradual steps, satire permits us to discover that we are reading, not what we expected but something else entirely. To this we cannot give a name (save "satire") because what we thought we were reading in the first place cannot quite be exorcised.

So as verbal technologies go, satire is a sophisticated contrivance indeed. "Technology" seems the term to employ. I am following Eric Havelock, who has taught us to think of alphabetic writing as itself a technology, loosely definable as something no Noble Savage would be likely to think of. "The ability to document a spoken language is itself a technological feat, one on which the cultures which preceded the Greek placed some reliance, and which has become essential in post-Greek cultures."[2]

Once people are used to *texts*—etymologically, things *woven*, as by the fingers—they have trouble imagining how words can exist in any way save textually. ("Freeing ourselves of chirographic and typographic bias in our understanding of language is probably more difficult than any of us can imagine," writes Walter Ong, himself entoiled in texty words like "bias.")[3] For textual man, reader and writer

---

[1]Whether *The Rape of the Lock* be satire is not something we'll quibble about, though whoever questions its genre ("mock-epic"?) plays satire's game. So did Pope's contemporaries when, as often, they disputed the authorship of something. For if a wit has written a transparent piece of duncery, then it is satire, but if a dunce, not.

[2]Eric A. Havelock, *The Literate Revolution in Greece and Its Cultural Consequences*, Princeton, 1982, 106.

[3]Walter J. Ong, *Orality and Literacy*, London, 1982, 77.

alike, words are external, "out there" in space. They are pointers to "things," likewise "out there." (Literate traversers of this page will think of the philosophers of Lagado, who economized breath by rummaging through bags of things.) Writers "arrange" them (in space), and certain distinctive arrangements are identifiable by eye: Sonnets (which look well on quarto pages), Pindarick Odes (elaborately indented), Works of Learning (small-print footnotes), latterly Novels (a hundred or more cubic inches of wood-pulp, with much conversation typographically marked). Other genres are recognized by conventions of titling, hence Swift's care for titles ("A Modest *Proposal* . . ."; "TRAVELS into certain remote Nations . . ."). Moreover the arrangement has been effected "by" someone; the key-word on a title page is "by." Whereas a book is naturally "by," spoken words are "said by" thanks only to the convention of the passive voice; for speech, the natural words are "Homer said." But, once book-ridden (on the analogy of bed-ridden), the *Iliad* is something "by" Homer. *It*, being here in our hands, has precedence over *him*. He is a "by-line." (Did he exist? Did Gulliver? Bentley said that "Phalaris" did not exist, and one prop of antiquity seemed hewn.)

From all that order of technology satire derives, and we should not be surprised to find it emerging in times of technological stress among the genres: in Rome, when the appropriation of Greek genres—the epic, the panegyric—was apt to raise questions concerning their applicability to what you might notice around you; in England, when the commercializing of the new commodity we aptly call "reading matter" could raise doubts concerning the authority of the page itself. What, we are bidden to ask by *A Tale of a Tub*, is verbal authority worth, if the work of any hack with adequate command of grammar can strike the eye and heft in the hand just like something substantial? That hacks and dunces preoccupied Swift and Pope is something that should not surprise us. By 98 percent of all empirical tests, the differences between Pope's *Iliad* and anything at all by Ambrose Philips are imperceptible. Even the inventory of words they "arrange" is as nearly identical as makes no difference. Words being normally printed, we can now *count* them, and count their component letters, and discern that "English" has its statistical norms. Those norms make half a writer's decisions for him.[4] (Try to write a page with no "e.")

A newly commercialized typographic culture, presided over by "booksellers" who, as today's undergraduates need informing, did much more than sell books,[5] was a milieu both Swift and Pope were acutely aware of. By one stratagem or another, they had had to connive a way into it; otherwise they would not have been allowed to exist as book-men. With some university press or other at his disposal by professional courtesy, the modern academic can have difficulty seeing why hacks and scribbling ninnies preoccupied them so.

Wyndham Lewis (1882–1957) likewise came to the 20th century book-world from the outside. By vocation he was a painter, his normal creative impulses flowing down the musculature of shoulder and arm into his strong fingers. It is not irrelevant that there were painters in his lifetime who called themselves *les fauves*, the wild creatures. Though a savage is not aware of being a savage, a painter in London or Paris can be aware how, like the savage and unlike the bourgeois, he spends his most vital time doing something physical. Lewis projected his savage heritage so eloquently his more articulate contemporaries could not fail to register it. "The thought of the modern and the energy of the cave man," wrote T. S. Eliot, astonished.

Not surprisingly, writers and readers, the producers of written words and their consumers, were always to the eye of this caveman a trifle strange. What a confidence-game! Someone scribbles, or strikes keys, or even dictates, and after an interval of technological processing gets acclaimed as a magician by thousands who hold in their hands a wood-pulp artifact, distinguished by ink markings.

That was odd, and what was odder was that Lewis all his life could make money at the writing game more readily than by his brush. (In later life he lived on advances for books, which the books seldom repaid though he wrote them meticulously.) That was because the arrangements for marketing pictures ensure that what gets marketed is a *name*, and require that at any one time no more than a very few

---

[4]Almost exactly half, a man who seemed to know once told me, but just what he was counting I did not find out.
[5]It was they for instance who chose the English Poets before Johnson wrote the Lives.

names of power shall be acknowledged. The list is kept by a sanhedrin of middle-men called dealers, and any name's presence on it seems wholly arbitrary. "Wyndham Lewis" was never in that arcane sense a "name," so painters less talented routinely fetched bigger fees.

Early in his career, needing money, he accordingly set out to write a potboiler, *Mrs. Dukes' Million*. By a characteristic miscalculation it brought him nothing because it went unpublished till after his death[6]—J. B. Pinker himself couldn't market it—but it is readable today and discloses an early preoccupation with provisional worlds. Very simply, the way to affluence and power is to make yourself be thought to be somebody else. The public world, reported in the newspapers, is a web of illusion—"the stunt of an illusionist"[7] was his brusque later phrase—and to inherit Mrs. Dukes' Million you have only to pass yourself off as Mrs. Dukes. A master illusionist in command of a company of actors has arranged for this to be effected, also for the real Mrs. Dukes to be bundled off to America, by 1908 convention the world's waste-basket.

An actor they are recruiting is told about "the prime difference between our theatre, which has the world for its stage, and the theatre that you are used to":

> We improvise. No pieces are written for us. The actors act the part as they go along. That is what I myself always wanted to do when I was acting. . . . I wanted to see actors no longer bound by the "piece" they had to play, but to *act* and *live* at the same time. . . . [For us] the play goes on sometimes in several places at the same time. One of the present players in my company is playing his part six thousand miles from here, without audience, but none the worse for that.

That 1908 illusionist spoke for Lewis, who sensed, and ever more strongly as he grew older, that the "real" was always appearance: was contrived. When we have worked our way up the hierarchies of *The Human Age* to God, God, in the only fragment of Part IV that survives,

[6]By The Coach House Press, Toronto, in 1977. The typescript had vanished into England's Sargasso Sea of discarded papers, to surface after nearly five decades in a London junkshop. See my essay in Jeffrey Meyers, ed., *Wyndham Lewis: A Revaluation*, 1980, 85–91.
[7]From a letter to T. Sturge Moore, 1941, in W. K. Rose, ed., *The Letters of Wyndham Lewis*, New York, 1963, 293.

is "the old magician of the cloudy wastes of heaven." That God is a *benign* magician goes without saying (though in 1919 Lewis called the Universe "a gigantic and, from every point of view, dubious concern");[8] but as the levels get lower magicians get more and more corrupt: precisely, Apes of God. At the levels we inhabit, the "reality" accessible to our casual sight has been contrived in reputation-factories where the staff can seem inextricable from the product: pressmen, politicians, Famous Writers, "authorities," film stars, gossip stars, yes, art dealers.

Something else to notice about *Mrs. Dukes' Million* is the way its "reality" has been imported from the fin-de-siècle novel: from *The Sign of the Four*, from *The New Arabian Nights*, from *The Prisoner of Zenda* and *The Man Who Was Thursday*. Apart from some genial detail about boardinghouses and their perky landladies, it tells us little about what Lewis had seen and heard, much about what he had been reading. That is unsurprising in an avowed potboiler, but arresting when we consider how *Mrs. Dukes* foreshadows what Lewis the committed publicist and satirist would later have us believe about reality's texture. "The best-seller," he was to write years later, "is like the camera, it cannot lie." He was saying that it could not lie about what its readers took for granted; but to the best-sellers of his young manhood, with their mystifications and charades of mistaken identity, Lewis seems to have attributed an insight into what God, "the old magician," had contrived: a "reality" that was *always* provisional. Only the artist, "older than the fish" as he memorably said, can draw on "the fundamental slime of creation."

> The creation of a work of art is an act of the same description as the evolution of wings on the sides of a fish, the feathering of its fins; or the invention of a weapon within the body of a hymenopter to enable it to meet the terrible needs of its life.[9]

That attempts, with Darwin's help, to constate the authentic: the authentic is whatever meets needs, "terrible needs." Art, so we are

---

[8] *The Caliph's Design*, 1919; reprinted in Walter Michel and C. J. Fox, eds., *Wyndham Lewis on Art*, London, 1969, 153.
[9] Michel and Fox, *Wyndham Lewis on Art*, 152.

being told, does likewise. All else is spurious, commencing perhaps
with the Universe (what need did *it* serve?) and including certainly
best-sellers, sonnets, grammarians, six-shooters . . .

> It was inventions of this order—the musket, pistol, and breechloader,
> not to mention the fire-water—which enabled the European to over-
> run the globe a few centuries ago. And what good has it done to him or
> anyone else? . . . For in most of the places where the White Man went
> with his little gun, his polo-ponies and gangster-films, he has de-
> stroyed something finer than himself. . . .[10]

—something Older than the Fish, in fact. How readily we get hypnotized by the spurious! And by the pretense that our alphabetical
scratchings on paper can convey anything save the conventions
within which they operate.

For here is Bestre, a Breton inn-keeper; and our first thought may
be that the barbarian in charge of the pen has not the least idea how to
go about a description. Yet the barbaric surface has been carefully
contrived—"Bestre" went through two recastings, the first one seismic, between 1909 and 1927—and the words Lewis finally joined say
chiefly this, that sentences as they flow from a normal pen can tell us
nothing at all about a creature at once so primitive and so agonistic.

> His very large eyeballs, the small saffron ocellation at their centre, the
> tiny spot through which light entered the obese wilderness of his body;
> his bronzed bovine arms, swollen handles for a variety of indolent little
> ingenuities; his inflated digestive case, lent their combined expressive-
> ness to say these things; with every tart and biting condiment that eye-
> fluid, flaunting of fatness (the well-filled), the insult of the comic, im-
> plications of indecency, could provide. Every variety of the bottom-
> tapping resounded from his dumb bulk. His tongue stuck out, his lips
> eructated with the incredible indecorum that appears to be the
> monopoly of liquids, his brown arms were for the moment genitals,
> snakes in one massive twist beneath his mamillary slabs, gently riding
> on a pancreatic swell, each hair on his oil-bearing skin contributing its
> message of porcine affront.[11]

[10]"Power-Feeling and Machine-Age Art" (1934), in *Wyndham Lewis on Art*, 1969.
[11]*The Complete Wild Body*, Bernard Lafourcade, ed., Santa Barbara, 1982, 78. "Bestre," a
rewriting of a 1909 sketch, achieved its present form at some time between war's end
and its publication in *Tyro #2* (London, March 1922, the year of *Ulysses*).

We were all taught to write *sentences*, subject, subject > verb > object. Lewis attacks that assumption at the root. Sentences map actions, but Bestre is a restless stasis, like a picture. Accordingly, amid empty deferral to syntactic conventions, this paragraph's unit is not the sentence but the phrase, each one a surreal snapshot: "the obese wilderness of his body"; "snakes in one massive twist"; "gently riding on a pancreatic swell."

We all believe too in sleek organic integrity, when the object of our attention is a Man, someone "human" like our fine selves. But this man is built up of parts, of oddly assorted phrases, and the order of the components, from "his very large eyeballs" to "each hair on his oil-bearing skin," seems nearly random. (Are we ourselves more random than we suppose?) A long sentence, a short, a long: their catch-all rhythms govern. When we read "Bestre," as we must, against something we carry in our heads, the uncodified but substantial tradition of personal description, all that novelists have learned from one another about ways to convey the look of people, then we may suspect a chasm between affrontive reality and literature's suave procedures. Bestre is not so much ushered onto the page, as relentlessly *looked* at, between discharges of metaphoric shells.

In his 1950 *Rude Assignment* Lewis explicitly connected "Bestre" (1922 or earlier) with his celebrated *Apes of God* of 1930.[12] He was accurate. Here is the *Apes'* Lady Fredigonde, veteran gossip star, getting herself upright from a chair:

> . . . The unsteady solid rose a few inches, like the levitation of a narwhal. Seconded by alpenstock and body-servant (holding her humble breath), the escaping half began to move out from the deep vent. It abstracted itself slowly. Something imperfectly animate had cast off from a portion of its self. It was departing, with a grim paralytic toddle, elsewhere. The socket of the enormous chair yawned just short of her hindparts.

Next, she sinks into another chair two rooms away:

[12]Lafourcade noted this in *The Complete Wild Body*: "Out of Bestre . . . grew . . . the aged 'Gossip Star' at her toilet" (220).

> She lowered her body into its appointed cavity, . . . ounce by ounce—
> back first, grappled to Bridget, bulldog grit all-out—at last riveted as
> though by suction within its elastic crater, corseted by its mattresses of
> silk from waist to bottom, one large feeble arm riding the billows of its
> substantial fluted brim.

Finally, she speaks:

> There was a great bustle all at once. Her head was lived in once again.
> A strong wheezing sigh, as the new air went in and the foul air went
> out, and then she realized the tones of a muted fog-horn to exclaim—
>   "There will come a time Bridget when I shall not be able to move
> about like that!"[13]

Quickly riffled, the pages of *The Apes of God* say "novel"; do they not
display "conversations"? More closely examined, these conversations prove synthesized. "There will come a time Bridget when I shall
not be able to move about like that": this string of words lacks the two
crucial commas that would designate a human utterance. Here we are
deep in the technology of writing, to which alone commas pertain
(there are no *spoken* commas); deep too in the layered conventions
that would have us intuit from the commas, were commas here, a
warmth toward Bridget, soul calling unto soul, without our even having to voice the sentence. Reading silently, we do not so much as pretend to be reading aloud; yet having interiorized print—the chief
project of our early education—whenever we scan it we adumbrate
reading aloud. So lifelong habit makes us want to have Lady Fredigonde's voice solicit a person, Bridget, and the missing punctuation
will not let us.

Here, likewise, is a minor heroine the words will not let us warm to:

> A lovely tall young lady it was, of a most drooping and dreamy pres-
> ence—most modest of *Merveilleuses* that ever stepped upon a palpitat-
> ing planet screwed into position by a cruel polarity of sex—in conse-
> quence compelled to advertise a neck of ivory, nipples of coral, a
> jewelled ankle of heart-breaking beauty-line—extremities, for the rest,

[13]*The Apes of God*, London, 1930, 22–24. I am using the beautiful 1981 Black Sparrow
Press reprint.

superbly plantigrade—a miracle of blunt-heeled—metatarsally-dominant—proportion—under the arch of whose trotter a fairy coach made out of a cobnut could be readily driven.[14]

We do well not to warm; "she" is Daniel Boleyn in drag. Still, the parodic mechanism repays inspection: all those paratactic dashes, where custom would enjoin subordinate structures; that palpitation, attributed to a planet; the word "palpitating" in connivance with the word "screwed"; the lascivious focus on the *feet*, "a miracle," its ecstasy dashed by the pork-butcher's word, "trotter." This sentence goes about its analytic business—the burdens "cruel polarity" can lay on a girl—all the while recalling, but refusing to endorse or duplicate, much homage to loveliness lying about in books for any literate reader to supply in paraphrase:

> Her azure veins, her alabaster skin,
> Her coral lips, her snow-white dimpled chin. . . .[15]

One writer Lewis knew thoroughly was Shakespeare; and—"azure," "alabaster," "coral," "snow"—by convention, Shakespeare's Lucrece is complimented by the seeming assertion that such are her components. We may entertain a momentary suspicion that such a convention is exceedingly odd; does it not protect a Lucrece as synthetic, on the page, as was Bestre? What a baroque agglomeration is Lucrece!

It was by pretending not to understand the literary conventions of English, and the normal ways to construct or punctuate English sentences, that Lewis cast doubt on the normal world they conjure: the world of jolly Jack Falstaff, bluff Sam Johnson, heroines with coral lips, Lloyd George the Welsh Wizard, Lord Peter Wimsey, Lady Chatterley. "That Johnson was a sort of god to his biographer we readily see. But Falstaff as well is a sort of english god, like the rice-bellied gods of laughter of China. They are illusions hugged and lived in; little dead totems. Just as all gods are a repose for humanity, the big religions an immense refuge and rest, so are these little grotesque fetishes":[16] so he put that part of his case in 1927, in the course of

[14] *Apes of God*, 455.
[15] *The Rape of Lucrece*, ll. 419–20.
[16] *The Complete Wild Body*, 151. Subsequent references will be abbreviated CWB and will be given parenthetically in the text.

rephrasing his 1917 "Inferior Religions," an essay T. S. Eliot had called "the most indubitable evidence of genius, the most powerful piece of imaginative thought, of anything that Mr. Lewis has written."[17] That had been at the outset of the "modernist" enterprise in England, when they were trying to write English as knowingly as if it were a foreign language—the way Flaubert had written French—and part of Eliot's polemic strategy had been to call (in vain) for someone with a first-hand opinion of Shakespeare. One kind of first-hand opinion would be an intelligent barbarian's. But "little dead totems": such are the deliverances of canonized literature. Educated minds are furnished with little else.

Great danger lay in the inability of educated minds to distinguish these cherished totems from more sinister abstractions. "Media creations," we are accustomed now to say of people who woo votes and wield power. Lewis preceded us by two generations in seeing how literature and its totems create the habits whereby anyone who has learned to read apprehends public reality. He distrusted "romantic"—i.e. literary—celebrations of the primitive; he distrusted D. H. Lawrence. But the genuine primitive, in fact the illiterate: that was the "something finer than himself" that the White Man had destroyed "with his little gun, his polo-ponies and gangster-films"; in particular, Lewis might have added, with his newspapers.

So he expended his literary energies on letting us watch the strange behavior of the civilized. A man of the polo-pony set named Sigismund, who keeps a bulldog called Pym and believes in "breeding," can conduct a courtship not in the gall-wasp's disciplined way or the caveman's but only in so grotesque a fashion as this:

> She fell into his arms to signify that she would willingly become his bride. In a precarious crouch he propped her for a moment, then they both subsided on to the floor, she with her eyes closed, rendered doubly heavy by all the emotion with which she was charged. Pym, true to type, "the bulldog" at once, noticing this contretemps, and imagining that his master was being maltreated by this person whom he had disliked from the first, flew to the rescue. He fixed his teeth in her eighteenth-century bottom. She was removed, bleeding, in a titanic faint. (CWB, 164)

[17]Reviewing *Tarr* in *The Egoist*, September 1918; quoted in *The Complete Wild Body*, 148.

Burlesque? But observe the decorum of the even sentences, their analytic detachment. "Her eighteenth-century bottom": that is an aspect the prose thinks worth noting, and it is "eighteenth-century" because she is a woman distinguished, like Pym, by documented
"breeding." (Her faints are "titanic.")

A caveman's finesse would likely have improved on Sigismund's.
Yet Sigismund, should he try to think of a caveman, would no doubt
be guided by the literary abstraction of a grunting boor. For here is Sigismund's circle, as perceived by his bride:

> They smoked bad tobacco, used funny words, their discourse was of
> their destiny, that none of them could have had any but the slenderest
> reasons for wishing to examine. They very often appeared angry, and
> habitually used a chevaleresque jargon: ill-bred, under-bred, well-
> bred; fellow, cad, boor, churl, gentleman; good form, bad form, were
> words that came out of them on hot little breaths of disdain, reproba-
> tion, or respect. (CWB, 164)

That reads like an ethologist's field-notes: *homo domesticus*, as perceived through a lens. "It is difficult," Lewis observed, "to see how the
objective truth of much that is called 'Satire' can be less true than the
truth of lyrical declamation, in praise, for instance, of a lovely mistress."[18] Elsewhere he stated roundly, "Wherever there is objective
truth there is satire." That is to say, whenever the externalizing inherent in the habits of written language so alienates us from our human
interior as to permit us to see what it is that words are saying, then it
will prove less creditable than we expect. *All* writing, in short, is satire, except insofar as it has acquired the tricks whereby nothing gets
said. These are called, collectively, "style." Let us inspect a few sentences lacking in top-hatted style.

> An animal in every respect upon the same footing as a rat or an ele-
> phant, I imagine you will agree—man, except for what the behaviour-
> ist calls his word-habit, is that and no more. . . . So really *the word*—in
> contrast to the sound or image—is the thing most proper and peculiar
> to him (the word, and laughter perhaps). That we are merely *talking*
> monkeys—rats, elephants, bullocks or geese—is obvious. It is a very
> peculiar situation! (MWA, 288)

[18]*Men Without Art*, London, 1934, 122. Subsequent references will be abbreviated MWA
and will be given parenthetically in the text.

It is indeed, and especially so since these categories are inseparable from literacy, which insists that we perceive ourselves from "outside," the outside where the written word exists, and where it situates readers, telling them "about" what cannot be *us*. (For each of us is an interior, an "I.") Perceived from outside, our activities are value-less, not to say valueless. "Regarded as great herds of performing animals," the way literature at bottom would regard us were it faithful to the logic whereby it exteriorizes the word (so enabling us to think of "species" including the human), we can not be deemed to evince any more distinction than might be observed among the whooping cranes.

Yet one of our species wrote,

> Where'er you walk, cool Gales shall fan the Glade,
> Trees, where you sit, shall crowd into a Shade:
> Where'er you tread, the blushing Flowers shall rise,
> And all things flourish where you turn your Eyes.

And he also wrote "Satires," full of "objective truth." It is not the "Atticus" or the "Sporus," but Pope's "beautiful" passage, that is most thoroughly contrived, gales, trees, and flowers obeying the fact of her presence; and she, if we search back through preceding lines for the pronoun's antecedent, is a "Nymph"! "Come, lovely Nymph, and bless the silent Hours. . . ." Why, the intelligent barbarian might ask, must an upholder of western civilization, just when he is evoking its delights, *pretend* so much?

We know that the way to answer is to invoke one of western civilization's arcane strands, the Pastoral Tradition. Lewis knew that as well as any of us. But the way of the satirist is apt to be relentless; one thing he will never let us do is appeal to a history that must be learned. (Is not "learning" a set of excuses?) Had Gulliver known a little more of history he would have been less discomfited by the Houyhnhnm objections; but Swift accords him no functional knowledge of the past—he is an archetypal barbarian—and Swift's readers are apt to have difficulty recalling the historic customs that, summoned to their aid, might enable them to be diverted instead of vexed.

Lewis likewise contrives to have us spooked by literary history, as we thrash our way through one of his arresting barbaric paragraphs.

For we are agreed that our being civilized entails the fineness of imagination that can contrive such a cadence as "Where'er you walk. . . ." You would never divine, though, Lewis insinuates, the presence of that agreement among us, if you were to watch us simply spending our time. Examine the talking monkeys, and what do you see?

> A good dinner, accompanied by as good wine as we can get hold of; a pleasant spin in the fresh air in as satisfactory a petrol-wagon as we can afford; a nice digestive round of golf; a flirtation accompanied by the rhythmical movements prompted by a nigger drum, purging us of the secretions of sex—a nice detective volume, which purges us pleasantly of the secretions proper to us in our capacity as "killers" and hunting-dogs. . . ; all these things are far more *important* than anything that can be described as "art." (MWA, 290)

Those sentences help press Lewis's reckless case home. Yet is not the barbarian observer, by definition, himself just such a creature as he observes? If these field-notes on our animal behavior describe our days well, then what can be said of the "arts" on which we vaunt ourselves? Yet if "art" is nothing for the creatures, it can also be nothing for him, or nearly nothing: he is a "creature" too. The fine arts become merely "the very fine manners of the mind," and Lewis performed the satirist's leap when he said in the next breath, calmly, that he took their value for granted. For how could that be?

It could be so in the perspective of a whole unwritten literature, from whose energies value might leap incontestably. Such a literature—vast scintillant tracts—his practice from time to time bids us imagine.

It is normal for us to imagine non-existent literature. Now and then, for a few lines at a time, poetry can hint at more than we are used to encountering, and we have all in our heads an intuited spectrum of verbal delight which but a few glints have prompted. Had we the habit likewise of canonizing rare prose paragraphs, the one I shall next quote could not be excluded; nor could anyone fail to notice how dissimilar it is not only to the prose we chew daily but to prose we are exhorted to admire.

It is a barbarian's extravaganza, composed by a newly recruited professional killer. That is to say that in 1917, newly enlisted as a bombardier, Wyndham Lewis, aged 35, is writing "Inferior Religions," no doubt by lamplight, in a Dorset army camp in 1917, and, far from his studio and from all he feasts on, is drawing for a rare moment on his deepest passions.

> But life is invisible, and perfection is not in the waves or houses that the poet sees. To rationalize that appearance is not possible. Beauty is an icy douche of ease and happiness at something *suggesting* perfect conditions for an organism: it remains suggestion. A stormy landscape, and a pigment consisting of a lake of hard, yet florid waves; delight in each brilliant scoop or ragged burst, was John Constable's beauty. Leonardo's consisted in a red rain on the shadowed side of heads, and heads of massive female aesthetes. Uccello accumulated pale parallels, and delighted in cold architecture of distinct colour. Korin found in the symmetrical gushing of water, in waves like huge vegetable insects, traced and worked faintly, on a golden pâte, his business. Cézanne liked cumbrous, democratic slabs of life, slightly leaning, transfixed in vegetable intensity. (CWB, 153)

"It remains suggestion": true of painting, that statement is true also of such writing. Even in Lewis, there is very little else like it. It suggests what writing might be in another cosmos: preempting, it goes without saying, the flaccid respect we have for our literary heritage. Its authority seems to emanate from beyond that heritage: from a world of *fauves* who do what they wish with paint, and accumulate icons of their satisfactions: not "subjects," but qualities, timeless, tirelessly reaffirmed. That is the world of the eye: the world to which writing aspires, but from the riches of which it is debarred.

Vision, wrote Merleau-Ponty, "vision dissects."[19] So it does, and when writing delivered language to the eye it rendered all words dissective: analytical: Aristotelian. They slide: they unravel: they are systems of self-deceit. Dissection, turned against Man, is a terrible thing; and, once they are moved into the domain of scrutiny, written words have an ineluctable proclivity for showing man up as a talking ape. But "style"—a shared system of agreements not to notice the bleak thing written language implies, has for centuries served to conceal so

[19]Quoted by Ong, *Orality and Literacy*, 72.

stark an outcome. And "style" is a set of conventions derived from history.

But the eye denies history: what it sees is *now*. "A philosophy of the EYE," was how Lewis described his satirist's approach; "the wisdom of the eye, rather than that of the ear" (MWA, 118, 128). The true barbarian is an ear-man, illiterate. Lewis's barbaric pose ("older than the fish") was that of a literate, sophisticated eye-man, seeking homeopathic remedy for distortions introduced by the eye.

It distorts, but it need not. History may be an excuse, but it need not be. The root problem is time, in which history is embedded; death-bound, we lack time. If "Wherever there is objective truth there is satire," that is because imperfect man, whenever, pen in hand, he is being objective, cannot long sustain such a vision as phrased "red rain on the shadowed side of heads" or "cumbrous democratic slabs of life"; or, for that matter, such an acoustic delicacy as ". . . all Earth flourish where you turn your Eyes."

1984

Going to Hell

DANTE: THE DIVINE COMEDY, *a new verse translation by C. H. Sisson. Manchester: Carcanet New Press Ltd, 1980. 455 pp.*

DANTE'S PURGATORY, *translated with notes and commentary by Mark Musa. Indiana University Press, 1981. 373 pp.*

DANTE ALIGHIERI, THE DIVINE COMEDY, *translated, with commentary, by Charles Singleton. 6 vols. Princeton University Press, 1970.*

DANTE, INFERNO, *a new verse translation by Allen Mandelbaum. University of California Press, 1980. 307 pp.*

One of this century's more improbable sellers was a pocket-sized book that J. M. Dent of London published at a shilling the year before the century opened: *The Paradiso of Dante Alighieri* on 418 small pages, Italian text on the left, an English crib on the right, with many diligent notes. You must search through fine print at the back to discover who made the translation: a clergyman named Wicksteed, who claimed nothing for it save that it would guide you through the Italian whether you knew Italian or not. A little Latin would do, or a little French.

He and his publisher calmly supposed that they were meeting a demand, and they were right. *Inferno* and *Purgatorio* soon followed, then reprint after reprint: 1900, 1901, 1903, 1904, 1908, 1910, 1912 . . . These were not schoolbooks; their sale graphs a passion for Dante, which did not begin to slacken until after the Great War. Were the passionate numbered in thousands or tens of thousands? How large were those printings? J. M. Dent won't say. Such information, they huffily rejoin, is kept confidential "between publisher and author." This implies that royalty statements go annually to Ravenna, where the author's bones have now moldered for 660 years.

For make no mistake, the Temple Classics Dante is Dante's book, not Wicksteed's (who himself, for that matter, has been dead for fifty-four years). Wicksteed merely holds your hand while you ponder words Dante wrote in a tongue you may never have studied.

L'amor che move il sole e l' altre stelle: just a little school French lets you be persuaded by Wicksteed that this, yes, says, "the Love that moves the sun and the other stars." *L'amor* can recall *l'amour* (*toujours*), and *il sole* something solar, indeed the weatherman's Old Sol, and *stelle* would be stellar things, stars . . .

That's not a game you can play with Homer, whose Greek remains perfectly impenetrable unless you undertake its cold-blooded study. As for Virgil, not even three years of Latin grammar prepares most students for his crossword puzzles, no word in its expected place. Dante is unique: the great poet whom enthusiasts who lack his language are apt to feel they can almost read.

The young T. S. Eliot was such an enthusiast. At Harvard he taught himself Dante out of the Temple edition, and would recite aloud whole cantos of *Paradise* he did not know how to pronounce, "lying in bed or on a railway journey." This was a self-study substitute for the famous Dante course that Harvard offered for more than a hundred years. Its first professor (1836) was Longfellow the poet, and the main business of its students was to read through the *Divine Comedy* in a year, whether they understood Italian or not. (Like Eliot, they mostly had high-school French and Latin.)

Eliot came to think Dante "extremely easy to read," though for reasons unrelated to his language, which a larger acquaintance with Italian eventually persuaded him was far from being as simple as it looked. No, Dante was accessible because not quirky: he wrote with a peculiar directness, one clear visual fact succeeding another, and he wrote in an intellectually unified Europe when poets were not expending energy to demonstrate their own way of differing from all other poets. American poets—look at Emily Dickinson—have always tended to do that, and it was easy for Eliot, an American who sought a neutral idiom, to indulge in groundless nostalgia for a lost unity.

Translators no longer assume that what you want is help with the Italian. What you want is Dante-in-English, and it is also widely assumed that getting him into English, though a lot of work, is in principle straightforward. Fidelity will give us poetry.

We may call this the Eliot Illusion, and C. H. Sisson is one who entertains it. A British poet who first encountered Dante in Eliot's 1929 essay and subsequently carried the Temple *Inferno* in his wartime knapsack, he has now published what is billed as "a new verse translation" of the whole *Comedy*, in which he relies on Dante's left-to-right syntax and on his own willingness to put lots of syllables into one line, not so many into another.

Sisson asks us to believe that Ulysses exhorting his crew could have sounded like this:

> "Brothers," I said, "who through a hundred thousand
> Dangers at last have reached the occident;
> To this short vigil which is all there is
>
> Remaining to our senses, do not deny
> Experience, following the course of the sun,
> Of that world which has no inhabitants.
>
> Consider then the race from which you have sprung:
> You were not made to live like animals,
> But to pursue virtue and natural science."

Printed as prose, this would be lamentably contorted, and being printed as verse doesn't help it. And the diction! "Natural science," forsooth. Would that be physics and chemistry? No, Dante's *cano-*

scenza is just "knowledge," what you pursue with your mind, the way *virtute*, the conduct becoming to men, is what you pursue with your will. But Mr. Sisson wants us to know that he knows about theological knowledge as well, and knows, too, that the pagan Ulysses wasn't after that kind.

And no seaman ever said "occident." Though Dante's word in a language descended from Latin is *occidente* (it remembers *sol occidens*, the setting sun), in English we say "west."

Not that Sisson is deaf to idiom. He contemns the idiomatic vagaries of one of his predecessors, Laurence Binyon, who permitted himself words like "poesy." Sisson was alive and adult, he says, in 1934, when Binyon's *Inferno* appeared, and "can testify that this was not the language of the period." True, people in 1934 didn't say "ye." Yet Binyon gave these words wings:

> "Brothers," I said, "who manfully, despite
> Ten thousand perils, have attained the West,
> In the brief vigil that remains of light
> To feel in, stoop not to renounce the quest
> Of what may in the sun's path be essayed,
> The world that never mankind hath possessed.
> Think on the seed ye spring from! Ye were made
> Not to live life of brute beasts of the field
> But follow virtue and knowledge unafraid."

Today Binyon's infelicities ("brief vigil that remains of light / To feel in") are brandished to horrify us with the messes that a decision to reproduce Dante's rhyming can get a man into, but when his version works, as it does hereabouts, it's the rhyme that enables it. In sounding the line endings, rhyme can zone off the phrases, tell you where to pause, assert emphasis, show how a speech is articulated. Lacking both rhyme and a decisive meter, versions like Sisson's leave you perpetually groping after cues to the shape of the sentence, never mind that the translator has felt free to write down simple words in a simple order.

Dante was the greatest of rhymers, and rhyme these days is in bad repute. Mark Musa, whose *Inferno* of 1971 has just been joined by a *Purgatorio*, thinks rhyme is no good at all. The very thought of it makes him sound like Cotton Mather shunning a gin mill, expressing "horror" at its "paralyzing potentiality." Avoiding it, he (alas) felt free to pour over his pages sentences like this:

> The day was fading and the darkening air
> was releasing all the creatures on our earth
> from their daily tasks, and I, one man alone,
> was making ready to endure the battle
> of the journey, and of the pity it involved,
> which my memory, unerring, shall now retrace.

"Our" is a line filler, so is "daily," so is "it involved"; and hark to the buzz of monosyllabic midges, which can clutter English so perceptibly when verse puts the single words on exhibition! Far better Charles Singleton's unpretentious prose: "Day was departing, and the dark air was taking the creatures on earth from their labors; and I alone was making ready to sustain the strife, both of the journey and of the pity, which unerring memory shall retrace." The word count shrinks by 20 percent; the sentence is firm.

Professor Singleton, in volumes published a decade ago by Princeton University Press, does us Wicksteed's kind of service, guiding us through an Italian text that has benefited by the best modern editing, and though today's costs price his services at $30 the volume, against Wicksteed's shilling, Dante is surely worth the outlay: $180, including three volumes of wondrously erudite commentary.

Dollar for dollar, Princeton/Singleton fetches you more than the Indiana/Musa *Purgatory* at $27.50, for which you get notes but no Italian, just a translation that tells less about Dante than about the difficulties of being straightforward in English.

All those little dead words! Yet they can be avoided. Allen Mandelbaum avoids them.

> The day was now departing; the dark air
> released the living beings of the earth
> from work and weariness; and I myself
> alone prepared to undergo the battle
> both of the journeying and of the pity,
> which memory, mistaking not, shall show.

"Prepared" is better than Musa's "was making ready," better because shorter. "Both of the journeying and of the pity" has a dignity and balance absent from "of the journey and of the pity it involved." Small matters, but readability is the sum of numerous small felicities.

As for "work and weariness," that phrase unpacks *fatiche*, which contains both of them. As for "I myself alone," it stand for *io sol uno*, which Mandelbaum designates "the first triple repetition of an 'I' that we have in Western writing." He adds that it is "steeped in the certainty of fame."

That is important. Mandelbaum's Dante is not Eliot's at all: not the impersonal scribe of a long-gone unity, but an affirmer of the supremeness of his own supreme fictions, "the swiftest and most succussive of savants, forever rummaging in his vast and versal haversack of soughs and rasps and gusts and 'harsh and scrannel rhymes'" for just the studied inelegance that will grate on our senses and certify like a cat's scratch to his credibility.

This sense of his author is what quickens Mandelbaum's reach for the opportune.

> Just as the lizard, when it darts from hedge
> to hedge, beneath the dog days' giant lash,
> seems, if it cross one's path, a lightning flash. . . .

Wait, did a rhyme flash? Yes, it did. Was "lash" a word patched in to set up the rhyme? No, it's Dante's *fersa* exactly. Does Mandelbaum rhyme consistently? No, just when it suits him. Examine his opening:

> When I had journeyed half of our life's way,
> I found myself within a shadowed forest,
> for I had lost the path that does not stray.
> Ah, it is hard to speak of what it was,
> that savage forest, dense and difficult,
> which even in recall renews my fear:
> so bitter—death is hardly more severe!

"Way"/"stray," "fear"/"severe"; and the consonance of "forest" and "was." On the same page there are assonances ("rise," "lithe," "hide," to terminate successive lines), off-rhymes ("spent" and "present"), alliterative stitchings, devices to clutch words into expressive clusters and persuade us of studied but living speech. If everyone else can display one detail or another done better, still Mandelbaum's seems for now the English Dante of choice.

Inferno (with the other two parts scheduled within eighteen months) is priced at $24.95, and there'll be three volumes of commentary too, setting the "California Dante" squarely in competition with Princeton/Singleton and Indiana/Musa. The strife of three universities for his fame, on a continent not yet dreamed of when he died, must gratify Dante's restless, emulous shade. To augment its fortune in the quality of its translation, California offers what it can do, when it likes, better than any other American press, a piece of sumptuous book design, embellished with forty-two splendidly mannered drawings by Barry Moser, a New England artist whose "Cerberus" can make your flesh creep.

Nothing, needless to say, beats the Italian. For help with it go to Singleton. For a decent substitute try Mandelbaum. But do not suppose that, contrary to Ezra Pound's caution, by any route you will get through hell in a hurry.

1981

Beckett at Eighty

Beckett can invade your mind with a single phrase: "You go dumb as well and sounds fade." Those vowels, that pacing, weave Coleridgean magic. I'd no sooner met just those eight words on the second page of *Molloy* than I knew I must write a book. He's had a like effect on many people; Beckett Books accumulate like Napoleon Books. There are likely more words written about Sam Beckett than about any other living man. I'll refrain from estimating how many of them make profitable reading. The point is, they all seemed necessary writing.

It's not as though he were a public personality. As everybody knows, he won't be interviewed. He eschews "the literary life." Even Joyce ("indifferent, paring his fingernails") seems garrulous by contrast. Joyce had tropes and schemes to expound; to explain that he was writing a book based on the *Odyssey* was one way to keep the curious a safe distance from the emotional core he cared about. Beckett, though, has no such periphery. He writes, he'd have us believe, in a kind of anguished trance; far from being contrived, the fine symmetries grow secretly.

"Happiness, too, yes, there was that too, unhappily": that wears a look of Archimedean engineering, the first word foreseeing the last, the very hesitations calculated; but he likely couldn't tell you how it was done.

"I preferred France at war to Ireland at peace": that's one of his famous phrases. "I made it just in time." He made it back to France, that is to say, just before the gates of Occupation clanged shut. Looked at from one angle, the maneuver has a Buster Keaton look: a deadpan rendezvous with disaster. But your man of genius makes no mistakes. It was in wartime France that he found his material. His real career starts post-war. *Waiting for Godot* is very nearly a fable of the Occupation.

People sleep in ditches and aren't surprised to be beaten. A man and his servant, laden with possessions, are in flight from somewhere to somewhere. Everything was different "a million years ago, in the nineties." And two people are to meet a third whom they know only by a single name, a code-name as it were; they don't know why they're to meet him, but it matters. If the assignation fails they're to try again in 24 hours, meanwhile hanging about as inconspicuously as possible. It takes little insight to recognize details from some tale about Resistance groups, where the less anyone knew the better for all concerned.

Beckett played a modest role in a Resistance cell, which was compromised when someone broke under inquisition. That's easily connected with one of his obsessive situations, the man talking in the presence of shadowy inquisitors who will only relent when he finally says the right thing. (Can he dream up a lie they'll accept as the right thing?) *The Unnamable*'s "I can't go on, I'll go on" would be a natural thought for someone in that spot. In *Play* three people are led over the same story again and again, under spotlights. Gestapo grillers reputedly made much use of such lights. Yet *Play* was rebuked for imperfect contact with reality.

For, seeing a Beckett play, reading a Beckett text, no one thinks, "The Occupation!" The "power of the text to claw"—another of his quotable phrases—arises precisely from his way of unhooking it from historical particulars, leaving something as vivid as a bad dream, as oppressive, as inescapable. In a corner of the dreaming mind lurks awareness of what it dreams about; the agony of the nightmare consists in being tormented by such knowledge, unsustained by hope of making contact with it.

Beckett's situations, likewise, seem time and again almost literally transcribed from experience, public experience; yet they wear the look of perverse and unmoored fantasies. And a part of the mind says, No, this is how it is. Much of life is waiting. Much of talk is *making* talk. Much of living is a long dying. "I shall soon be quite dead at last in spite of all," commences *Malone Dies*, almost jauntily. Later, "I have lost my stick. That is perhaps the principal event of the day." Everyone has known such days, and such events.

His voice is both mellifluous and metallic, his sentences are careful and beautiful, his courtesy is unfailing. Back when I first got in touch with him, in 1958, on my very first trip to France, he'd become so much the prisoner of his own scrupulousness that all mail went unanswered; for to make a start by answering today's correspondent would compound his neglect of all the preceding ones. And to begin at the bottom of the pile, with the first letter he'd neglected long ago, and work his way up to today's mail at the top, was something he could not face. So he was doing nothing at all about his mail. He might have been one of his own characters. How to get in touch with him?

As it happened, I'd bethought me to revive fading idioms by reading something French on the plane; in the Montreal airport I'd bought a French crime novel. On an early page, by way of local color, its author alluded to the *pneumatique*. That was news to me: a system of tubes running through the famous sewers, linking postal depot with postal depot. You bought a blue form, it seemed (the novel set out the words you'd use, and the fee); your message rode in a cylinder through the tube to where a boy with a bicycle could hand-deliver it. And—my heart leaped up—the boy would ask, Was there to be any reply?

That seemed the way to circumvent Sam Beckett's accumulating guilt-inducing stack of mail. At a PTT, I recited the phrase from the book and tendered the coins. The form was duly produced, and I was soon watching a tube gulp my message to Sam. Back at my hotel I awaited some consequence: what came was a responding *pneu* with a telephone number to be rung at 5. At 5:01 I rang it. (The very digits were Beckettian—0011). A firm voice asked, would I come by, or would I like him to come to me. Naturally I elected to visit him in his habitat. And that, for me, was the beginning of that.

What I'd done was trust fiction as a guide to life: improbable fiction at that, come to think of it. The tubes, the boy on the bicycle, the Cartesian number: such a web, with a man at the center too scrupulous to answer his mail, seems just such a dream-universe as Beckett might have invented. But it hadn't needed inventing. It was all true, and someone's fiction about part of it was coherent enough to rely on. To transform it all into one of Beckett's worlds you have only to subtract the rest of Paris, the way he subtracted the War from the world of *Godot*.

And that is the way Beckett's works achieve their coherence. Feeling little need to invent, he disorients by simply omitting. All of Ireland (or is it France?) has been omitted from *Molloy*, save for a few hills and roads, a wood, a shore, a bicycle or so, a police station—features like those, with no visible community sustaining them. In a Beckett book you'll not chance upon helpful facts such as I found in the *roman policier*: he leaves little just lying around. Frequently he will subtract the entire universe save for the contents of one bleak room. The resulting plight seems unthinkable.

Yet his plights are always thinkable somewhere, if only in some Gulag. Yes, the procession of men crawling through mud in *How It Is*—even that is thinkable, as you realize if you imagine it signed "Solzhenitsyn." Beckett simply (simply!) gives it to us sans Gulag. The work he saves by not inventing worlds goes into the austere phrase, the shapely period: the domain of order humans can still control when all else is uncontrollable—when all is death outside the "shelter" (*Endgame*), when the earth has seemingly ceased to revolve (*Happy Days*), when day after day Godot neglects to come. Solzhenitsyn, at least as seen through his translators, pays little heed to local elegance. Beckett is *all* local elegance. "What's keeping us here?" cries the actor playing Clov; and the actor playing Hamm replies, "The dialogue." You can't improve on the accuracy of that. (And they'd be positively tortured by a long run—by "success.")

That by and large what seems to matter is uncontrollable would

seem to be his working assumption. So he busies himself with the local order of language, and with pertinent ancillary detail. Its minute
ordering grows oddly comic, as though on the sinking *Titanic* door-
knobs went on being polished. (The planet of *Happy Days* crumbles,
and Winnie fusses with grammar.) One night he was worrying aloud
about a production of *Endgame* he would soon oversee in London. The
trouble was, the stage was far bigger than he had conceived. That
would spoil the trapped feel of things? I ventured. No, he said, you
can get claustrophobia in a big place as well as a small. (That was
something he seemed to *know*.) The trouble was with Clov's speech as
he moved his ladder from window to window. With the windows set
further apart, there were, as Sam saw it, three options. Clov could run
out of words before he ran out of steps. Or he could be supplied with
more words. Or he could speak the existing words more slowly. It
would have to be one of those three, and each of them altered an equilibrium.

I don't know which he elected. But it exemplifies thousands of
problems he's put to himself, in just that analytic way. And however
he solved it, there will have been spectators present who stirred to a
precise depiction of the human condition, and two or three who may
even have started writing books. They'll have supposed he was peer-
ing deep into man's plight. No, he was pondering a symmetry of
words and paces. That may mirror man's plight just as well as any philosophy, in that every solution has unsatisfactory aspects. And if it's
trivial, then so is the *Divine Comedy*, worrying at its threes and its
thirty-threes and its threefold reversion to stars.

1986

POSTSCRIPT

August 28, 1989. Sam is in a nursing home. I've been prepared for the
worst. He has always belittled (a) his health; (b) his state of literary
preparedness. As to his health, he proves to be a very spry 83-year-
old, mind perfectly clear, body no more sparse than I've always remembered it. *Stirrings Still* has just been published, in a hideously expensive Limited Edition. A trade edition is to come. It's palpably a

meditation on his own death. ("Oh all to end": its last words.) It has
1,906 words exactly, and he was born on Good Friday the Thirteenth,
1906. Sam smilingly denies having counted the words, notwithstanding that the count came out to 1,906 thanks to a dropped hyphen
once in one hyphenated expression to make it two words just once.
Sam could be exasperatingly denying.

He's made a French translation (*Soubresauts*), and he talks about
the difficulties with that. "Bourne" in English makes you think of
Hamlet's soliloquy:

> That undiscovered country, from whose bourne
> No traveller returns. . . .

He'd used the word, with that intent, in *Stirrings Still*. But "borne," a
French word, says nothing of the kind: just boundary, margin. Sam
had always been most at ease talking technicalities. (Though he
didn't say what, if anything, he'd done about "bourne.")

We make plans (now empty) to meet the coming summer. We chat
of this and that. Chat gets round to Yeats (Jack), one of whose paintings Sam once owned and prized. From Jack we drift, inevitably, to
William Butler. William Butler Yeats, the Great Founder! Ireland's
greatest poet, also the creator of an establishment in which the author
of *Malone Dies* would have had no room. And, suddenly . . .

I'll remember this all my life. Sam Beckett's gaze is fixed upward, to
my right. His voice thins and lightens: "Now shall I make my
soul. . . ." I respond, "Compelling it to study." And Sam, a gentle
smile on his face, continues, line by line, requiring no prompting:

> In a learned school
> Till the wreck of body,
> Slow decay of blood,
> Testy delirium
> Or dull decrepitude,
> Or what worse evil come—
> The death of friends, or death
> Of every brilliant eye
> That made a catch in the breath—
> Seem but the clouds of the sky

When the horizon fades;
Or a bird's sleepy cry
Among the deepening shades.

That is Yeats, in 1926, meditating on his own death, which seemed to impend. (He would soon be critically ill with something called Malta fever, but he recovered.) And Sam is not performing, not reciting. (I never, ever, heard him perform, recite, even quote.) His gaze elsewhere than on me, he is communing with the words, calling them in one by one, stating them in that thin rhapsodic voice, feeling his way syllable by syllable to those deepening shades.

We say Good-bye, and alas, it *was* Good-bye. We were to have met again in June. But the man who was born on Good Friday the Thirteenth '06 was buried the day after Christmas Day '89.

Oh—something he imparted that last day—there's no longer a *pneumatique*.

1990

Sweet Seventeen

LETTERS HOME *by Sylvia Plath, selected and edited with commentary by Aurelia Schober Plath. Harper & Row, 1975. 502 pp.*

As a high-school senior Sylvia Plath was already selling verse and fiction to *Seventeen* and *Mademoiselle*. She was writing in her diary sentences like, "Never, never, never will I reach the perfection I long for with all my soul—my paintings, my poems, my stories—all poor, poor reflections . . . for I have been too thoroughly conditioned to the conventional surroundings of this community . . ."; and also, "*Now, now* is the perfect time of my life."

That sounds like the heroine of a *Seventeen* story on a jag of affirmation, and also like a million adolescent diarists. In 1950 it wasn't her fluency that set Sylvia Plath apart, nor her (quite commonplace) intensity of feeling, but that knack for commercial fiction and the quite exceptional persistence that learned from countless rejections not so much how to write as what the magazines were buying.

An unusual girl, but not altogether unusual. She might have grown into a good, tough, middle-aged soap-opera scripter; there are worse destinies. She'd have remembered how to "do" the girl she once was, a valuable character to have on tap.

No, what is unusual is to find her, at 24, by then a graduate of Smith, in Cambridge (England) on a Fulbright, still pouring out the *Seventeen* idiom: "Oh, mother, if only you knew how I am forging a soul! . . . I am fighting, fighting, and am making a self, in great pain, often, as for a birth, but it is right that it should be so, for I am being refined in the fires of pain and love."

One looks round in bewilderment for signs of the pain, but she seems effervescently, even relentlessly, outgoing. As to that: "I am glad that I am outgoing and open and intense now, because I can slice into the depths of people more quickly and more rewardingly than if I were superficial or formal."

This suggests that if you didn't want your depths sliced into you'd keep clear of her, but nobody seems to have. She was a happy, gregarious girl. She wasn't, evidently, slicing. She merely cherished the belief that she was. She cherished every belief that appalling idiom embalms: that a man she met in Greenwich Village was "the most wonderful, brilliant man in the world," that a Smith prof was "the most brilliant, enchanting man I've ever known," that an editor at *Mademoiselle* was "the most brilliant, clever woman I've ever known," that one afternoon at Cherbourg shows you "why the French produce painters: all pink and turquoise, quaint and warm with life"; that *The New Yorker* for verse and the *Ladies' Home Journal* for prose were Platonic norms of literary aspiration; that Phyllis McGinley even was a poetic norm, not incompatible, apparently, with "my beloved Yeats"; and much, much more. Nabokov should be writing this story?

But it's a tragic story, everybody knows: more poignantly so than Scott Fitzgerald's, whose suicide took him decades. One strand of the tragedy, imperceptible till we had this book of letters, was the absolute coextensiveness of her thoughts and feelings with an immature style in which she could be fluent, and not in adolescence merely but right up to her thirtieth year.

Writers grow up because they cannot say what they feel, and need to learn how; in learning, they do not simply acquire an instrument, they educe and shape unguessed rigors of feeling as well.

But what if some unholy symbiosis between New York editorial professionalism and the Great American Teenage Aspiration has fabricated for your use a brilliant Lego-block idiom in which you can really, truly, at every moment, feel confident that your words are sincere? What if Daisy Miller had possessed both genius and a charter subscription to *Seventeen*? And met and married that remarkable man Ted Hughes? (Not even Sylvia's mother was a more extraordinary person than Ted Hughes.)

What happened between Sylvia Plath and Ted Hughes is none of our business, though we can't help guessing a little. He took her verbal skills in hand, evidently, and she gained access to whole provinces of language (later, alone, she would draw on their riches). She had notions that she was taking *him* in hand: "To find such a man, to make him into the best man the world has seen: such a life work!" The marriage lasted six years. When he suddenly left she was a few months short of thirty. We can see no sign, till the very moment he has left, that anything is wrong.

No sign. The household Ted was to find intolerable is theme for Sylvia's usual unmodulated burble. She recites the *Canterbury Tales* for twenty minutes to a field full of cows. She worries about Strontium 90. They settle into a thatched cottage in Devon. They write, they attend the Anglican chapel evensong, Ted puts up shelves . . . Did he suddenly tire of being trapped in a *Seventeen* story? It's none of our business; I mean that. He leaves.

And just as suddenly, alone, Sylvia Plath undergoes the mutation that enforces the claim of this story on our attention. She takes to rising at four and working on poems till eight ("a poem a day and they are terrific": appallingly exact word). She renounces the old slick norms ("It is much more help for me to know that people are divorced and go through hell, than to hear about happy marriages. Let the *Ladies' Home Journal* blither about those").

The poems would one day be published in a book called *Ariel*: a book unlike any other in the language: an equivocal work of genius: cunningly shaped, seemingly the long shrill cry from the white flame at the heart of the crematorium. (That was 4 A.M. work. Afternoon letters burble still: "I want to study, learn history, politics, languages, travel. I want to be the most loving and fascinating mother in the world.")

She and two children moved back from Devon to London, to a flat in a building in which (this was important) Yeats had lived: a flat with pine bookcases, rush matting, Hong Kong chairs, a little glass-topped table, straw and black iron, even a lilac hyacinth: also the gas oven into which, on Lincoln's birthday, 1963, she thrust her head.

1976

Nabokov
(Tyrants Destroyed)

TYRANTS DESTROYED AND OTHER STORIES, *by Vladimir Nabokov. McGraw-Hill, 1975. 288 pp.*

Like Oscar Wilde and Charles Kinbote, Nabokov plays—has been playing now for many decades—a game to which self-appreciation is intrinsic. His invented selves even appreciate one another. John Ray, Jr., Ph.D. in his foreword to *Lolita* tells us how to admire what Humbert Humbert accomplished in the 69 chapters of the narrative proper: "How magically his singing violin can conjure up a tendresse, a compassion for Lolita that makes us entranced with the book while abhorring its author!" Then Vladimir Nabokov, closing the huge parenthesis, supplies for our retrospective delectation in an afterword an inventory of the more magical bits: not the "good parts" of a porn novel—that's the list he's parodying—but Lolita playing tennis, or "the tinkling sounds of the valley town coming up the mountain trail (on which I caught the first known female of *Lycaeides sublivens* Nabokov)."

(If we want to know where that trail *really* was, incidentally, we shall have to track down the museum where that specimen is kept with its locality label. He drops the hint, cites two possible museums, and prompts us to imagine "some twenty-first century scholar with a taste for recondite biography" who shall devote a career to such errands.)

Ada concludes with a lyrical blurb for itself. The introduction to a reprinted *Bend Sinister* lists allusions no one seems to have noticed the first time around. The introduction to a revised *Speak Memory* prompts us to turn up a sentence deep in the book—"The ranks of words I reviewed were again so glowing, with their puffed-out little chests and trim uniforms. . . ."—and discern buried there "the name of a great cartoonist and a tribute to him."

All reviewers, it seems, missed that one. Reviewers—torpid folk, and with deadlines—don't pick up Nabokov sentences one by one, as they're meant to be picked up, nor marvel at their iridescences, tap them for false bottoms, check them for anagrams. His only fit reader is finally himself ("It is only the author's private satisfaction that counts"), and the rest of us should wait to speak until we're spoken to—as we are being, constantly, by all those notes and prefaces.

Now on with the motley: *Tyrants Destroyed*, 13 stories scooped out of the past, 12 of them out of his remote Russian-language past when he went as "V. Sirin"; and lo, a foreword apprises us that his *oeuvre* has been accorded a full-dress bibliography and reminds us (cryptically) that he also wrote *Lolita*. The bang-you're-dead reviewer will lower his cocked index and think twice before pronouncing stories so sponsored dismayingly empty, especially as Nabokov has more than once slipped in ahead of him, anticipating doubts but leaving them equivocal.

For instance, the fourth story, "Music," is called in its headnote "a trifle singularly popular with translators." This phrase conceals several false bottoms. Translators fall for my trifles. You are about to read a story that has been—so to speak—around. You are about to see a *real* job of translating ("by Dmitri Nabokov in collaboration with the author"). And since I present "Music" here with a certain amount of circumstantial fuss, including the date of its Russian-language appearance in a Paris émigré daily, you will understand "trifle" correctly; I, who also wrote *Ada* and *Pale Fire*, am entitled to call this story a trifle.

The story? Some 2,000 words about an unmusical man at a concert who spots his former wife and while they sit silent, 20 feet from each other, must let the music—formally meaningless to him—shape his reliving of a past he had shut away. Phrases like "How long ago it all seemed!" and "What bliss it had been" and "We can't go on like this" suggest a trifle indeed, unworthy of the master illusionist. Then she slips away, and then the name of the piece of music is revealed: "'What you will,' said Boke in the apprehensive whisper of a rank outsider. '*A Maiden's Prayer*, or the *Kreutzer Sonata*. Whatever you will.'"

Careful—Beethoven's sonata shares its title with a Tolstoy fiction. Check *that* out, O researcher of the twenty-first century. And Beware of the Labyrinth.

So it goes. These are, generally, trick stories with a twist at the end, of the old-fashioned magazine kind. One—"The Vane Sisters," already several times printed—has an acrostic in the last paragraph, implanted there by two dead girls of whose collaboration the narrator is supposed to be unaware. The headnote apprises us to watch for it. "This particular trick can be tried only once in a thousand years of fiction. Whether it has come off is another question." (But by prompting us, the sly author has *made* it come off.)

In another, dating from 1926, a lady devil offers a timid voyeur all the girls he shall covet between noon and midnight, gathered and placed at his complete disposal, provided only that the total number be odd. (Trick ending: His tally is 13, but one girl got counted twice.) Nabokov, anticipating groans, passes this tale off as "a rather artificial affair, composed a little hastily, with more concern for the tricky plot than for imagery and good taste." Lest we hasten to agree he also remarks that it therefore "required some revamping here and there in the English version," readers of which are being spooked into discerning imagery and good taste.

A readier way to profit from this story ("A Nursery Tale") is to discern in its plot, albeit half a century old, the Nabokov Theme full-bodied, a theme that has sustained story after story, novel after novel. A way of stating it, almost but not quite too general to be of use, is this: *A man almost possesses what he seeks, but loses it because of a quirk in the conditions.* (The Tithonus story, or a fairy-tale plot; no wonder it can be made to seem Protean.)

In the story the quirk was simple: The Devil meant an odd number of girls, the man toted up an odd number of encounters. In the novels it is apt to be more complex. The quester changes, or his object (*Lolita*). He becomes enmeshed in a larger design of his quarry (*Pale Fire; The Real Life of Sebastian Knight*). Or the author has contrived an unthinkable exaction: the unpayable price of Pnin's tenure (*Pnin*) would have been service under a long-ago trifler with his fiancée.

The *Pnin* case is instructive. Since this parvenu is also the novel's narrator, unmasking his steely smile in the final chapter, there to dispose of Pnin's destiny much as the author does, he very nearly fuses with the author, or with what the author has called elsewhere "an anthropomorphic deity impersonated by me." ("I have finished building a world," says the novelist Sebastian Knight, "and this is my Sabbath rest.")

Those beautiful involuted sentences, which are Nabokov's hallmark, are ways to build a world, not ways to describe one. "Without any wind blowing, the sheer weight of a raindrop, shining in parasitic luxury on a cordate leaf, caused its tip to dip, and what looked like a globule of quicksilver performed a sudden glissando down the center vein, and then, having shed its bright load, the relieved leaf unbent. Tip, leaf, dip, relief. . . ." Between book covers, there is no leaf and no raindrop until the creator has done all that.

And as a narrator who fuses with V. Nabokov effects the destiny of Pnin, so what *happens* in these big and little worlds is what V. Nabokov has decreed shall happen, right down to the passage of an "inquisitive butterfly" across a tennis court in "Champion, Colorado," between Humbert Humbert and Dolores Haze; in a paragraph all to itself.

It is he, Nabokov, who is Humbert's "McFate"; he (not a dead girl) who planted the acrostic in "The Vane Sisters"; he who arranged the arithmetical misfortune of the timid voyeur; he who has equipped such a roster of his creatures with faulty hearts, and decreed that the heart of Ivanov in the story "Perfection" should fail when it did (for particulars see the story). Grown bolder, he has recreated space and time: The spaces and times of *Ada*, where old Russia's hegemony includes the North American continent, and where *Anna Karenina*, as though written by a counter-Tolstoy, opens with a sentence exactly inverse in sense to the sentence the earthbound Tolstoy wrote. Meddling with the future also, it is he who gives instructions to a twenty-first century scholar (who will surely obey them, if he shall happen to exist).

It is he: That is what all the self-appreciation is really about. It is also why the stories in *Tyrants Destroyed* are so empty: the slight amusements of "an anthropomorphic deity," arranging small systems, like chess problems, to suit himself.

This deity will allot himself, say, 3,500 words, and will contrive within that limit to place the lost wife whom Luzhin is seeking on the very train where Luzhin works as a waiter, and have them not meet, have him even not find the ring she lost in the diner, have him go through with his plan to kill himself while the train bears her away toward Cologne. "A Matter of Chance," it's called. Chance is seldom so hollowly neat. No, a better title would be "The Whims of Nabokov," iron whims.

By a fraudulent deity's tricks, he contrives to keep patterns trim within narrow limits. To the deity responsible for your life and mine, the minimum intelligible system appears to be the universe itself, and excerpts have a certain random look. Sensing this principle, V. Nabokov now inclines to refer every excerpt to its universe, which is The Complete Works of V. Nabokov. That is what is really going on in *Tyrants Destroyed*: less the promotion of some negligible stories than their careful assignment to year and month and room and weather and journal, the reinvention of an aspect of the author's past, a pendant to *Speak Memory*.

For his chief work is finally himself, as it was Hemingway's, as it was Huysmans's. Joris-Karl Huysmans (1848–1907) is a *point de repère* Nabokov's appreciators seem to have shunned. Contemplators of *Ada*'s lush verbal jungle (now sleeps the nacreous petal, now the gules) might adduce with advantage the creator of Des Esseintes, whose tortoises were bejeweled, and who tired of flowers, and indulged in artificial flowers, and then tired of those and sought out real flowers so exotic they could pass for artificial.

1975

Lisping in Numbers

Remove number from the Creation, said St. Augustine, and everything would perish. As empirical a man as Isaac Newton, needing seven colors for his spectrum, fudged that total by inserting Indigo between Blue and Violet. For there had to be as many colors of light as there were notes in the scale (also, days of Creation). The Genesis account of Creation affirms six days of work, one of rest. That makes seven; and adding $7+6+5+4+3+2+1$ gives us 28, which is (roughly) the count of days in the month according to the moon. Never mind that adjusting the lunar month to 28 days exactly gave astronomers headaches for centuries: God was plainly imparting a strong hint as to what He was about. So man, busied at his humbler creative activities, would be remiss in attempting less. A creator? A counter. What gets counted and why is an age-old theme for attention.

The link of number with music is a commonplace as old as Pythagoras; and by the evidence of the oldest poems we have, poets since the dawn of the art have been continually counting something. Homer, as everyone knows, had a habit of counting by sixes, though what it was he counted is surprisingly difficult to say. If you have an answer ready, that is thanks to the tradition of the classroom, which has borne to us from far back a terminology of "feet" and "spondees" and "dactyls," in my experience resisted by most students, and learned, if at all, out of acquiescence in the game whereby mastering a jargon earns you a grade.

For let us imagine the tradition somehow obliterated. Now here is a committee of astute scholars, and they have before them a few hundred consecutive words of the *Iliad*. And since when the *Iliad* was first written down no one had yet thought to divide it into "lines," we'll imagine too that the words simply run from side to side of the page, the start of a new line having no special significance. Now someone has proposed a hypothesis, to the effect that *counting* somehow underlies this utterance. A Nobel Prize awaits whoever can be most persuasive about how the lost system works: in particular, about what is being counted. I'd expect a small chance indeed of the committee reaching any agreement whatever, let alone of someone discerning more or less the metrical system we've been taught to take for granted.

But of course our hypothetical committee is staring at a silent text, whereas our metrical terms were devised when Greeks could still hear the *Iliad* chanted aloud, to the rhythmic twang of a lyre. The scribes who first arranged it into "lines" were supplying a visual aid: a very strong hint that what got displayed on one line contained the system of counting. Then a spondee—two successive "long" syllables—and a dactyl—a long plus two shorts—proved handy analytic tools for dividing a line into "feet"; and the foot was what there always proved to be six of. We'll skip over the somewhat complicated rules for assigning length to a syllable, and ponder instead the sheer physicality implied by such terms. For the word "foot" hints that verse is somehow on the march, or perhaps beating out the measure of a dance. And a dactyl? That means a finger.

Liddell and Scott have some choice lore about *daktulos*. The word is akin, they tell us, to the Latin *digitus*, which means a finger but also came to mean a unit of counting, a digit; and their very first Greek citation is from Herodotus, *epi daktulon symballesthai*, to reckon on the fingers. A *daktulos* was also the smallest Greek measure of length, the breadth of a finger; in a pleasant aside, we're told of modern Greek seamen still measuring the sun's distance from the horizon with the hand held at arm's length, an ever-available dactylic sextant. As for dactyl the metrical foot, the Lexicon's first citation sends us to the *Republic*, 400b, where Socrates is enumerating some feet his friend Damon has collected, and the dactyl is one he sees no need to explain.

The word *sponde* is quite as interesting. It means what the Romans meant by a libation: a solemn drink-offering. You hallowed what you were about to drink by pouring a little of it out for the gods. The plural, *spondai*, meant a treaty or truce, an occasion ritually solemnized by spondaic offerings. "Slow solemn melodies," the Lexicon adds, were proper to such ceremonies; the meter that fitted those melodies came to be called spondaic.

So Homer's hexameter is, at some distant remove, an affair of libations and fingers: of slow offerings to the gods, and deft hands fingering the lyre-strings. We're a long way by now from the blackboard. Alas, it's back to marks on a blackboard that such physicalities have a way of collapsing, and it's hard to fend off the idea that a set of rules is being expounded, laid down by some invisible tribunal to the end that poets may be taught their business. Pope in the *Essay on Criticism* puts this misapprehension as neatly as he puts most things:

> But most by Numbers judge a Poet's Song,
> And Smooth and Rough to them are Right and Wrong.

He seems to have been pestered by coffee-house sages who'd keep counting on their ten fingers and expect a crisp rhyme always on the tenth. Milton's preface to the second printing of *Paradise Lost* snarls at surly browsers who've been complaining that "the Poem rhymes not," the line-endings therefore often inaudible amid the disruptions caused by his strong caesurae. That's a way of saying that the poet hadn't taken enough trouble to justify their spending money on his book; it's instructive that the complaint came to Milton by way of the Bookseller, who'd had all too many occasions to observe folk closing the big tome and walking out of the shop. The fuss about "free verse" likewise, now almost a century remote, seems entoiled in an obscure grudge against so-called poets who simply weren't working at a poet's prime job, i.e. counting. The *Cambridge Review* in 1909 pronounced, concerning some early work of Pound's, that poetry's three elements were "thought, words, and metre. . . . That is the begin-

ning and end of the whole affair," so let us have no more "unmetrical
sprawling lengths." That review is signed by Rupert Brooke, who
would soon be getting himself known as a scrupulous counter. He
counted in fours for choice:

> In Grantchester their skins are white;
> They bathe by day, they bathe by night.

That was one riposte to such American nonsense as

> Eyes, dreams, lips, and the night goes . . .

with, however you counted *that*, nothing else in the poem answerable
to a like count. (It's a dactyl between two spondees, but never mind.)

Homer's counting was seemingly internalized, cued by heard or
unheard music, the way the rowers of triremes were cued by the
gong. He'd likely have blinked in dismay at our talk of dactyl and
spondee, conveniences that satisfy our itch to fit what lies silent on
paper with analytic marks. Having no paper, he'd have had no way to
count lines, let alone words. Indeed the very concept of the word was
unavailable to Homer: it is alien to the unwritten. *Logos?* That means
something like "whatever is said or spoken," and Liddell and Scott
warn us that it never means "name." "Name" is *onoma*, which turns
up only twice in the *Iliad*. Unlike *logos, onoma* is detachable from the
flow of speech, because it's what some thing is called, so you might
point to Hector and say just "Hector," to his horse and say just "hip-
pos." To do that is to onomatize; we do it constantly to help young
children. So the Greeks were familiar with *names* standing all by
themselves, but not, in our way, with *words* standing all by themselves, the way a dictionary isolates them, or a scribe. The scribe isolates word from word by inserting spaces; the space was the last symbol of the alphabet to be invented, and the moment it was invented
the word was, and we could say that things we can't point to have corresponding words, such as "red" or "cold" or "evening." Likewise,
once lines were there you could count lines, and lines weren't "there"
till scribes started putting them there, to help us grasp the rhythm by
eye.

One reason for scribes to do that was the way the lyric poem had of repeating a rhythmic pattern over and over, so as to recycle a tune shorter than it was. Each time that happens we have a "stanza," and the stanza's way of following the tune is analyzable into lines, the lines furthermore into words. What existed as mouthfuls of air is being analyzed by a graphic technology we so take for granted we assume Sappho thought likewise. But she didn't, nor did the Troubadours of Provence, whose stanzaic prowess was formidable. Like Sappho, they were accepting the guidance of a tune, conceived once, then repeatedly submitted to. It was a triumph, the fifth time round, to get out of your tune what it hadn't at all seemed to promise the first time.

What for Homer, so we may guess, was wholly interior, an embodied sense of how a line got its shape, like a carpenter's sense of how to hit a nail; what music helped Sappho and the Troubadours to interiorize, so that her stanzas seem crystalline growths, theirs the outcome of intricate but exact calculation: all that, laid flat on paper by scribes, or by poets holding pens, could come to resemble a draft to be worked over. The poet for whom paper is natural—is primary—can see many things to count, many countable symmetries, and knows of readers who can see them too. That's a new level of poetic communication. So much does it elude what we can take in by ear that it's been called "Silent Poetry." It coexists with the poetry that's shaped by breath, breath uttering sound.

So behold, in 1916, William Butler Yeats, counting. He has undertaken his elegy for the men England executed after the Easter 1916 rebellion, and by adding to the Dublin firing-squad victims one man hanged in England and another in Cork he's been able to make the total come to sixteen. Sixteen martyrs for 1916! He is careful to point that up in a pendant poem called "Sixteen Dead Men." Then, "I have met them at close of day," he commences the major poem, and by the time its first stanza is done we have, yes, sixteen lines.

Sixteen lines the third stanza has likewise, but the second and the fourth have twenty-four, almost as though we're to think of sixteen as an incomplete twenty-four. Twenty-four? By one of admittedly several estimates there were twenty-four millennia of earth-years in the

Platonic Great Year, much on Yeats's mind at the time, that restores all things under the moon to their first condition. Though that is what revolutions also expect to do, their success is never more than partial. The most they may achieve is to give birth to a terrible beauty (and this one, alas, ultimately would midwife De Valera: in Oliver Gogarty's words, "that cross between a corpse and a cormorant").

There's a more immediate relevance of 24 to 16. The Rebellion erupted on April 24, having been postponed a day from its scheduled date, the 23rd of April, tercentenary of the death of William Shakespeare. Sure enough, "Easter 1916" encodes its date exactly, 24/iv/16, the 24 and the 16 being line-counts, surrounding the count of stanzas. As always, such observations move us beyond any ability to say to what extent what we can count reflects any counting of the poet's. Draw rein, draw breath; take note, move on.

His large plan laid out, Yeats now fills it with precisely mapped details. The recurrence of "A terrible beauty is born," climaxing stanzas one, two and four and by its absence marking out the third as a hushed meditation, is but the most evident of the symmetries. Three lines from the end of the first stanza we're reminded of a past when all Irish people "But lived where motley is worn." Three lines from the end of the last we're bidden look to a present and future "Wherever green is worn." Stanza two likewise lists one-time anonymities: "this woman," "this man," "this other," even "a drunken vainglorious lout," while in stanza four names leap into cymbal-clashing specificity: "MacDonagh and MacBride / And Connolly and Pearse" (and the "lout" is MacBride, accorded moreover the dignity of a rhyming position). Likewise, the Yeats we glimpse seven lines before stanza one ends—hitting on "a mocking tale or a gibe" to amuse someone at the Kildare Street Club—is transmuted, the same distance exactly before the end of stanza four, into the bardic Yeats transubstantiating those names: "I write it out in a verse." "I" was the first word of the poem: back then, a confessional "I," now an "I" proudly affirmative.

It's by way of the gridding, the counting, the numerical symmetries exact and free, that "Easter 1916," slowly and repeatedly reread, attains its stature as one of Yeats's major achievements. Rightly, it contains a numeral in its title. Yeats was coming to think of the count of years as a countdown. Just eighty-four years till the next millennium! Rough beasts were commencing to stir, preparing to slouch.

And if Yeats was a counter, other Irishmen have been great counters. George Boole, whose Truth Tables of True and False are employed every day by every computer programmer, he was Irish. So was William Rowan Hamilton, who discovered conditions under which the result of a multiplication might depend on which number you looked at first, and wrote his formulae on the side of a Dublin bridge. The Synge family were such counters they could regard the playwright John Millington Synge as their black sheep; Synges are embedded in the history of mathematics, and one of them is at this moment attached to the Institute of Advanced Studies at Princeton. So it's unsurprising that James Joyce for instance was a counter. He conceived what he was doing with his pen as a giving of complex instructions to printers, so he tended to count printerly creations, paragraphs and words and letters, the isolate items on the printed page.

Joyce's most magical of numbers was eleven, the one that begins anew when a decade is exhausted. It also signals, though, that something has ended. So eleven is his number of hope, of potentiality: and yet also of death, since new potential can only dislodge potential unfulfilled. "Time has branded them," thinks Stephen Dedalus of events that are not to be thought away, "and fettered they are lodged in the room of the infinite possibilities they have ousted." So Paddy Dignam's funeral is scheduled for 11 A.M.; it's young Patrick Aloysius Dignam who'll be Paddy Dignam henceforward. Rudy Bloom died at 11 days, and in Bloomsyear, 1904, his death was 11 years past: 1893. Since then there has been no real sexual fulfillment for Leopold Bloom and Molly. But on Bloomsday, 16 June 1904, Marion Bloom (her real name, and 11 letters) has a tryst with Hugh E. Boylan (also 11 letters), and when that occurs, offstage, it's in the 11th episode of *Ulysses*. Hard though this betrayal is on Leopold, he gleans hope from his encounter with Stephen, unwashed bard and possibly surrogate son. And Stephen's age is 22: two times 11.

Nowhere, parenthetically, is this coincidence of potential with extinction more poignant than in the last moments of *Finnegans Wake*. As that book of cyclic rebeginnings ends, Anna Livia the river is merging into nonidentity, into the sea. She'll be drawn up to fall once more as rain in what we're assured is a renewing cycle; and yet here's the end of her too, the book's last words, an unfinished sentence: "A way a lone a last a loved a long the": no final period, but eleven words.

Very possibly Joyce in his browsings among the Fathers had caught sight of St. Augustine's preoccupation with the numbers 11 and 22. Eleven, Augustine explains, is the number of sin, because it goes beyond (transgresses) the 10 of the Law, the number of Commandments. Joyce was less negative about sin than was Augustine—he thought it might be a "portal of discovery"—so his 11 has its upbeat side. As for 22, Augustine took a cue from Homer, whose *Iliad* and *Odyssey* have each of them as many books as the Greek alphabet has letters: 24. The language of God being Hebrew, with a 22-letter alphabet, Augustine arranged his own *De Civitate Dei* in 22 books. And something similar could befit a big book about a wandering Jew in Dublin, a book in which the first words spoken by anyone quote a Latin translation from the Hebrew.

Accordingly, by mid-1915 we find Joyce reporting that he is at work on a 22-episode *Ulysses*, with a three-part grouping 4, 15, and 3. Some time before May 1918, though, he'd changed his scheme, though it still drew virtue from 11. The tripartite grouping had now acquired a symmetry: three episodes, eleven, three again, and the first three are egocentric versions of the last three: narrative (young) versus narrative (aged), catechism (personal) versus catechism (impersonal), monologue (male) versus monologue (female). But seven months later 3–11–3 got supplanted by 3–12–3, Joyce having decided on an unforeseen episode, one moreover not guided by the *Odyssey*, Wandering Rocks. That wildcard conferred on the book many benefits needless to enumerate here. Notably, in moving its successor episodes forward by one, it made Boylan's conquest of Molly coincide with a count of eleven. That left Joyce with a total of 18—by good fortune, the number of letters in the *Irish* alphabet. And though both 22 and 11 had now been discarded, he was careful in other ways to accord 22 due homage. By coincidence, 22 had been his own age—hence, Stephen Dedalus's—on the day in which the book is set. The

Universe, Guy Davenport has remarked, seems to have been arranged for Joyce's convenience.

Ulysses begins the way a book so titled should begin, with a ringing Homeric hexameter:

Stately I plump Buck I Mulligan I came from the I stairhead I bearing

—though with a spondee in the fifth foot, where the Greek bard avoided spondees. Following, though, to the end of the sentence, we find counting on a different principle: "Stately, plump Buck Mulligan came from the stairhead, bearing a bowl of lather on which a mirror and a razor lay crossed." That sentence not only swings from "Stately" to "crossed," from "The Imperial British State" to "The Holy Roman Catholic and Apostolic Church" Stephen Dedalus will cite as his "masters" just a few pages later, it does so in a canonical 22 words. The second sentence, like the second part of the book, lapses into what Mulligan and Stephen would deem Bloomish indistinction. Fourteen words, what meaning has that? But sentence three of this three-parted work reasserts numeric principle. "He held the bowl aloft and intoned: *Introibo ad altare Dei.*" That's exactly 11 words. Twenty-two, [fourteen], eleven. Yes, our author is counting. He is counting too, much later in *Ulysses*, when he enumerates Leopold Bloom's books. For behold, Bloom owns 22, including a *Useful Ready Reckoner* and a *Short Yet Plain Elements of Geometry*. (Yes, the list runs to 23 titles, but one of them isn't Bloom's; it belongs to the Capel Street Public Library and is an ominous 13 days overdue.)

Elsewhere he will bestow his counting skills on another typographic artifact, the paragraph. The 14th episode of the book (but the 11th of its central section) takes place in a Maternity Hospital and concerns itself with themes of Birth. Birth is an "11" motif: a new beginning, something unlikely—or perhaps not—for Leopold and Molly. Lo, the episode in question, called "Oxen of the Sun," takes 11 paragraphs to get Leopold into the hospital; keeps him there for 40 paragraphs; then spends an 11-paragraph coda outside. Those 40 interior paragraphs we may ascribe to the 40 weeks obstetricians reckon for normal gestation. So the 11 initializing paragraphs can correspond to the spermatazoon entering the ovum, and in the 11 exuberant final paragraphs something has been delivered into the outer air. What has been delivered? Why, in this book of words, just talk, the street-slang of 1904, emitted by, yes, 11 people. Deprived of the stylistic guidance we've been depending on for many pages—pastiche after pastiche of recognizable conventions—we find we can't readily be sure who's saying what to whom, or why. That is not unlike our trouble interpreting the cries of the newborn. The episode ends just after the stroke of 11. And it's the episode in which Bloom, having finally met Stephen after two near-misses, begins to persuade himself (wrongly) that he's acquired a surrogate son.

Another number recurrent in *Ulysses* is 32, the number of the ur-Christian event, the Fall. That is because a falling body accelerates by 32 feet per second per second (it's less tidy in the metric system). Exactly how the formulation goes is something Bloom struggles to recall all day; that, and the mnemonic for the seven colors of Newton's spectrum, seem the two chief things that linger from his high school days. (He attended the same high school, by the way, as W. B. Yeats. But its two most famous graduates never met.)

Nor did Joyce's dealings with these numbers cease with *Ulysses*. In *Finnegans Wake* we find, recurring end to end, "1132," which often looks as if it were a date but is chiefly just 11 and 32, the recurrence-number, the fall-number, placed side by side. In the *Wake*, moreover, Joyce is even counting letters. That was early divined, and readers were long assured by critical consensus that the famous ten thunder-words have 100 letters each. Then some more scrupulous counter discovered, correctly, that the last of them has 101. That yields 1,001 for a total, the same number as the night-time tales of Scheherazade, just what we ought to have been all along suspecting of a Joycean night-book.

We'll turn lastly to yet another Irish counter, Sam Beckett, born in 1906, on, he says, Good Friday the 13th. That has to be April 13, since Easter by definition cannot fall before March 23. The twentieth century calendar affords only three April 13 Good Fridays—the others are dated 1979 and 1990—and Beckett has been a long time pondering whatever fate its unlikelihood implies.

One thing he did was count his way through the alphabet to the 13th letter, "M," and for years thereafter give non-hero after non-hero an M-name: Murphy, Molloy, Malone, Mercier, Mahood. One time he inverted "M" and got "W" and called a book *Watt*. Watt's name has four letters and his book has four parts. Beckett likes M's and W's for heroines' names as well: thus in *All That Fall* Mrs. Rooney's name is Maddie, and in *Happy Days*, amid what seem the final throes of the planet, indefatigable cheerfulness emanates from a Winnie, who's married to a Willie.

Then there's the four-member cast of *Endgame*, named Hamm and Clov and Nagg and Nell. Hamm for hammer; and Clov and Nagg and Nell deform *clou* and *Nagel* and *nail*, what a hammer smites in French and German and English. One hammer, then, three nails: just the needful equipment, Guy Davenport once remarked, for the event we remember on Good Friday, a crucifixion.

Or, to end with, there's *Stirrings Still*, a text Beckett published only a short time ago. There are signs that it may be (after all) his last, and it is certainly a meditation on his own impending death. It is in three parts, and its first feature of interest for our purposes is its inventory of sentences. These total 120 exactly, and the parts distribute them in a diminishing sequence: 90, 20, 10. Ten, we may guess, might be a child's life span, 20 an adolescent's, 90 an old man's (Beckett is now 83). As for 120, in the Renaissance it was recorded as the ideal duration of a good life. Whoever is still unconvinced that Beckett was counting may undertake the trouble of counting the words. He was born, you remember, in that year of the fateful Good Friday, 1906. One thousand, nine hundred and six. And the number of words in *Stirrings Still*, counting the two-word title? Yes, you've guessed it. Beckett seems to have made that happen by a last-minute fiddle, taking the hyphen, just one time, out of "half-hour" to make it count, just once, as two words, not as one.

Silent Poetry indeed, since it exists in a dimension inaccessible to what Beckett called in another connection "the power of the text to claw." The count of words, 1,906, simply lies there mutely to be found, and might never be found; or might be found, and not convey anything at all in the absence of information about our century's first Good Friday the 13th, and our author's attachment to that year. It's like a message in a bottle, cast into sound's roiling seas; or like a cry for help, borne all the way from Arcturus, so encoded that Earthians are almost sure to miss it. How many such messages other writers may have sent it's impossible to guess, such etherial dimensions has number acquired since Homer's hexameters brought voice and breathing and numbered acoustic weight to eager ears in Greece. One of Beckett's motives for sending it, though, he hinted at years ago, in *All That Fall*. Blind Dan Rooney is indulging his habit of counting the stairs he climbs. Three . . . four . . . five . . . it jars Maddie's nerves. She begs him to stop. And Dan is like Sam in declining to be repressed: "Not count? One of the few pleasures in life?"

1989

Self-Similarity,
Fractals, Cantos

. . . In nature are signatures
needing no verbal tradition . . . (87:573)

Ezra Pound's *Hugh Selwyn Mauberley* has two parts, the first longer (twelve poems and "Envoi"), the second shorter (four poems and "Medallion"). Similarities between them are easily observed.

—Thus words like "Colourless" and "lacking the skill" (poem I of part 2) echo details like "out of key with his time" and "Wrong from the start" (poem I of part 1), though they characterize two different men.

—Thus the phrase "For three years . . ." initiates both poem I of part 1 and poem II of part 2. In each poem the next phrase offers a musical analogy: "out of key with his time"; "diabolus in the scale." Thereafter verbal divergence increases rapidly, though thematic congruence remains detectable.

—Thus part 1 commences with an epitaph, while part 2 nearly ends with one.

—And how part 1's terminal "Envoi" and part 2's terminal "Medallion" correspond is something we needn't labor; nor how the cameos and medallions that dominate part 2 reject the "mould in plaster" an "age" had "demanded" in part 1.

Self-Similarity, Fractals, Cantos

A good phrase for the relationship between the two lobes of *Mauberley* might be "self-similarity." It resembles sung poetry's oldest device, a tune recurring, carried by different words. It differs in that the metaphorical "tune"—here, not repeated sounds but a set of structural relations—recurs on a smaller scale; much as the "Mauberley" of part 2, with his passion for the tiny and the exquisite, exists on a smaller scale than the "E. P." of part 1, whose poetic took on things Mauberley's couldn't face, even the War itself.

("Not repeated sounds but a set of structural relations." But music *is* a set of structural relations. We'll be returning to that.)

What we find in *Mauberley* we find everywhere in Pound: structures repeating themselves on ever varying scales. As *XXX Cantos* gets under way, I is a journey to the underworld, II a set of metamorphoses. At the start of the *Pisan Cantos*, LXXIV locates us in a secular underworld, the DTC; whereupon LXXV bids us contemplate the metamorphoses of a musical theme, from birds to Janequin's voices to Munch's violin. But LXXIV is much longer than I (25 pages, against 2½); LXXV much shorter than II (against five pages, only 36 words, plus wordless scored music with "per metamorfosi" handwritten at the top).

Again: XI, Italy; XII, the Americas; XIII, Kung's China. (Italian Columbus, en route to China, bumped into America; in a way it's that simple.) Then, on a huge scale, China (LII–LXI), America (LXII–LXX): Italy always a tacit presence. Then, on a smaller scale to commence *Section Rock-Drill*, China, 85–6; America, 87–8. . . . You're seeing the idea.

So, throughout *The Cantos* we find motifs recurring in similar sequences but on different scales. In II, many huge cats precede a manifestation (of the god, Dionysius): one page (2:8).[1] In LXXIV, one small cat precedes a manifestation (of a woman, "La Donna"): nine lines (74:427).

Scaling up, scaling down. Back in '49, new to *The Cantos*, I found myself writing of a "nodal point," which I attributed to "every great writer," where "the diversely collected rays meet and are brought under simultaneous control.

[1] References to *The Cantos of Ezra Pound* cite Canto and New Directions page number.

"Every great writer operates from some such node. It is the point—to change the metaphor—at which the local operation of words in lines and passages becomes continuous with the operation of passages in the main design, and of whole works in the poise and thrust of a lifetime's output." I went on: "To see . . . a hierarchy of parodies in the sentence as in the situation, in the situation as in the book, in the book as in the cycle, is to occupy the point of leverage in the work of James Joyce." And, "Pound has made it especially easy to locate this point in his own work, by telling us repeatedly what and where it is."[2]

I now think that with a sleepwalker's accuracy I got something profoundly right, though I hadn't grasped the pages where Pound really tells us. Nor had I guessed how much more deliberate than anyone else's was his use of self-similarity at varying scales. At 26 you may simply be lucky.

———

The phrase "self-similarity" is promoted by the mathematician Benoit B. Mandelbrot, to describe configurations that, viewed from varying distances, seem imitations (not duplicates) of themselves. His famous examples include (1) the coastline of Britain, comparably irregular whether we examine a full mapping, a 500-mile sample, or the wavering line we can trace around an inlet's pebbles; (2) the jagged mountain whose any detail is jagged likewise; (3) the spiralling eddy which (Leonardo knew) is made of the similar sub-spirals we miscall "turbulence." Mandelbrot makes claims for "the fractal geometry of nature," "fractal" being his term for a look of irregularity that turns out to be self-similar at varying scales.[3]

As to why that turns up in the arts: well, they imitate nature, don't they? In a 1981 contribution to the British periodical *Leonardo*, Man-

[2]Hugh Kenner, *The Poetry of Ezra Pound*, 1951, 14.
[3]For the benefit of readers who confine themselves to the literary, I'd better dilate on Mandelbrot's eminence. The fourth chapter of James Gleick's *Chaos: Making a New Science* (New York, 1987) isn't a bad introduction; or look at his own *Fractal Geometry of Nature* (New York, 1983), or at Peitgen and Richter's *The Beauty of Fractals* (New York, 1986). Like Buckminster Fuller, though a far deeper mathematician, he's a student of large-scale patterns. His "fractals" display self-similarity's ordering of seeming chaos, from huge scales in to tiny. He finds them in cotton prices, alpine contours, clouds; also in the variation of sunspots, undersea currents, the fluctuating levels of rivers. An IBM Research Fellow, he has even professed at Harvard.

delbrot asks us to "consider the role of scaling in representational fig-
urative and nonfigurative pictures"; it "could well be influenced by
the role of scaling in nature."[4]

And "scaling"? That's Mandelbrot's term for the Alps, or a building like the Paris Opera, both of which repay attention at whatever
viewing distance. ("Stylistic homogeneity" is lit-crit's way of saying
the rewards are self-similar.) But the "scaling" work is to be distinguished from the "scalebound," exemplified by a Mies van der Rohe
box, which can please as a whole but has nothing new to offer in close-
up. Get close to the Opera, and chances are you examine ornament-
ing stone; close to a Mies, you confront some blankness of glass. The
Great Pyramid is eminently "scalebound." (So, for that matter, are a
salt crystal—mostly sheer facets, and the solar system—mostly emp-
tiness. Nature doesn't *abhor* the scalebound, but artists have been
drawn to her scaling themes.) But, clear down to knee-high elephants
and a two-inch Venus-face, Sigismundo Malatesta's Tempio in Rimini
is "scaling." The story of the building of the Tempio runs through
Cantos VII–XI, and in its wonderful miscellaneousness, exquisitely
detailed, the Tempio is manifestly one of the poem's models for itself.

But, partly because of a burden imposed by novels, lit-crit is more
at home with the scalebound. It likes plans, overviews; it likes diagrams later "filled out," paint-by-numbers. Subordinating details to
some Big Picture, it identifies "form" with a schema, and cries havoc
when a schema seems not producible. (Understanding that well, the
ever-cunning Joyce produced a *Ulysses* schema retroactively.)
"Form"? That's what it was for Mies, a diagram.

But let us consider reality; Mandelbrot's categories do group artists
plausibly. To concentrate, with him, on the visual: Mondrian, Brancusi, yes, Picasso: all scalebound. Come close, see less. Agostino di
Duccio, Van Gogh, Pollock: scaling, with rewards for distance, other
rewards for closeness. The yokings are odd: you'll find one favorite of
Pound's in each of those trios. Yet by and large he was drawn to the
scaling: the skew ringlets of Botticelli's Venus repeating her slanted
stance; Mantegna letting the fringe of a courtier's cape rhyme the trim

[4]Benoit B. Mandelbrot, "Scalebound or Scaling Shapes: A Useful Distinction in the Visual Arts and in the Natural Sciences," *Leonardo*, Vol. 14, 1981, 45–7.

of his cap, or abstracting 20 roundish heads of the Gonzaga family into rows of stone loops on a painted wall behind them. And don't forget Excideuil, with its "wave-pattern cut in the stone." Remembered near Pisa (80:510), that detail mimed not the contour of its castle but one contour of the poem it's embedded in. Fortunes rise and fall like the lunar cycle ("Que tous les mois avons nouvelle lune"); people fade and die ("Nancy where art thou?"; "Orage, Fordie, Crevel too quickly taken"); artifacts like the *Rubaiyat* wane, then wax:

> lay there till Rossetti found it remaindered
>   at about two pence
> (Cythera, in the moon's barge whither?
>   how hast thou the crescent for car?) (80:510)

—where self-similarity works down to the vowels of "how" and "thou," "barge" and "car." And the reach of that theme extends to remoter parts of the poem, as to

> wave falls and the hand falls
> Thou shalt not always walk in the sun . . . (42:210)

"A scaling object," writes Mandelbrot, "includes as its defining characteristic the presence of very many different elements whose scales are of any imaginable size. There are so many different scales, and their harmonics are so interlaced and interact so confusingly, that they are not really distinct from each other, but merge into a continuum."[5] (That can clarify early responses to *The Cantos*.)

And: "For practical purposes a scaling object does *not* have a scale that characterizes it. Its scales vary also depending upon the viewing points of beholders. The same scaling object may be considered as being of a human's dimension or of a fly's dimension." (So concentrate on three lines, three pages, three Cantos.)

Mandelbrot also observes that "a nontrivially scaling object" will have its blank areas. (When it hasn't, art critics reach for the word "busy.") In a typical Renaissance portrait there are draperies and skies, to approach which is to see less, and "finely detailed areas (in-

[5]Mandelbrot, "Scalebound or Scaling Shapes: A Useful Distinction in the Visual Arts and in the Natural Sciences," 45–7.

cluding background landscapes that may seem to lack any other purpose)." The blander parts total, perhaps, one- to two-thirds of the whole. In nature, too, "a typical scaling pattern selected without systematic bias tends to include substantially featureless portions." (Was that what Poe intuited, about blank spots in an epic? Why Pound moved between rhythmic intensity and stretches of "prose"?)

For in literature? Though here Mandelbrot doesn't guide us—he's a geometrician, a *visuel*—we may venture instances. Dostoevsky in translation, powerful but scalebound, the individual sentences unlikely to hold our interest (a translator's hands are full just managing the story). Scott likewise scalebound, albeit in his native tongue. Then think of *Ulysses*, scaling, where a closeup scan yields wonders like "The felly harshed against the curbstone: stopped," or even "Mrkrgnao!" (spoken by a cat). "Scaling" connotes interesting detail at varying ranges: *Hamlet*, one scene of *Hamlet*, one soliloquy, one image. The Shakespeares, the Flauberts, the Joyces scale; the Walter Scotts do not. And gradations may be calibrated. Pope scaled more than Dryden, Browning more than Tennyson, Eliot more than Auden.

Intuition, personal proclivity, the felt example of nature? Any may prompt one "scaling" worker or another. I'm proposing that Ezra Pound had glimpsed the principle itself, and that (beginning with "Mauberley," 1920) he scaled deliberately, to get details organized into larger forms, defined in turn by the contour of the details.

————————

He teases us with hints of "major form." Ford's *A Call*—I remember him lighting up: "That had *form!*" He'd adduced its "form," too, in *ABC of Reading*. Though I do wish I'd pressed him, I'd not likely have received the stone tablets. For our talk was of literature, whereas (I now realize) the supremely scaling art, to his mind, was music,[6] his express passion in the 20's and 30's when he was working out the way

[6]Mandelbrot tells us how for a long time he'd thought classical Western music scalebound, till the work of Richard Voss convinced him otherwise. He refers us to Martin Gardner's exposition of Voss ("White Music, Brown Noise, Fractal Curves and One-over-f Fluctuations," *Scientific American*, April 1978, 17 ff).

of the *Cantos*, and his sole connected exposition of the "scaling" principle is the "Treatise on Harmony" of 1924.[7]

The thrust of the Treatise has tended to be overlooked amid doubts about its application to Harmony, much as The Chinese Written Character's relevance to Poetry gets lost amid expert assertions that Chinese Doesn't Really Work That Way. But be guided by Mandelbrot; adopt a suitable viewing distance. (That advice is pertinent in Poundian terrain *passim*.)

The fundamental idea of the Treatise is simple and breathtaking; it invites us to imagine *all* of music, from the single note outward to the symphony, as a complex systematic modulation of time, always subject to a principle Pound had evidently glimpsed though a half-century would elapse before Mandelbrot named it "scaling." For pitches are vibrations-per-second, following one another in performance at intervals of beats-per-minute, and self-similarity, a phrase Pound might have had uses for, requires some relation between pitch and interval. Hence the manifesto on the first page of the Treatise:

> AND YET the simplest consideration of the physics of the matter by almost the simplest mathematician should lead to equations showing that A SOUND OF ANY PITCH, OR ANY COMBINATION OF SUCH SOUNDS, MAY BE FOLLOWED BY A SOUND OF ANY OTHER PITCH, OR ANY OTHER COMBINATION OF SUCH SOUNDS, providing the time interval between them is properly gauged; and this is true for ANY SERIES OF SOUNDS, CHORDS, OR ARPEGGIOS. (Schafer, 296)

In 1961 the Canadian composer R. Murray Schafer asserted that "the total number of contributions to the science of harmony in our century is three"; he listed Arnold Schoenberg's *Harmonielehre*, Heinrich Schencker's *Harmonielehre*, Ezra Pound's *Treatise*.[8] Elsewhere Schafer adds, "no modern book on the subject so cogently forces us to see harmony as a study in movement" (Schafer, 294). Thus Pound, on prelapsarian musicians:

[7]First published in *Antheil and the Treatise on Harmony*, Paris, 1924. Accessible in R. Murray Schafer, ed., *Ezra Pound and Music*, 1977, 296–306, cited hereafter as "Schafer." Subsequent references will be given parenthetically in the text.
[8]R. Murray Schafer, "Ezra Pound and Music," *The Canadian Music Journal*, V-4, 31.

It never entered their heads that people would make music like steam ascending from a morass.

They thought of music as travelling rhythm going through points or barriers of pitch and pitch-combinations. (Schafer, 297)

And: "There is nothing whatever in music but a combination of frequencies, microphonic and macrophonic" (Schafer, 304).

Anyone whose curiosity has been piqued concerning Pound and music should consult Schafer's admirable anthology and notes. Here we'll stay with the evident fact that the "Treatise on Harmony" implies the "self-similarity" Mandelbrot would long afterward attribute to what he'd call "scaling" works—works with something of interest to offer at varying scales of attention. Moreover, when Pound talked emphatically about music, he was saying how he meant his *Cantos* to hang together. For as events in time pass below the threshold of audibility they become not clusters of vibration but discrete objects of attention. First pitches, then related notes, then phrases, then structural members: then the whole work. The difference is one of scale, as we stay alert for the self-similar. "The percussion of the rhythm can enter the harmony exactly as another note would. It enters usually as a Bassus, a still deeper bassus; giving the main form to the sound" (Schafer, 303).

In 1924 he was hinting, and by 1938 proclaiming, a corollary of this: that the pace at which a composition is performed is dictated by its inner relationships. For each piece of music, self-similarity dictates a single right tempo (Schafer, 476–9). This he called the "Great Bass": the lowest of all notes, timed by seconds and minutes, and simply the measured recurrence of the larger elements. "Self-similarity" can help us make sense of that.

As early as 1910 Pound had introduced the term "absolute rhythm," clearly the Great Bass in a much earlier guise. It's in the introduction to his Cavalcanti translations of that year:

Rhythm is perhaps the most primal of all things known to us. It is basic in poetry and music mutually, their melodies depending on a variation of tone quality and of pitch respectively . . . but if we look closer we will see that music is, by further analysis, pure rhythm; rhythm and noth-

ing else, for the variation of pitch is the variation in rhythms of the individual notes. . . . When we know more of overtones we will see that
the tempo of every masterpiece is absolute, and is exactly set by some
further law of rhythmic accord. Whence it should be possible to show
that any given rhythm implies about it a complete form—fugue, sonata, I cannot say what form, perfect, complete. Ergo, the rhythm set
in a line of poetry connotes its symphony, which, had we a little more
skill, we could score for orchestra. (Schafer, 469)

"The variation in pitch is the variation in rhythms of the individual
notes": that is exactly what he would say in 1924, relating the frequency of each note's pitch to the tempo of the composition. This 1910
statement should warn us against supposing that "the fugue," to
which he would later relate *The Cantos*, was in fact a primary model.
True, the fugue's principle is self-similarity: subject and counter-
subject reintroduced, restated. But when Pound introduces this analogy in letters he tends to hedge it with qualifications. It looks as
though the fugue was but a producible instance of something more
general that he had somehow grasped very early. His recurrent reference to mathematics is indicative; though he lacked its discipline,
he intuited its eventual command of something more fundamental
than musical orthodoxy: here see especially Schafer p. 309, where
Pound is suggesting "a geometry applicable strictly and solely to the
conditions of music," yet "as suggestive, and ultimately as useful as
the constructions of Euclid or Descartes." Yes, he's fishing for fractals;
is even predicting a geometrician who'll discover them.

"The tempo of every masterpiece is absolute": what did Pound
mean by that, in a 1910 discussion of poetry? By 1938 he meant it literally, of musical performance; aged 25, he's still unsure what he
means literally, what analogically. Yet by and large there's nothing
there he'd want to take back. Small units, when they have integrity,
imply wholes. Self-similarity is a good name for what he's intuited. At
25 you can be lucky.

———

He's often been deemed to have had either no powers of construction
or no interest in it. Yet T. S. Eliot told me in 1964 that the ordering of the

poems in *Prufrock and Other Observations* came from Pound, to whom
he ascribed great gifts of sequencing. The University of Wisconsin,
Milwaukee, has letters in which Pound is advising Margaret Anderson how to order items in issues of the *Little Review*. He was always
confident in discerning a whole implied by its parts. The original *Cathay* of 1915 (minus four poems *Personae* later appended) begins with
a war-poem, then places another midway and another at the end; the
three are of graduated starkness. The intervening poems present re-
grets, nostalgia, leave-takings; and with "Exile's Letter" he juxta-
posed, of all things, the Anglo-Saxon "Seafarer" of comparable date,
sensing that *Cathay*'s self-similarities could absorb it. *Cathay*, a response to the war that had just erupted, was his first ambitious sequence, *Homage to Sextus Propertius* (1917) his next, *Mauberley* (1919–
20) far more ambitious. Then came *The Cantos*, still apt to be read as
"bits." Their wholeness needs a new look.

For the premise of *The Cantos*, a "poem including history," is that
history's stuff, human experience, is self-similar. (So *Cathay*, in its
khaki-colored covers, could tacitly pertain to the 1914 war, loneliness
in cold Flanders trenches being analogous to guard duty on the north-
ern frontier of old China.) As late as 1960 he was telling Noel Stock that
the "method" of *The Cantos* was to present "the transient, recurring,
and enduring."[9] A like triad of terms recurs in his letters of the 20's and
30's, and he once tried to explain their scope to Yeats with the aid of the
Schifanoia frescoes in Ferrara. That time he also invoked the fugal
analogy, and later complained that Yeats muddled the exposition
through inability to distinguish a fugue from a frog.

Transient, recurring, enduring: terms for our experience of a "scaling" work of art such as a fugue. Transposed into spatial terms, they
apply to the isolate accents, the manifestly self-similar passages, and
the massed form of a Mantegna, of a Tempio.

History has no finale; analogously, self-similarity imposes no
norm of completeness. The Alps (as Mandelbrot would have us observe) are self-similar, from skyline clear down to boulder. And had a
few mountains never been formed, we'd not deem the Alps "incomplete." Nor, in the absence of some capillaries, would a human circu-

[9]Noel Stock, *My Life in Brief with a Memoir of Ezra Pound*, Columbus, 1987, 91.

latory system be demonstrably imperfect. It's been noted too that a fugue may simply stop. It "regenerates itself constantly from its own motivic material, according to the invention of the composer," and when he's done a pedal will close it.[10] Self-similarity in general confers the liberty to stop without incompleteness. *The Cantos* and *Paterson* stopped when their composers lost the will to go on. They aren't "un-finished," nor is the fractal composition of mountains, islands, clouds.

1988

[10]Schafer, in his Introduction (22). It's a perfectly orthodox observation; and the various "recipes" for a fugue all pertain to ways of getting it started.

Riddley Walker

RIDDLEY WALKER, *by Russell Hoban. Summit Books,*
1982.

The bad time, when the flash from the Power Ring turned night to day, was two or three millennia ago. "Then every thing gone black. Nothing only nite for years on end. Playgs kilt peopl off and naminals nor there wernt nothing growit in the groun. Man and woman starveling in the blackness looking for the dog to eat it and the dog out looking to eat them the same. Finely there come day agen then night and day regler but never like it been befor."

That happened not long after 1997 A.D., the last date anyone has found on any stone. It is now 2347 O.C. ("our count"), but no one knows how many years were missed before they started counting again. So it may be as late as the forty-fifth century A.D. In "Inland" (England), people live in fenced farm hamlets, beset by packs of dogs. A band of hunters with spears brings back a boar. Kids chant rhymes about the "Ardship of Cambry."

As the Humpty Dumpty you've heard of was King Richard III of York, so the Ardship, as no one remembers, was the archbishop of Canterbury. *Riddley Walker* builds on the fascinating premise that nothing prior to the time in which you and I are reading is remembered at all. A.D. has been heard of but is thought to mean "all done" (1,981 years all done), the cultural heritage (Anno Domini) and the religious one (in the year of our Lord) having been wiped out equally. The etymologies have vanished from language, leaving "explain," its Latin root lost, to turn into "as plain." Picking our way phonetically through Riddley's narrative (and take courage, it gets quicker with practice), we have ample time to ponder how much of our comfort with familiar English stems from the intricate past it remembers. This is something most of us are barely aware of till a magician like Russell Hoban takes it away and leaves us to puzzle out what plain words about plain doings can be saying.

Not that doings can ever be plain. Deprived man lives by ritual even as do we, and this semi-nomadic civilization of loosely gathered tribes assesses events for patterns of significance; surrounds occasions, like coming-of-age, with ceremony; and scrounges among rhymes, riddles, and the wrecks of long-buried machines for clues to the lost time of boats in the air and pictures on the wind.

Folklore preserves "the Littl Shynin Man the Addom"—"atom" fused with a lost vestige of "Adam"—and linguistic flotsam like "blip" and "input" can tantalize. People live through their keen senses and by their hunches, and deem the turn toward counting and computing that preceded the Bad Time a sort of original sin. Bolder ones, nonetheless, ache for means to repeat it, not guessing at intricate interdependent technology but persuaded the right spell would suffice could they but find the right materials, the right words.

Mr. Hoban has written a number of children's books that assume that even quite young children enjoy complex satisfactions. *Riddley Walker*, in requiring adults to sound out the words, puts them where they've not been since they were children: in a state of active attention to printed pages that hint at all manner of things conjuring up the recognizably strange. There's no weirder moment in recent fiction than the one that brings onto these pages a leaf of twentieth-century writing for forty-fifth-century men to puzzle over. It's been laboriously copied from the caption below a fifteenth-century painting in Canterbury Cathedral, and they are convinced that it pertains to the physics and chemistry of "the Littl Shynin Man the Addom."

"At the bottom of the painting St. Eustace is seen on his knees before his quarry, a stag, between whose antlers appears, on a cross of radiant light, the figure of the crucified Saviour."

Is that stag not the Hart of the Wood, and being "crucified" must mean something that's done in a crucible, and "Saviour" means savor, salt, and as for that radiant light, it is surely the Addom. So, no doubt, do we ourselves misinterpret Minoan depictions of bulls.

The sponsor of that particular interpretation will before long be ceremonially blinded by the cultists of a different set of meanings. To read signs, to ponder meanings, to be convinced by pattern and analogy; also to do violence to others in the name of certainty: These, in Hoban's story, are inescapable human traits. So is the capacity for awe, such as Riddley feels, and such as we share when we realize where he is—inside the buried Cathedral of Canterbury:

"Stoan branches holding up the over head and growt in to it. Stoan branches unner a stoan sky. A stoan wood unner the groun the hart of the wood in the hart of the stoan in the woom of her what has her woom in Cambry."

Them as made it, he thinks, "musve put ther selfs right." Russell Hoban, for his part, has put many things right, just right, in a book where at first sight all the words are wrong, and at second sight not a sentence is to be missed.

1981

Keys to the Kingdom

THE OXFORD ENGLISH DICTIONARY, *Second Edition,*
prepared by J. A. Simpson and E. S. C. Weiner. Oxford
University Press, 1989. 20 volumes; 21,728 pp.

So here it is at last, the distinguished thing; and at 11.5 cents a page
not really overpriced. For these pages average 2,400 words. Thus the
likes of Stephen King's hardback publisher are charging more per
word for phrasing far less meticulously thought out.

("Meticulously"? That contains Latin "metus," fear, and it used to
connote timid fussing such as you'd smirk at. But the OED's dated citations permit you to watch as in the 20th century meticulousness
slides toward the admirable: "careful, punctilious, scrupulous, precise.")

All four of those words apply to any OED entry. Take "Adamant,"
which my favorite one-volume dictionary, Webster's Ninth New Col-
legiate, disposes of in six lines. At Oxford they accord it half a page,
from which we learn that its Greek root means "untamable," that
Greeks and then Romans applied it to the hardest substances they
knew of (ultimately the diamond), then that "early med.L. writers"
got hung up on "adamare," Latin for "to love deeply," and took to using "Lapidem Adamantem," the Attracting Stone, for the new-

fangled magnet. "With this confusion the word passed into the modern languages"; that's why you can hardly feel sure what Shakespeare, for one, means by it.

> You draw me, you hard-hearted Adamant,
> But yet you draw not Iron, for my heart
> Is true as steele.

—which is *Midsummer Night's Dream*, and virtual nonsense. But the sense of unyieldingness somehow prevailed, and by 1936 we find Adamant meaning just plain stubborn (though the point at which it slid from noun to adjective is "not determinable"). The OED's final citation is from a 1961 London Sunday Times: "'When it's a girl her mother should be the one interviewed,' he stated adamantly." And we've drifted far, far from diamonds. It is by such means, entry after patient entry, that the huge work offers us keys to the kingdom of English.

In the first edition, the citations for "Adamant" stop at 1878, well before anyone was stating adamantly. That was because Oxford published the first part of "A" as long ago as 1884, and thereafter kept it locked in type. From then clear to 1928 the work emerged piecemeal, in units of (normally) 64 pages, collected by thrifty folk for future binding. By the time the whole Dictionary was available in a 12-volume set (1933), so much new material had flooded in that the earlier portions were already obsolete. So the same year saw a supplementary volume; and when a second (four-volume) Supplement got added (1972–86), meticulous users found themselves consulting three alphabets. It was time, they decided at Oxford, to consolidate.

Briefly: with generous help from IBM-UK, the whole huge bank of knowledge got computerized, the supplementary entries now integral with what they'd once supplemented. Henceforward, no more of tacking new stuff on at the end. A novelty inserted in its proper place now nudges everything to its right further rightward. In the process some 5,000 new words (and new senses of old words) got added: acid rain, daisy-wheel, Amex, Visa, CAT, brain-dead, dingbat; the computerisi's sense of Pascal, the mathematician's of set.

(And hang on, we'll be getting back to "set." No review may slight so eccentric a tour de force.)

I've made that all sound easier than it was. The keyboarding, sub-contracted to a firm in Fort Washington, PA, took 180 people 18 months. Custom software nicknamed Oedipus Lex (*OED Integration, Proofing and Updating System*) got written in England, while at the University of Waterloo, in Ontario, they devised the database code to keep track of structural "tags," more or less the elements typography sorts out on the page: pronunciations, etymologies, sub-divisions of senses, instances ordered by date. At one stage the eye-glasses of fully five dozen proofreaders were being wiped with unreckonable Kleenexes. (Kleenex, 1925: "the proprietary name of an absorbent disposable cleansing paper tissue": and ten citations from, e.g., *Trade Marks Journal*, Noel Coward, Gypsy Rose Lee, Graham Greene). The result is so up-to-now it's even captured "fax" (v.t., 1979, with examples down to 1986).

So a certain Victorian aroma has evaporated from the OED. (Those four-letter words, even: yes, they're now treated in full. That began as long ago as the Supplements.) It is still, though, recognizably the work Sir James Murray shaped and guided for 38 years, with no more resources than pen, paper, and pigeon-holes. Murray, whose grand-daughter Elisabeth's life of him, *Caught in the Web of Words*, ranks with the most entrancing of biographies, had been exactly the man (stern, Scottish, fanatical) to organize the fumblings of the Philological So-ciety, a loose gathering of zealots who thought it a national disgrace that there was no decent English dictionary.

The Society had been aroused by Richard Chenevix Trench, Dean of Westminster, later Anglican Archbishop of Dublin, who wrote in 1851 that "Many a single word . . . is itself a concentrated poem, hav-ing stores of poetical thought and imagery laid up in it." Trench had read in Ralph Waldo Emerson's "The Poet" (1844) about all language being "fossil poetry." The job of a Dictionary should be not to legislate usage but to display a tongue's slow unfolding word by word from its stubborn roots. To capture that process, for the whole of the docu-mented language, was the project Murray was rash enough to undertake and stubborn enough to bring as far as the letter T, amidst which, *Trink to Turndown* just issued, he died in 1915 at 78.

Even fifty years earlier the enterprise would not have been thinkable. For one thing, the Great Consonant Shift (Jakob Grimm, 1822) was then undreamt of. Now it could explain countless perplexing matters, as how English "fish" was connected not only with Saxon "fisc" but with Latin "piscis." That made usable Sir William Jones's conception of an Indo-European language family, to which English belonged and to which Sanskrit was a main clue. (Sanskrit! Sam Johnson had made do with Latin, Greek, Hebrew.) Also, printed books had been growing plentiful. Steel pens (1831) had superseded goosequills. And a decent postal service was in place, steam-driven, to bring the penned findings of countless readers to Oxford.

For the vast project depended on many hundred readers, combing through book after book for each word that struck them, filling out a "slip" with word, book, page, quotation. Slips by the hundreds of thousands rained in on Murray. As eleven little Murrays one by one grew literate, they earned pocket-money alphabetizing.

The great task, though, was organizing what the alphabet could bring together; which leads us to "set." "The language," wrote Murray in 1881, "seems not to contain a more perplexing word." By then an assistant had spent 40 hours organizing it. Thirty-something years later—time to confront the S's in earnest—"set"'s final ordering would consume 40 days.

Part of the trouble inheres in the Teutonic structure of the earliest English roots. But what a German dictionary can regard as "separable prefixes"—ersetzen, entsetzen, versetzen—and banish to different alphabetical places, an English lexicon must treat as instances of plain "set"—set up, set to, set forth, set out (verb plus tag)—to be managed all in one entry. That seems to entail pretending that "set" has a core meaning for every particle in the language to somehow modify, and assigning such a core meaning is nigh impossible.

The final arrangement of "set," achieved under the by then septuagenarian Murray, is perhaps lexicography's Eroica Symphony. The noun occasions two movements, one related to "seat" (as, where the sun sets), the other to "sect" (as, "a sett of avaricious Hucksters"). In both movements the orchestra does grow agitated; the first "set" is soon evoking (I.10.d) "Of a woman: a determined attempt to gain a man's affections" and (I.19.b) "The slight lateral deflexion in opposite directions of the alternate teeth of a saw," while the second divagates into such areas as (I.4) "The number of persons required to perform a country dance," or (II.9.b) "The complement of teeth (natural or artificial) with which a person (or animal) is furnished."

It's "set" the verb, though, that really runs amok. Its categories include sitting, then descending. But soon they start a frantic revel, till we're getting "Of a rabbit: To be resting," or "Of a soft-nosed bullet: To expand on impact." While Conductor Murray keeps on staunchly beating time, his measures visit the tympani, flutter in the strings, exhaust and even re-exhaust the alphabet *con brio*—in one instance from "a" to "z" and from "aa" clear to "rr"—while the look of barely comprehensible order, imposed here and there by recourse to even Greek-lettered sequences, contends with utter semantic wildness: "to arrange the pleats of a gown"; "to prepare woad for dyeing"; "to flow in the reverse direction"; "to soil the next leaf or sheet." Anything in the universe seems ready to turn up under "set." A lifetime feels insufficient for grasping the grand design of those 60,000 words, a fettered anarchy fully four-fifths the length of Milton's *Paradise Lost*. And hadn't Milton undertaken the easier task, relying as he could on a plot? If the OED is the Victorian epic poem, is its "set" not perhaps the Georgian *Finnegans Wake*?

(In the first edition, the ratio between "set" and *Paradise Lost* was closer to 2/3; that gives an idea of what the language has been up to in seven decades while the OED waited and watched.)

We next confront the vexing fact that the words that cause the most trouble—words like "set" and "black" and "water"—are just the ones least likely to be looked up. You might turn to a dictionary to learn what "borborygmus" means (bowel rumble), and find a definition some clerk wrote in five minutes. What turned a James Murray's hair white you're unlikely to scan at all. The earliest dictionaries were merely lists of hard words; it was only when the quest for completeness started reaching for the common words too that lexicography became a calling for saints.

Another rule of the intricate game the editors have agreed on is that they'll use no pictures, not a one. My Webster's has a fine striped aardwolf on its very first page. The OED, which doesn't reach the aards (-vark, -wolf) till as late as page 7—though Lord! its dealings with plain "A"!—makes do with "A South-African carnivorous quadruped (*Proteles Lalandii* St. Hil.), of the size of a fox, occupying an intermediate position between the dogs, hyenas, and civets" (citations from 1833, 1847). Webster's wording, even, is more visual than that: "A maned striped mammal (*Proteles cristata*) of southern and eastern Africa that resembles the related hyena and feeds chiefly on carrion and insects." Clearly, the OED assumes a client who's far from asking what an aardwolf *looks* like: no, one athirst for such taxonomic insight as it's austerely willing to provide.

But *Lalandii* vs. Webster's *cristata*: that discrepancy does fuel one's suspicion that the science in some older entries remains a mite old-fashioned. A need for resident scientists on the staff wasn't felt till as late as 1967, when the editor paid an eye-opening visit to Merriam-Webster's offices. Earlier, *Webster's Third* of 1961 had documented an explosive development of English outside of England. That disturbed a good deal of complacency, and the reach of the Second Edition extends everywhere you can think of.

You'll find "Faulknerian," for instance, and "bluegrass" (the latter documented from 1751, but missed by Murray's team completely). You'll find the Ezra Pound of 1909 cited as the first authority for "persona" as the role played by a writer in his work. You'll find coinages like Eliot's "polyphiloprogenitive" (1919) and Joyce's "riverrun" (1939). On that theme, Prof. Frank Tompa of Waterloo University, who helped devise the retrieval software, needed about 10 seconds* at his console to scan 350,000,000 characters and advise me that the OED now sports an astonishing 184 citations from darkest *Finnegans Wake*.

One, of course, is under "quark," where "Three quarks for Muster Mark" bears out physicist Murray Gell-Mann's assertion that he named those elusive particles with Joyce's aid. Where did Joyce,

---

*And most of that time was consumed in typing. The actual scan is performed in an amazing four-fifths of a second.

though, come upon the word? Speculation has ranged pointlessly far, as far even as the Swiss-German name for cottage cheese. But Joyce's "quarks" are emitted by sea-birds. And what's this, higher up on the same page? "Quark: to croak," with an 1893 citation, "The herons quarked harshly." That entry dates from Murray's time, and Joyce's.

So the "quark" that helps certify scope and up-to-dateness for the OED's Second Edition got there via *Finnegans Wake*, the book of a tireless dictionary-fan who in all likelihood had skimmed "quark" originally from a source he's known to have frequented, the First Edition of the OED.

———

I wrote the above for the *New York Times Book Review* (16 April 1989) against a ten-day deadline. A second thought amid some leisure: the updating, albeit impressive, is mysteriously spotty.

Impressive: the entry for "rathe" ("prompt, eager, earnest, vehement"—it's the long-lost positive form of "rather") records not only its flourishing after 1400 and its disappearance some two centuries later, but its resurrection in 1949 ("E. POUND *Pisan Cantos* . . . 'Pull down thy vanity, Rathe to destroy, niggard in charity.'"). That does bespeak vigilance. So does the exhumation of a sentence to illustrate one nuance of Buckminster Fuller's "tensegrity." They found it in the obscurest of my own books, *Geodesic Math and How to Use It*; and when the *Scientific American*'s reviewer of Kenner on Fuller composed a sentence to shed yet further light, Oxford scooped that up too.

Still, spotty: the last citation for "graffito" (pl. "graffiti") is as old as 1886. That's long before spray-can statements were testing a boundary between contempt and art. And "epiphany" in the Joycean sense is missing, despite its having become the too-frequent recourse of all manner of critics, even unto dance critics. And . . . but let's forego a longer list.

Can the current inflections of "graffiti" and "epiphany" have eluded the net that caught "teen age" surfacing (1921) in the Victoria (British Columbia) *Daily Colonist*? Is that net perhaps riven with gashes? (The process is fallible by definition, relying as it does on no one's assuming that *this* usage has surely been reported already.) Or, confronted by a sheer tonnage of new citations, did the editors just run out of time? Of space? Of attention? There are hints of a Third Edition, perhaps early in the 21st century. Meanwhile, yes, OED-2 does have superb value to offer for anyone's $2,500.

1989

Design by David Bullen
Typeset in Mergenthaler Palatino
by Wilsted & Taylor
with Michelangelo Titling display
Printed by Maple-Vail
on acid-free paper